The Peasants of El Dorado

The Peasants of El Dorado

Conflict and Contradiction in a Peruvian Frontier Settlement

Robin Shoemaker

Cornell University Press

Ithaca and London

Copyright © 1981 by Cornell University Press

All rights reserved. Except for brief quotations in a review, this book, or parts thereof, must not be reproduced in any form without permission in writing from the publisher. For information address Cornell University Press, 124 Roberts Place, Ithaca, New York 14850.

First published 1981 by Cornell University Press.
Published in the United Kingdom by Cornell University Press Ltd., Ely House, 37 Dover Street, London W1X 4HQ.

International Standard Book Number 0-8014-1390-7
Library of Congress Catalog Card Number 81-9742
Printed in the United States of America
Librarians: Library of Congress cataloging information appears on the last page of the book.

Contents

Tables

7

Figures

Acknowledgments

In the course of their research, anthropologists often contravene the principle of reciprocity by asking of individuals and institutions more than they can offer in return. Much to my discomfort and chagrin, I still have no answer to the question that my informants often asked when they agreed to give me their time and cooperation: "What good or benefit will come to the Satipo colony as a result of your study?" Surely what they had in mind was not a book about themselves, written, alas, in a foreign language. Nor would they find much consolation in the fact that this book is intended not as a contribution to the esoteric pursuits of an academic discipline but as a policy-oriented quest for information and understanding.

Thus for several years I have been a gift receiver more often than a gift giver. Various individuals and institutions in Peru and in the United States have given me their time, their money, their advice, and, finally, their patience in awaiting the results. Here I shall try to acknowledge most of these gifts, without purporting to mention them all. In so doing I accept the maxim that in gift exchanges the status of the giver is enhanced while that of the receiver is diminished. Whether or not I regain my status depends largely on how the persons named below judge the quality or, as the colonists would say, the usefulness of this book.

My fieldwork in Peru, which was carried out between November 1973 and March 1975, was made possible by a grant from the Department of Anthropology at the University of Chicago. For this grant and for the financial support I received from the University of Chicago in the early stages of my graduate work I offer my thanks.

On arriving in Lima my wife and I called on several Peruvian friends who had been foreign exchange students during our undergraduate years at the University of Texas. They assisted us in finding a place to live and introduced us to people who would be interested in my research. I thank in particular Carlos Aramburú and Alejandro Camino for the many favors they performed in our behalf and Donald and Gladys Tarnawiecki for their help and their company during our intermittent sojourns in Lima. César Barrios and Adela Tarnawiecki de Barrios kindly allowed us to stay in their home whenever we needed to spend a few days in the capital city. Arnaldo and Ana María Rubini were also hospitable and generous Limeños to whom we extend grateful thanks.

While in Lima I had many opportunities to discuss my work with the staff of the Peruvian government agency CENCIRA (Centro Nacional de Capacitación e Investigación para la Reforma Agraria). I thank the members of CENCIRA's research division and its director, Pedro Ortiz, for sharing with me their ideas concerning the role of colonization in Peruvian development. Their assistance in the selection of a field site is also gratefully acknowledged. I alone, however, am responsible for the opinions and conclusions expressed in this book. My evaluation of the present crisis in the Peruvian colonization movement should not be seen as a reflection of CENCIRA policy.

My greatest debt is, of course, to the people of Satipo. As settlers in a land of unfulfilled promise, they shared with me their anxieties and their frustrations as well as their hopes for a better future. I am especially indebted to a few close friends who served not only as informants but also as intellectual companions who listened to my tentative explanations of local development problems and steered me away from unsound and over-simplified conclusions. To Julio Díaz, Dámaso Paredes, General Rómulo Merino (retired), Carlos Boto Bernales, Andrés Lanyi, Evaristo Llacza, and Leoncio Ledezma I offer my heartfelt thanks. Much of what I learned about Peruvian frontier society was taught to me by these men. Any errors of fact or judgment in this book should be attributed not to their teachings but to my imperfect comprehension of what was taught.

I am also indebted to the people who oversaw my training and development as an anthropologist and who provided guidance and encouragement throughout the various phases of my Peruvian research project. Shepard Forman was an extremely helpful teacher and adviser who aroused my interest in Latin American colonization efforts. His help in getting me into the field is much appreciated. During the often slow and always difficult task of writing this book, Ralph Nicholas served as my chief consultant. His sometimes sympathetic, sometimes goading remarks have been a constant source of inspiration. I appreciate his careful reading of the manuscript and his several suggestions for improvement. Manning Nash has also been an accessible and patient adviser who has applied his critical insights to many of the complex issues raised in this book. Finally, the advice of Friedrich Katz has been invaluable in defining its theoretical and substantive concerns.

I have had the good fortune, furthermore, of receiving the full support, both moral and, on occasion, financial, of my family. Without the help and encouragement of my parents, step-parents, and parents-in-law, I probably would have given up this project long ago. As for my wife, Martha, thanks are hardly appropriate. From beginning to end this research project was a joint endeavor. We experienced the peaks of joy and the valleys of depression together. What we learned is only partially told in the following pages. To all of my family and in particular to my beloved daughter, Carolyn Paige Shoemaker, I dedicate this book.

ROBIN SHOEMAKER

Houston, Texas

The Peasants of El Dorado

Societies of this sort—where outworn and embryonic forms of organization indecisively contend, where instability is the rule rather than the exception, and where feverish activity and boundless ambition combine with deepening immobilism and bitter despair—are often called transitional. But when there is no reason to suppose that such conditions may not continue to exist for a very long time and when whatever equilibrium, dynamic or otherwise, the system may be moving toward is entirely obscure, the term seems—like "underdeveloped" or "emerging"—merely wistful.

 —Clifford Geertz, *The Social History of an Indonesian Town*

1

Sundays in Satipo

Sunday is market day in Satipo, a time when the lonely, tedious life of the jungle settler is momentarily relieved by a trip to town. In the early morning colonists begin to converge on the one regional highway where they await transportation to Satipo on a bus or truck jammed with people but always with room for one more. Those who live in the most remote canyons have had to walk for several hours along muddy paths and logging trails to reach the main road. Other settlers, the lucky ones, have land near the highway and travel frequently and easily to town.

Satipo serves as the economic and social center for a widely scattered population of nearly 38,000. It is here that the colonists come to buy food supplies, tools, and medicine. Here also are located the branch offices of national banks, government agencies, and the farmers' cooperative. But on Sunday colonists go to town to do more than their routine business: they go to learn about recent local and national events, to see a movie, to watch a soccer game, to attend a dance. Town, in the language of the pioneers, is a place "to civilize oneself a little."

During the week the colonist family lives in solitude, rising each day before dawn and heading for the fields at first light. The work group consists of a man and his older children and perhaps a few hired laborers *(jornaleros)*. When farmwork is involved, cooperation or mutual assistance among neighbors in a frontier settlement is rare. Each man, as they say, goes his own way. In the course of a normal week settlers seldom see anyone outside of their own household. Many colonists say that the monotony and the oppressive isolation of farm life would be unbearable if it were not for Sundays in town.

For the anthropologist studying the colonization process Sunday also provides a welcome change. Because of the highly dispersed pattern of settlement, most of my time during the week was spent walking the narrow trails and back roads that connect colonist huts to each other and to the main highway. The effort expended in reaching the settlers often seemed enormous in proportion to the data collected. In addition, the visits I paid to colonists on their farms tended, despite my efforts to the contrary, to acquire a formal or businesslike flavor. I was properly received, my questions were dutifully answered, and my departure was politely awaited so that they could get back to the pressing tasks of the farm. Occasionally in the late afternoon or early evening a more relaxed, spontaneous interview might be had. But Sundays in town offered the only certain opportunities for informal conversation and participant observation, the principal methods of social anthropology.

Colonists whom I had seen during the week on their farms would often return the visit at my house in Satipo on Sunday. They came to discuss whatever was on their minds, to ask questions, to seek advice, to request a favor. During their visits, when the roles of anthropologist and informant were frequently reversed, a set of themes emerged that was repeated consistently throughout the course of my study. These themes, reflected in the following examples of Sunday conversations, form the axis around which my analysis of Peruvian frontier society revolves.

One man, a former mayor of Satipo who was at one time a

fairly prosperous coffee grower but who has become heavily indebted to the bank, comes to tell me of the latest catastrophe that has befallen him. Every year in January or February he hires an *enganchador* (a labor recruiter) to go to the central Andean highlands (about a day's travel by bus from Satipo) to contract with thirty or forty peasants to harvest coffee on his farm, about thirty kilometers from town. This year (1974) he hired a man who appeared to be trustworthy and who seemed to know the techniques of recruiting migrant labor. As he had always done before, he gave the enganchador 25,000 soles (about $500) in cash to pay for the workers' transportation and to give them a small advance on their wages. The enganchador had left with the cash over a month ago and had not been seen since. Not only had the colonist lost the money; he faced the possibility of losing most of his coffee crop for want of laborers to harvest it. The colonist, a light-skinned *criollo* who came to the jungle from the coast of Peru, says that the enganchador is a "filthy Indian" from the *sierra* (highlands). These Indians were once subjected for their own benefit to the power of the *patrones,* he explains, but the agrarian reform and a "communist" military government have changed all that. The Peruvian Indian, according to this former patrón, was once honest and obedient but has now been irrevocably corrupted. The "old system" and the social order it imposed have now been destroyed.

Another man, who has a small farm located in a steep canyon approximately eight kilometers from town, pays a visit to ask if I understand and can explain to him the national law of cooperatives, which sets rules for the formation and operation of farmers' cooperatives in Peru. With hat in hand and head bowed he apologizes for bothering me and says that, unfortunately, he was born the son of an Indian peasant and, unfortunately, finished only two years of school and never learned to read or write. Recently he was elected by the colonists of his canyon to represent them at the biweekly cooperative meetings held in Satipo. Since he became a delegate he has learned that the chief administrator and the managers of the cooperative are stealing money from the institution. Most of these directors, he explains, are Satipo's former patrones or their sons. They are the ones who founded the cooperative ten years ago and they have held control of it in spite of all the social changes that have taken place. The corrupt directorship remains in power because few colonists understand the law or have any concept of their rights as members of the cooperative. Most of today's settlers are of Indian peasant origin, he says, and they lack the "education and culture" necessary to oppose the management of their cooperative effectively.

A third Sunday visitor is a recent migrant to Satipo who is farming in partnership with his older brother on twenty hectares (roughly fifty acres) of land in the Sondobeni canyon, about fifteen kilometers from town. In April of the preceding year he and his brother applied for a loan from the Banco de Fomento Agropecuario (Bank of Agricultural Development, the only bank that extends credit for agricultural purposes) to finance the clearing of five hectares of land and the planting of corn. The bureaucratic procedures involved in acquiring the loan were so complex and time-consuming, he says, that they almost decided to give up. Finally, in late October, their loan was approved. By that time the rainy season was about to commence and it was too late to clear and burn the jungle land (according to standard slash-and-burn practice) to prepare for planting. Still, they decided to proceed with their plans despite the risk, because they badly needed the money to make it through the next year. After they had cleared the land, however, the rains began, and the vegetation did not dry out sufficiently to make a good burning possible. They planted the corn under these unfavorable conditions and the crop that resulted was a disaster. Not only did they fail to realize a profit, but they were unable to cancel their debt and have been blacklisted by the bank. They will not be granted any further credit until the previous loan (with interest) is completely paid off. The colonist claims that the bureaucracy is responsible for his crop failure and that the employees of the bank exploit farmers rather than help them. Almost all of the small farmers of the Satipo region are, he contends, slaves of the bank. If one has power and influence and is willing to offer a gratuity to the bank officials, one's loan application will be processed rapidly and efficiently. But the small farmers are trapped by the bureaucracy because of their poverty and their lack of social contacts and personal influence.

A final visitor is the headman of a Campa[1] settlement called Cushibiani, a legally recognized "native reserve" located in the Río Negro Valley, approximately eight kilometers from town. He comes to ask for my assistance in confronting a sawmill owner who has refused to pay the Campas for lumber taken from their reserve. The arrangement that they made with the lumberman was to sell logs cut on their lands for S/.5 per board foot. No formal written contract was drawn up, however, and when the time came to pay off the Campas, the sawmill owner said that he had promised only S/.3 per board foot. Furthermore, the lumberman cheated them on the measurement of the logs and on the calculation of their value, as well as on the original rate agreed to by both parties. According to the headman, it has been difficult for the Campas to adapt to the ways of "civilization" (a term he uses frequently), and as a result, colonists and lumbermen have always robbed them at will. The wealthy patrones (such as the sawmill owner) are bad people, he says, and the Indian peasants from the sierra are even worse. The Campas, moreover, have been unable to protect themselves because until recently they have not understood civilization and have often tried to run from it. But the headman has decided that this time he is going to present his complaint to local authorities and demand justice, though he believes there is little hope of achieving it.[2]

[1] The Campas are the aboriginal high jungle Indians who inhabited all of the Satipo region before colonization and who now comprise about 25 percent of the population in colonized zones.

[2] I did in fact accompany the headman (with whom I had become friends early in my study) to discuss his complaint with the sawmill owner, but to no avail. The lumberman was suspicious of my motives and accused me publicly of being "a communist and an agent of the CIA."

A Community and a Nation in Transition

To a North American prepared to find in Peruvian frontier
society a dynamic, ambitious force able to play a major role in
national development (the impression one gains from planners
and engineers in Lima), the Sunday experiences described above
represented a major setback. What I heard and saw was a new,
formative society riven by old antagonisms and divisions and
unable, in the midst of it all, to see the proverbial light at the end
of the tunnel. The Satipo colony is undoubtedly a society in
transition, but from what and especially to what is far from
clear—a situation that characterizes the Peruvian nation as a
whole. To say that the transition is from underdevelopment to
development would be to give an overly optimistic appraisal of
modern conditions in Peru. It would be more accurate and
realistic to say that Peru stands at a crossroads where many alternatives, including a hasty retreat or a prolonged period of
agonizing indecision, are possible. To forge ahead along one of
the several alternative roads to development is to undertake a
grueling, uphill journey, the sort of journey that only an organized and unified nation can survive. One thing, at least, is
certain: "developing" nations are not those that rush pell-mell
from an uninterpreted past to an undefined future. If Satipo
and Peru are to emerge from what is called transition but might
better be termed chaos, then there must come a day of ideological reckoning when crucial decisions and commitments are
made. As yet that time seems a long way off. The present course
of social reform in Peru resembles what Clifford Geertz
(1965:5), describing a similarly deadlocked nation, calls "an unbroken advance toward vagueness."

How, then, does one examine and analyze a community or a
nation in transition, where the actors are often as confused as
the observer, where anomaly is a dominant theme of social life?
Furthermore, how is the community–nation relationship to be
conceived in this context? The detailed study of a small part of a
larger whole is a venerable tradition in anthropology, one that is

followed in this book. But the conceptual formulas developed thus far to explain microcosm–macrocosm relations are crude at best, and crudest in the handling of transitional, disequilibrated societies in which interaction between microcosm and macrocosm is characterized by conflict and instability. Let us, for the sake of clarity and a proper perspective, take a closer look at the theoretical currents that have guided anthropology through the early phases of community–nation research.

Contemporary conceptions of rural communities in the underdeveloped Third World have been shaped and reshaped in the postwar period as the facts of change were accommodated and as new analytic directions were explored. The rethinking of the relationship of nation and community continues to be a central concern of social anthropology. From simple beginnings when the "little community" was acknowledged to be affected by outside factors (Redfield 1941), the microcosm is now studied by some anthropologists as an actual or potential setting for the takeoff to modernization and economic development (e.g., Geertz 1963b; Nash 1967). But while we seem to have come full circle in our thinking about the little community, many complex theoretical and methodological problems remain. Thus, although the rethinking process discussed below has led to a sharpening of conceptual focus, it has not led to the construction of a widely accepted model of microcosm–macrocosm integration.

"Distinctive, small, homogeneous, and self-sufficient" is the well known Redfieldian characterization of rural communities in the folk tradition. The notion of the isolated, self-contained human settlement, understood as a closed system of functionally interrelated parts, was formed in the ethnographies of primitive groups and was later borrowed by students of peasant societies. With Redfield, the "small whole" became part of a larger, compound social system while remaining a distinct entity intelligible primarily in and of itself. Functional equilibrium, which maintained and reinforced the traditional structure of the microcosm, served as the basic model around which anthropological description and interpretation were organized.

The impact of the modern world on the little community, one of Redfield's major concerns, is viewed as a linear process: the gradual unraveling of the tightly knit fabric of folk society. The penetration of urban life into the countryside leads invariably to increasing heterogeneity, diminishing solidarity, secularization, and individualization. The macrocosm is civilization and its heartland is the urban metropolis, where all change originates. The rural microcosm is seen as the passive element that receives and incorporates innovations from outside according to its degree of contact.

Such an approach is defeated by its own logic; once functional relationships are elevated to the status of a causal model, only two kinds of social change are possible: restoration of equilibrium or total collapse and disintegration. Either the macrocosm has no appreciable influence or it overwhelms the microcosm as the two come into contact. The former condition is generally referred to as "traditionalism" and the latter process is labeled "modernization." What this scheme fails to provide is an understanding of interaction between community and nation in a complex but unitary social system. Considerable rethinking of the Redfield model is required in order to explain the interpenetration of microcosm and macrocosm in various forms and in various degrees over time. The impingement or incursionist model of linkage posited by Redfield represents an initial, yet wholly unsatisfactory, attempt to account for the network of relationships that connect the part with the whole.

An even cruder formulation of the community–nation question is the "microcosm is macrocosm" theory of W. Lloyd Warner (1953) and his associates. The microcosm is seen as a miniature replica of the nation, or, conversely, the macrocosm is the small community writ large. According to Warner, the investigator's task is to find a "representative microcosm" (1953: 41), a community having all of the ingredients that went into the making of the nation. Warner felt that the racial, ethnic, religious, economic, and political composition of the microcosm should be the same as that of the macrocosm. The proportions would be equal or nearly equal; only the scale would be different. After a careful screening process, Warner believed that he had found a community that closely approximated the "ideal-typical expression" or the "central core" of American society. He gave this community an appropriate pseudonym: Jonesville.

The fallacies in Warner's reasoning are self-evident. The notion that a community could be an abridged version of the larger society to which it belongs betrays common sense and renders meaningless the question of the relationship of the part and the whole. Modern nations are many-stranded systems of relationships, not statistical aggregates that can be reduced to anthropologically manageable proportions. Enough indictments of Warner's model exist already, however; the point to be emphasized here is that the distinction between community and nation is qualitative, not quantitative. Microcosm and macrocosm are qualitatively different units of analysis, yet they belong within a single conceptual field.

Recent attempts to define this field have tended to focus on institutions and persons who play roles that serve to integrate or articulate various "levels" of socioeconomic organization. Eric Wolf (1956, 1967), for example, has studied the bonds that unite diverse groups at various levels of the larger society, with local communities representing the termini of this web of group relations. Mediating between groups and between "levels of integration" are "brokers" who "stand guard over the crucial junctures or synapses of relationships which connect the local system to the larger whole" (Wolf 1956:1075). Richard N. Adams (1970) has similarly analyzed the linkage roles of brokers and has delineated a set of "levels of articulation"—subcommunal, local, regional, national, and supranational—that are in continuous interaction, generating both conflict and accommodation. These levels of articulation, while generally applicable cross-culturally, take on locally specific forms that must be discovered and described in each empirical case. Finally, the study of "career mobility systems" (Leeds 1965), the tracing of individual movement across various levels of society, has added a new concept of linkage which complements that of the broker, who mediates between levels but does not move from one level to another.

The addition of "levels of integration," "brokers," and "career patterns" to the vocabulary of micro–macro analysis has infused new life in a field long dominated by folk–urban, *Gemeinschaft–Gesellschaft* thinking. Most important, the interactionist model questions the wisdom of anthropologists who continue to produce "bounded community ethnographies" in the midst of agrarian reform, expanding market networks, and even revolution. Instead of the traditional "ethnography of a locality," the interactionists propose a theoretically controlled form of research guided by a firm sense of problem and directed toward something more substantial and more specific than general cultural description. The locus and the theoretical objectives of a problem-oriented study are clearly differentiated and their relationship is defined in each empirical case. The "levels of integration" appropriate to the problem under investigation are also established case by case in order to accommodate the fluidity of group formation and disintegration in a complex, changing world. Thus the interactionist model provides a set of terms and concepts for thinking about microcosm–macrocosm relations in general as well as a research map for exploring particular dynamics at the empirical level.

The drawback of the interactionist model is that, despite its flexibility and openness, it often leads to a higher-order functionalism where accommodation, coherence, and integration govern relations among the levels of society. Sequences of action and reaction between microcosm and macrocosm generate equilibrium in a cyclical fashion. The result is a fixed morphology of levels and a mechanical view of interaction among levels. Conflict, contradiction, and structural change are not anticipated in the unfolding of events within this framework. Thus, frequently what begins as a well-intended alternative to the little-community model of functional integration ends as a projection of that very same model to the national level.

This lamentable state of affairs is due in part to the lack of a historical perspective on the shifting patterns of microcosm-macrocosm relations that would isolate and follow the interplay of causal forces through time. Anthropologists have rarely tested the waters of historical inquiry, preferring instead the terra firma of the ethnographic present. A growing number of anthropologists, however, have begun to use historical materials not simply to establish a pale background for a synchronic community study but to diversify their sources of data and to enhance their understanding of the relation of the part to the whole.

An example of this trend is John Cole and Eric Wolf's (1974) study of ecology and ethnicity in two alpine villages of northern Italy. The authors perceive both microcosms as the outcomes of two sets of historical forces, "ecological on the one hand, economic, political, and ideological on the other" (Cole and Wolf 1974:21). They proceed to analyze these two sets of causal forces as a complex dialectic, the interworking of thesis and antithesis over a period ranging from the early Middle Ages to the present. Patterns of "growth, crystallization, and demise" in the interaction of microcosm and macrocosm are carefully documented and explained.

Another noteworthy effort to examine the relationship of community and nation along historical lines is Shepard Forman's (1975) study of the social, economic, and political dimensions of peasant integration in Brazil. Forman (1975:6) contends that "to understand the nature of peasant integration in Brazilian society, history must be made to work for us, not merely by providing the backdrop for a particular village or group of people, nor even for the elaboration of specific situational sets of events, but by becoming the dynamic field in which particular events and relations are seen to transpire." Historically, the small peasant villages and plantation towns of Brazil have been affected by elite power struggles, by the vagaries of export-oriented commercial agriculture, by urbanization and industrialization, and by other macrocosmic forces. Forman shows that it is precisely the nature of the peasants' involvement in these national historical processes that explains their present dire condition. In arguing his point, Forman skillfully culls from 400 years of Brazilian history a set of themes that illuminate the essential features of microcosm–macrocosm integration.

The quest for more accurate and more comprehensive understandings of how small populations participate in larger, highly differentiated social systems has not been a fruitless one. Nor has the quest led anthropology away from what it has always done best, the detailed study of ordinary, everyday life in little communities. Rather, what happens in those communities has come to be thought about in terms of its possible broader implications, either as a stimulus or as a reaction to the changing complexion of the macrocosm. As recent history reveals, certain major social transformations have come from above while others have originated from below. Anthropologists, from their perspective, can focus on the local response to changes imposed from outside or, as the situation demands, turn their attention to the shape of movements generated at the microcosmic level. At the present stage of world history, this is a decidedly advantageous position to be in.

Anthropologists, then, look both inward and outward with respect to the microcosm. They do not, or at least not any longer, allow the little-community approach to obstruct their larger field of vision. Instead, complex forces of several kinds are seen to be at work simultaneously and the real challenge is to find a method of weighing or evaluating the unequal effects of the various factors that determine a given social configuration. In this endeavor history provides a kind of scale by which the long and the short strands of institutional development can be separated and their respective influences judged. This approach is not without its pitfalls, but the alternative of proceeding blindly in the ethnographic present is far less satisfactory.

In the study of a disequilibrated nation such as Peru, where an old order, vaguely defined, is being eliminated and a new order, even more vaguely defined, is being built, hindsight is an indis-

pensable analytic tool. In the new order much of the old persists
or is even revived, as in the strong identification of contemporary Peruvian nationalism with the country's Inca heritage. Little
of the anarchist bent for total uprooting and national rebirth is
to be found in Peru. At least in part, the key to the future is seen
to lie in the past. Thus the transitional period is one of self-
examination and historical stock-taking to determine what con-
stellation of old and new elements will guide Peru on the road to
development. Anthropologists are equally called upon to explore the temporal dimensions of the modern social transformations they study.

Fortunately, Andean historiography and ethnohistory are sufficiently advanced to provide the student of contemporary
change with some useful guideposts to the past. Taken as a
whole, the works of such scholars as John Murra (1956, 1961,
1970, 1972), Nathan Wachtel (1977), John Howland Rowe
(1947, 1957), Karen Spalding (1967, 1970, 1974), James Lockhart (1968, 1969, 1972), Virgilio Roel Pineda (1970, 1971),
Robert Keith (1971, 1976), Guillermo Lohmann Villena (1949,
1957), Jorge Basadre (1949), Frederick Pike (1967), and José
Carlos Mariátegui (1971) constitute an extensive, if somewhat
fragmented, account of Peruvian history. Overviews of Peruvian
history from pre-Inca to modern times are provided by Henry
Dobyns and Paul Doughty (1976) and David Werlich (1978).[3]
Equipped with a knowledge of the basic patterns of Andean
social history derived from these and other sources, the analyst
of modern conditions is less likely to be overwhelmed by the
dilemmas and contradictions that permeate community and nation alike.

My efforts to understand the dilemmas and contradictions of
the Satipo colony led consistently in two basic directions: backward and outward. I relied primarily on the memories of my
informants (some of whom had lived in Satipo since the region

---

[3]These works also contain excellent guides to the general literature on Peru.
For an assessment of the "state of the art" in Andean ethnohistory, see Murra
(1970).

was first colonized, in the late 1920s) to trace the development of Satipo backward from the present.[4] By examining marketing patterns and the workings of central government regulatory agencies I moved outward from the community to its controlling socioeconomic environment. Chapters 3 and 4 present the results of the microhistorical inquiry and Chapters 5, 7, and 8 are concerned with the processes of integration. Whatever explanatory power this study possesses should be attributed to the microhistorical and interactionist modes of analysis. Any less comprehensive research strategy would be inadequate to the task of understanding Peru's agonizing quest for development.

Whether or when a Peruvian road to development will be found is a complex question. There have always been, as there are today, the magical formulas, the get-rich-quick schemes of a desperately poor nation. Perhaps the most prominent of these panaceas is the colonization of the eastern jungles. A popular phrase heard repeatedly at all levels of Peruvian society is that "Peru is a beggar sitting on a heap of gold." The unconquered eastern frontier, long shrouded in the myth of El Dorado, symbolizes for many Peruvians that heap of gold. Adding to the mystique of El Dorado are the boom industries—rubber, coffee, lumber, oil—that flourish from time to time in the jungle region and bring fortunes to an adventurous few. Significantly, even the schemes for national development that make a point of debunking the myth of El Dorado assign a high priority to the settlement or "conquest" of the eastern frontier.

Indeed, transamazon development has become a byword for progress not only in Peru but in all of the nations whose ter-

---

[4]I searched in vain for archival materials relating to the aspects of Satipo's history with which I was most concerned. There are few historical materials of any kind for this area. The Catholic missionaries have kept records of their activities, and consequently more is known about the efforts of the Jesuits and Franciscans to "civilize" the Campas than about any other aspect of regional history. A chronicle of Franciscan missionary "accomplishments" in the central high jungle region of Peru can be found in two books by Father Dionisio Ortiz (1958, 1961). Anthropologist Stefano Varese (1973) offers an alternative view of these accomplishments in his stinging critique of missionary work among the Campas.

ritories include a portion of the vast South American rain forest. Although social-scientific research has not kept pace with the changing settlement policies and programs of these countries, there is a sizable literature on the colonization process. Since the publication in 1953 of Charles Wagley's now classic *Amazon Town,* a study of social and economic conditions among subsistence farmers and rubber tappers of the Brazilian Amazon, an ever larger community of scholars has concerned itself with issues pertaining to the conquest of the world's last great frontier.

The decade of the 1970s was a particularly fruitful period of research. Maxine Margolis (1973) studied Brazil's expanding coffee frontier and explained how the vagaries of weather and the world market affect the pioneers. Emilio Morán (1974, 1979) examined the adaptive system of recent immigrants along Brazil's transamazon highway. Allyn Stearman (1973) and Héctor Martínez (1969) studied, in Bolivia and Peru respectively, the adaptation of peasants from the Andean highlands to the harsh conditions of the tropical lowlands. Shelton Davis (1977), Norman Whitten (1976), and Stefano Varese (1972, 1973) exposed and analyzed the serious threat posed by colonization programs to the survival of the native peoples of the South American rain forest. Thus from several angles researchers probed the pioneer communities of the Amazon region in an effort to understand, and in some sense to influence, the course of frontier expansion.

I chose to study a frontier microcosm because I believed that the prospects for Peruvian economic development and social reform could be examined and evaluated in this setting. It seemed to me that the problems of a rapidly changing nation were vividly displayed in its frontier communities. This is perhaps the best definition of a "microcosm": a setting where the detailed, circumstantial analysis of common, ordinary people doing everyday things lends itself to broad-stroke interpretations of national life. Especially when, as in the Sunday conversations described above, patterns emerge in the most diverse problems of everyday living, the lines leading from particular to more comprehensive understandings can be drawn.

The frontier microcosm is also a setting where the more comprehensive process of development takes particular, concrete forms. In the heated debate on the general stages and aggregate indicators of economic growth, few scholars have bothered to assess and reflect on the local impact of development strategies. Although anthropologists are in an ideal position to undertake such an assessment, they have seldom worked with an eye toward understanding the actual or potential participation of their communities in the process of national economic development. In the study that follows I seek to arouse some interest in this dormant issue by evaluating the impact of government decisions, laws, policies, and programs on the Satipo colony. It is my belief that the scant attention paid to the problems of policy implementation at the local level explains the naiveté and unfounded optimism of much developmental theory.

Economists are correct in their assertion that late-twentieth-century development policy decisions must be centrally made and authoritatively implemented. The age of laissez faire development has yielded to the age of guided growth. But in this new age of broadly conceived goals and policies, the successful planners will be those who have at least an accurate, if not an empathetic, understanding of the specific realities they seek to transform. Development policies logically deduced from the axioms of modern economic theory are rarely successful. The formal elegance of economic theory belies the complexity of social, economic, and political change at the microcosmic level. A lack of flexibility and a strong adherence to the abstract principles of growth have kept the art of national planning at a primitive stage. Nonetheless, one fact is becoming clear to even the most cloistered architects of change: the microcosm is the final and decisive proving ground for development strategies.

Not all microcosms, however, are equally involved in the processes of national social and economic reform. Certain areas of a nation actively seek innovation and progress (often entailing considerable risks) while others maintain a conservative course.

There is no doubt as to which of these two paths Satipo has chosen to follow. This frontier microcosm stands at the forefront of national attention as a bold experiment that is expected to contribute significantly to the momentum of Peruvian development. Colonization has an important role to play in Peru's attempts to reach a stage of self-sustaining growth adequate to the needs of a rapidly expanding population.

But in light of present conditions, serious doubts must be raised with regard to the ability of colonization to play its assigned role. The manifold problems of the Satipo colony do not augur well for the future of jungle settlement in Peru. My purpose is not, however, to condemn the colonization experiment as a foolishly or maliciously conceived project that never had a chance to succeed. Rather, I want to show what went wrong, how, and why.

My search for answers to these questions begins with an analysis of the ecological crisis in Satipo (Chapter 2). I describe the process of environmental deterioration brought about by wasteful and destructive farming techniques. In Chapter 3 I turn to a discussion of the world market economy and other extralocal factors that, in effect, encouraged the settlers to use these improper methods of cultivation. Chapter 4 traces the erratic development of a small colonist community that shares and to a certain degree symbolizes the poverty, frustration, and despair of contemporary pioneer society. Chapter 5 explores the nature of social conflict in Satipo and exposes the barriers to concerted action. In Chapter 6 I present a series of individual portraits or vignettes in which seven of my closest informants relate and interpret their own life struggles. The final two chapters (7 and 8) offer, in turn, the empirical evidence of Satipo's economic stagnation and a theory that, in my view, helps to explain the present impasse in the colonization effort. Satipo's pervasive malaise is best understood, I argue, in terms of what has come to be known in social-scientific circles as dependency theory.

The Frontier as Hinterland

In recent years dependency theory has helped to demystify Latin American underdevelopment. The seminal works of André Gunder Frank (1967), Pablo González Casanova (1965), Aníbal Quijano (1971), Julio Cotler (1967–68), and Rodolfo Stavenhagen (1966) argue convincingly that development and underdevelopment are but two aspects of a single process. Disparities in levels of development are said to be attributable not to a time lag, as the theorists of modernization and diffusion assume, but rather to a parasitic relationship in which a developed sector grows and prospers at the expense of an underdeveloped sector. As Gunder Frank (1967:9) says, "economic development and underdevelopment are not just relative and quantitative, in that one represents more economic development than the other; economic development and underdevelopment are relational and qualitative, in that each is structurally different from, yet caused by its relation with, the other."

At the international level this pattern is seen in the relationship of the industrialized nations with the so-called Third World. The rich and the poor nations owe their respective statuses to the asymmetrical bonds by which they are joined. Quijano (1971) shows, for example, that Peruvian history is a history of domination by foreign capitalist powers (first Spain, then Britain, and most recently the United States). Far from being marginal to the dominant world economy, Peru has always had multiple links to this economy as a supplier of cheap raw materials and as a consumer of finished goods. Trade with and investment by the developed nations define and maintain Peru's subordinate satellite position vis-à-vis an external developing metropolis. Ronald Chilcote and Joel Edelstein summarize the dependency view of foreign trade and investment as follows:

> More foreign investment does bring an expanded gross national product, but it does not create self-sustaining economic development. Outside control is enhanced. Outward capital flows increase. Investment decisions continue to be based on plans for improved profitability and balanced development of multina-

tional corporations rather than domestic employment and production needs. Economic growth does not even reduce poverty since few jobs are generated by the new technology, while less advanced domestic competition is eliminated. [Chilcote and Edelstein 1974:27-28]

This web of dependency, once formed, entangles the underdeveloped nations in yet another dilemma. The tendency, according to Gunder Frank (1967), is for the internal contradictions of dependency to be replicated at the domestic level. Thus an underdeveloped nation such as Peru comes to have a metropolis–satellite structure of its own. The urbanized center of national power and wealth (in this case Lima) assumes the role of a metropolis that develops at the expense of a backward and underdeveloped rural hinterland. Rather than assuming that progress will come about through the spread of modern ideas and technology to backward, traditional areas, the dependency school contends that increased penetration of the periphery by the center only leads to greater exploitation and underdevelopment. As Chilcote and Edelstein (1974:27) conclude, "the countryside is poor not because it is feudal or traditional but because it has enriched the cities."

Thus, according to dependency theorists, the domestic structure of inequality tends to mirror the international structure of inequality. The national metropolis, which is a dependent satellite of the industrialized nations, in turn increasingly dominates its hinterland by preventing any accumulation of wealth or any growth of political autonomy in the interior regions. In this manner the economic, social, and political life of an underdeveloped nation is permeated by the contradictions of the world capitalist system. The implication for corrective action is, therefore, that improvements will be made not by intensified relations either between the city and its hinterland or between the rich and the poor nations, but by the overthrow of capitalism and creation of a socialist context for development.

Dependency theory and the model of internal colonialism are, as the above outline suggests, crudely formulated hypotheses in need of further testing and considerable refinement. Yet it is hard, especially for one who has studied and pondered microcosm–macrocosm interaction in Peru, to deny the kernel of truth that these concepts contain. There is and, at least since colonial times, always has been a structure of internal domination in Peru. The growth and prosperity of Lima and the stagnation and depression of the rural provinces is a pattern that has been noted by observers of Peru for centuries. Henry Dietz, in an essay on Peruvian urbanism (1978:206), says that "when Lima was founded on the Río Rimac in 1535 as 'The City of the Kings,' certain patterns in Peru's development were sealed, and have persisted to the present time: the coastal–sierra dichotomy, the flow of interior wealth and natural resources toward the coast for export rather than for internal refining, processing, or consumption, and the mutual dependent relationship between Lima (unable to produce raw materials for itself) and the rest of Peru (unable to generate local developmental autonomy)."

Once the hub of Spain's colonial empire, Lima continues to function as the center of foreign influence and domination. At the same time Lima has emerged as the controlling headquarters, the administrative apex, of Peruvian society. In this capacity Lima has drained the resources of the interior and appropriated them for its own economic development. Thus today Lima has the most and the best of everything: banks, hospitals, roads, schools, factories, and numerous other facilities and services.[5] This monopoly is a product of Peru's internal colonialist system.

An important question, then, is whether frontier expansion in Peru constitutes a break with or a continuation of the historical processes of dependency and internal colonialism. Does the settlement of jungle lands merely add to the hinterland or does it signal a new direction in national growth? It is my judgment,

---

[5]Doughty (1976) has assembled the most impressive evidence of Lima's disproportionately large share of the "good life." He uses these data to explain the swelling ranks of migrants leaving the Peruvian hinterland for the capital city. Cotler (1967–68) and Dietz (1978) also document the increasing concentration of economic and political power in the nation's capital.

after much research and reflection, that Peruvian colonization is initially spontaneous and autonomous but that the frontier is soon absorbed as a dependent hinterland of the national metropolis. Absorption occurs when frontier industry and agriculture begin to produce a marketable surplus. Once the commercial potential of a colonization zone has been demonstrated, the forces of economic and political absorption are set in motion. Roads are built, branch banks are opened, merchant-creditors arrive, and government regulatory agencies are established. But progress, the colonists rapidly discover, comes at a very high cost. In return for a few paltry symbols of modernization, the colonists are forced to surrender control of their emerging community to a host of government bureaucrats and enterprising middlemen. It is these modernizers from the capital city who, by regulating commerce between Lima and Satipo, reap whatever profits are to be made from frontier industry and agriculture. The agents of national development effectively prevent any local accumulations of economic or political power that might enable Satipo to become a focal point of regional development. Thus the frontier merely provides more grist for the mill of internal colonialism.

In the course of this book I shall attempt to explain how the Satipo colony acquired its hinterland status. I must make clear from the outset, however, that I did not undertake this research with the intention of applying dependency theory to a Peruvian frontier settlement. I began with only a vague sense of dissatisfaction with the prevailing view of rural Peruvian communities as somehow separated in time and space from the mainstream of national life. This view, associated with modernization theory in general and with the anthropological literature on Peru in particular, is contradicted by the political and economic history of the Andean region.

From the Spanish conquest to the present, Peruvian history has had only one, albeit unsteady, current. This single current has carried with it city and country dwellers, rich and poor, highlanders and lowlanders, farmers and bankers, fishermen and miners. The notion of multiple currents, of separate or dual or plural societies, distorts the realities of Peruvian history. There are no outsiders, no unincorporated masses seeking entry to national life. The protests and rebellions of dissident groups in Peru have been directed against the existing framework of integration, not against a lack of integration or involvement with the larger society. The poor fit between the historical facts and the conventional model of Andean social organization calls for a rethinking of the relationship of community and nation in Peru. My research is intended as a contribution to this rethinking process.

As I explained above, however, my study of social and economic change in a frontier settlement was not guided by any particular model of microcosm–macrocosm integration. I had read the works of dependency theorists and modernization theorists and I was aware of the issues that separated them. But I had no *a priori* commitment to either of these perspectives. I wanted to take a fresh look at the problems of rural development in Peru and to formulate my own conclusions. I was eventually drawn to dependency theory because the data I gathered revealed a consistent pattern of domination of the Satipo colony by the capital city. Through the collection and analysis of economic data I came to realize that the terms of trade between Lima and Satipo are heavily biased in favor of the metropolis. In subsequent chapters I shall retrace the path that led to this realization. In the final chapter I shall summarize the data that convince me (and perhaps will convince the reader as well) that frontier development is shackled by an intranational system of dependency and exploitation.

I hasten to add that my research does not lead me to endorse dependency theory without qualifications. Even though I employ the model of internal colonialism in my analysis of frontier expansion, some aspects of the dependency approach I find objectionable. For example, dependency theorists, in their eagerness to establish a comprehensive yet parsimonious theory of underdevelopment, tend to ignore the variety and complexity of social, political, and economic conditions in the contemporary Third World. Dependency theorists overemphasize the similarities and uniformities of experience in the recent histories of Africa, Asia, and Latin America. They do not address themselves adequately to such issues as the varieties of colonial experience, the diversity of cultures, or the complexities of political change in the underdeveloped nations. In a critique of Gunder Frank's writings on Latin America, John Walton (1976:49) claims that the dependency thesis "included an overly monolithic view of some complex forms of dependency" and that "it underestimated the importance of those variable internal circumstances of the underdeveloped countries that articulate with the interests of the metropolitan centers." Norman Long (1977:89) also finds Gunder Frank guilty of oversimplifying the relationships of dependency and concludes that "it is important therefore to try to specify the conditions under which different types and degrees of structural dependency or domination exist."

Peru, perhaps more than other Third World nations, represents a special case of dependency and underdevelopment. Following a coup d'état in 1968, the Peruvian armed forces surprised the international community by announcing the formation of a "revolutionary" government that would carry out an ambitious program of social and economic reform. The military government, through a series of expropriations and nationalizations of foreign (primarily North American) holdings, demonstrated its desire to alter the metropolis–satellite relationship between the developed nations and Peru. In taking over the Peruvian properties of such powerful multinational corporations as Standard Oil, ITT, W. R. Grace, Cerro de Pasco, and Starkist, the regime led by General Juan Velasco Alvarado captured international attention and received the acclaim of many Third World countries. By 1975, when the revolution shifted from a radical first phase to a far more moderate second phase under a new president (General Francisco Morales Bermúdez), Peru no longer exhibited the classic features of dependency and underdevelopment. Both the degree and the form of dependency had changed, a fact that the all-or-nothing philosophy of dependency theorists cannot adequately explain.

The special circumstances of the Peruvian revolution reveal yet another flaw of dependency theory. As we have seen, dependency has both an external and an internal dimension. Internal colonialism is said to be a product of external dependence (Fernández and Ocampo 1974). Yet the Peruvian case indicates that internal colonialism has a dynamic and a structure of its own and that it is not merely a product or corollary of external dependence. The data from Satipo and from other rural areas of Peru show that while the bonds of external dependence were being loosened by the Velasco regime, the bonds of internal colonialism were being tightened. The movement toward greater national autonomy was not accompanied, as dependency theorists would predict, by greater internal or regional autonomy.

Thus the net result of reforms in the land-tenure and internal marketing systems of Peru was a dramatic increase in central government control over the economic and political life of such farming communities as Satipo. The avowed purpose of the reforms carried out by central government agencies was the elimination of "capitalist exploitation" in the Peruvian countryside. But the domestic policies of the revolutionary government, far from being viewed in a favorable light, came to be seen by the colonists as a new form of political and economic domination. The settlers contend that for each obstacle removed from the path of local development, a new obstacle was erected. The state proved to be no less skilled in the abuse of power than the traditional oligarchy. This, at least, is an opinion often voiced by frontier settlers who have been affected by the government's reforms in the landholding and internal marketing systems. It is an opinion that challenges the dependency thesis that internal colonialism is a problem whose solution lies in the transformation of external dependency relationships.

The subject of colonist opinions leads me to make a final,

general criticism of dependency theory in its present form. From an anthropological point of view, the most serious limitation of dependency theory is that it has not been informed and shaped by the beliefs and ideas of the very people whose plight it seeks to explain. In charting the patterns of foreign domination and internal colonialism, dependency theorists use aggregate data on capital flows, import-export ratios, labor absorption rates, sectoral income breakdowns, and taxation structures (Walton 1975). While these figures offer an impressive statistical profile of dependency, they fail to show how the contradictions of underdevelopment are perceived and experienced in microcosmic settings. Almost hidden behind the numbers and the increasingly technical vocabulary of dependency theory lies a human tragedy beyond measurement. Wasted lives, thwarted ambitions, and hopeless poverty are the dominant themes of this tragedy. The actors are men and women much like the colonists of Satipo.

In the following pages I try to reveal what the hinterland function means in terms of human frustration and despair. I offer a personal, not a statistical, profile of underdevelopment. The concept of internal colonialism will not be mentioned again until the final chapter. In the interim, the reader will be able to judge whether or not the data I present are suited to the analytic framework of dependency theory. In formulating my own views I have sought, above all else, to be consistent with the views of my informants. Conversations with Sunday visitors and other settlers provided me with ample clues as to the source and the nature of Satipo's developmental crisis. With the aid of these clues I hope to resolve, at least in part, the puzzle of frontier stagnation.

2

Population and Environment

For years observers of the Peruvian nation have dwelled on the highly variable Andean landscape and its presumed sociopolitical consequences. The received wisdom, in essence, is that Peru's geography is tripartite, consisting of a narrow coastal desert (*costa*), the Andean highlands (sierra), and the Amazonian tropical forest *(selva)*. These zones constitute three parallel strips of land running from north to south along the entire length of the country (Ford 1955, Sauer 1950). It is said that this bold environmental configuration tends to retard communication and sociopolitical integration, a tendency that was overcome only during the brief span of the Inca state. After the fall of that glorious civilization the rugged terrain once again imposed its will, dividing and isolating the Andean population.

Recent research has begun to erode the foundation on which this conventional wisdom has stood. It is not that the traditional argument is totally inaccurate but rather that it is far too simplistic. John Murra (1972) and Stephen Brush (1977), for example, have shown that the patterns of ecological zonation in the Andes are much more complex than they were previously believed to

42

be. They argue that far more significant than the three basic divisions of Peruvian geography are the hundreds of micro-environmental niches created by subtle variations in altitude, temperature, rainfall, soil quality, slope, sunlight, humidity, wind intensity, and other factors. Within the space of a few kilometers one or more of these microenvironmental factors may vary greatly. Thus, according to Brush (1977), the key to understanding human ecology in the Andes lies in the study of microenvironmental adaptations. The data that Brush presents from his study of Uchucmarca, a peasant community that uses six different ecological zones in its subsistence cycle, amply illustrate his point of view.

Moreover, Murra (1972) shows that ecological diversity, far from being a divisive factor in Andean social history, has been an integrative force. Since each microenvironment is suited to a small range of crops, the people of diverse ecological zones can obtain a varied diet only by trading or exchanging their agricultural products. Murra (1972) uses the concept of "vertical control" to explain the economic strategy by which distant settlements at different altitudes are linked by means of food exchange networks. These networks are social and political as well as economic in nature.[1] Thus to speak of geographic "barriers" to sociopolitical integration in the Andes is entirely to miss the point. Survival in the Andes has always depended on vertical linkage and long-distance trade. The geographic "barriers" are, in fact, quite permeable.

Murra's ingenious (and well-documented) conception of the "vertical archipelago," a network of specialized communities or "islands" that produce different crops or other goods in different microenvironments and exchange these products over great distances, leads one to ask if the Satipo colony functions within such a system. Although Murra's concern is to explain the

[1]The linkage function of interregional trade networks in Peru is further discussed in a collection of essays edited by Giorgio Alberti and Enrique Mayer (1974). Each essay examines a particular form of exchange and its contribution to the social and political integration of the Andean population.

pre-Hispanic structure of Andean society, Brush believes, on the basis of his research in Uchucmarca, that "in spite of the tremendous upheavals caused by the Spanish Conquest, the patterns of vertical control which Murra has analyzed for the Andean highlands at the time of the Conquest have analogous patterns that operate today" (1977:15).

After much deliberation I have concluded that the data from Satipo do not, in fact, reveal a system of production or exchange that could be termed a vertical archipelago. The process of frontier settlement is geared to the production of cash crops (primarily coffee) for domestic and foreign markets. It would not be useful or productive, in my view, to apply the analogy of the vertical archipelago to the colonization zones of the Peruvian *montaña*. The dynamics of frontier expansion in Peru today are too complex to be adequately explained in terms of the model of vertical control.

Nevertheless, the following discussion of ecological relationships in Satipo owes much to this perspective on the Andean environment. In the traditional view, Satipo belongs to the selva or tropical forest region of Peru. My purpose is to dissect this broad and almost meaningless geographic category in order to discover within it the smaller and more significant units of ecological analysis. Subsequently, I seek to explain how two different populations, the aboriginal inhabitants and the recent immigrants, have adapted to the local environment. By comparing and contrasting two different adaptations to the same environment I hope to explain some of the complex problems of human settlement on the eastern slopes of the Andes.

The Mountains' Eyebrow

The eastern jungle region is the largest of the three basic divisions of Peru's geography. It extends from the eastern slopes of the Andes to the Brazilian border, covering 800,000 square kilometers or 63 percent of the nation's territory (CIDA 1966:5). The selva is nearly twice as large as Peru's other two major geographic divisions—a narrow strip of coastal desert and the Andean highlands—combined. Despite its size, the jungle has only 1.3 million inhabitants, about 10 percent of the total population of the country. Except in the one city, Iquitos, and several lesser towns, this small population is widely scattered along the major lowland rivers and the few roads that penetrate the high western fringe of the region.

In any discussion of the environmental features of the jungle it is important to recognize two distinct zones. The first is the *selva alta*, or high jungle, formed by the eastern slopes and foothills of the Andes. This mountainous area, where altitudes range from 1,500 to 8,000 feet, is also known as the montaña. The second zone is the *selva baja*, or low jungle, a vast flat plain below 1,500 feet in elevation that extends from the eastern edge of the montaña to the Brazilian border and beyond. Of the total jungle area in Peru, approximately three-fourths is selva baja and one-fourth is selva alta or montaña. In terms of population, however, 65 percent of jungle residents live in the montaña and only 35 percent in the selva baja (CIDA 1966:5).

The present study was carried out in a frontier settlement located in the lower part of the montaña, a zone known as the *ceja de montaña*, or mountains' eyebrow. (See Figure 1.) This area, covered by dense tropical rain forests, stands midway between the sierra and the Amazonian plain. Its proximity to the sierra is appreciated on any clear day, when from the town of Satipo, at the region's center, several snow-capped peaks of the central Andes range are visible to the west. Only seventy kilometers to the east of town a final low ridge of mountains gives way to the flat terrain of the selva baja. The geography, climate, and ecology of the intermediate zone, the ceja de montaña, are highly variable and complex.

Perhaps the environmental feature that most immediately affects the process of settlement is the high jungle topography. The contours of the land are extremely irregular and each minor variation has important ecological consequences. Basically, there are two kinds of topographic formations in the ceja

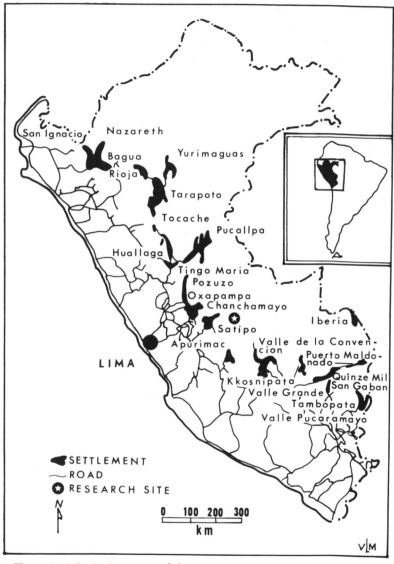

Figure 1. Colonization zones of the montaña. Adapted by permission from Wesche (1971b).

de montaña: *valles* (valleys) and *quebradas* (canyons). All major rivers and large streams form valles, and their tributaries, the innumerable small streams and rivulets of the region, form quebradas. The difference lies in the degree of slope of the river or stream channel and in the presence or absence of a floodplain. A valley has a gentle slope or gradient and at least a small terrace of flat or moderately inclined land surrounding the riverbed. A canyon, in contrast, has a steep slope with no appreciable floodplain. Clearly the difference is one of degree, but for the inhabitants of the area there is no confusion between the one and the other. The colonists of Satipo say that there are only a few valleys, formed by the Ipoke, Mazamari, Satipo, and Pangoa rivers, and that the remaining formations are canyons. Most important, these two zones stand in sharp contrast in terms of their agricultural potentials.

In general, the best farmland is located along the level terraces of river valleys, although canyon slopes are also suitable for cultivation. The primary variables that distinguish valley from canyon land are soil quality and susceptibility to erosion. When colonists evaluate the agricultural prospects of a piece of land, they tend to speak first of its soil characteristics. They define many categories of soil, using texture and color as the basic criteria. These finer distinctions are not important here; the wide range is covered adequately under three main headings. The first kind of soil is found on the alluvial plains of major streams and rivers and is considered high in fertility and suitable for intensive cultivation. The native term for this land is *pampa* and it refers to the flat areas of the valley bottoms. The second variety of soil is found on the low, gentle slopes of both valleys and canyons and is composed of a mixture of old alluvial and colluvial deposits. This type of land, locally known as *falda,* is irregular in fertility but is suitable for a limited number of crops. A third kind of soil is encountered on the *laderas* or steep slopes (having gradients of fifteen degrees or more) of canyons and certain valleys. This soil is entirely residual, is low in fertility, and can be used for only a small number of crops, including coffee.

Much ladera land is too steep to be adapted to any form of cultivation.

Table 1 (see also Figure 2) shows the percentage distribution of the various soil zones. From these figures it is clear that the best farmland is in short supply, representing only 10 percent of the total surface area. Furthermore, if we combine the final two categories we can see that 70 percent of the land is either moderately steep and of low fertility or too steep to be cultivated. In this ladera zone coffee is the principal crop, largely because it is almost the only crop that will grow there. Soil characteristics, then, represent one of the crucial variables in the ecology of crop production. Other environmental factors, to be discussed below, also constrain the overall development of high jungle agriculture.

One of the most serious obstacles to successful farming in the ceja de montaña is erosion. The region's heavy rainfall and its uneven, mountainous terrain make erosion a constant threat. Under natural conditions, the thick jungle vegetation acts as a deterrent to soil loss. But when the rain forest is cut down and burned to prepare for the planting of crops, the land is left completely unprotected and erosion inevitably begins with subsequent rains. As a rule, the steeper the slope of the land, the more rapid and devastating is the erosion process. The various

Table 1. Approximate percentage distribution of major soil zones in the ceja de montaña

Soil zone	Percentage of total land area
Pampa	10%
Falda	20
Ladera (cultivable)	35
Ladera (noncultivable)	35
All zones	100%

SOURCE: ONERN (1962:78) and Varese (1974: 25).

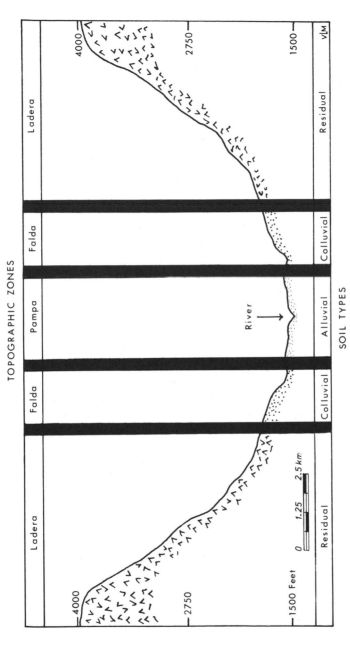

Figure 2. Topographic distribution of major soil types in the ceja de montaña.

49

Table 2. Degrees of susceptibility to soil erosion in the ceja de montaña and percentages of total land area affected

Degree of erosion	Approximate amount of soil loss (tons per hectare per year)	Percentage of total land area affected
Light	0–20	11.5%
Moderate	20–40	41.6
Severe	more than 40	46.9
All erosion		100.0%

SOURCE: ONERN (1962:85).

degrees of soil loss and the corresponding percentages of the total surface area affected are shown in Table 2.[2]

On the steeper slopes of the canyons and the upper valleys, where soil fertility is lowest, erosion is most destructive. This combination of factors severely limits the agricultural potential of the ladera zone. In fact, were it not for a few elementary measures employed by the farmers to impede erosion, the greater part of the ladera zone would be permanently destroyed by cultivation. Even with such measures (to be described later), the overall productivity of the land decreases year by year in a seemingly irreversible trend. The primary agent of this decline in soil fertility and consequently in agricultural production is erosion.

Another environmental variable that affects productivity and enters into the determination of ecological patterns is altitude. In the ceja de montaña altitudes range from about 1,300 to 5,000 feet above sea level. Over the short space of a few kilometers elevations may vary sharply, as between the lower and upper portions of a single canyon. Furthermore, even minor variations in altitude affect the kinds of crops that can be produced and may alter the growth cycle of the species. For example, corn can

[2]The table purports only to show different propensities for soil erosion when the forest is cleared and the land is exposed. The actual amount of soil lost varies not only according to the slope of the land but also according to the crop or crops planted.

be planted at any altitude but the growing period increases from three months at the lower elevations to six months in the higher zones. The longer maturation period is, however, compensated for by the fact that certain plagues and insects that attack the corn in low areas are absent at higher altitudes. Coffee, another basic high jungle crop, has the same annual growth cycle regardless of altitude but generally produces best in terms of quality and quantity at higher elevations. Bananas, in contrast, are better suited to cultivation in low areas, where temperatures are hottest.

Significantly, altitudes in all of the ceja de montaña are sufficiently low to free the area from the danger of frost. Above 5,000 feet occasional frosts occur, resulting in a totally different environmental configuration. Below the frost zone, temperature varies inversely with altitude, higher temperatures at lower elevations and vice versa, but the range of fluctuation is moderate. In addition, there is no appreciable seasonal variation in temperature. Thus altitude and temperature are constant, predictable elements in the high jungle ecology, a fact that helps the colonist to make decisions as to what to grow where and how. These kinds of stable, fixed environmental features are by far the easiest to deal with, even though they may limit agricultural development.

Not all environmental factors, however, are so consistent and predictable. Rainfall, one of the most critical variables in tropical forest ecology, is a case in point. Although a general rainy season–dry season cycle prevails in the ceja de montaña, as it does throughout the Amazon basin, irregular and unexpected shifts in this pattern frequently occur. Under normal conditions the rainy season begins in late October and ends in early April, with the most intense rains coming from December through March. The dry season begins in April and reaches its height in June, July, and August, eventually concluding in October. From December to the end of March there is seldom a day without rain, and often it rains for several days without stopping. During the dry season there may be one or two brief thunderstorms per week but mainly the days are dry and hot. This standard annual rainfall pattern can be seen clearly in the data presented in Table 3.

The definite rainy season–dry season cycle reflected in the precipitation data is not so consistent as might at first appear. For example, in any particular year the transition from dry to rainy weather may take place earlier or later than usual. Another common deviation from the "normal" situation is a rainy season that is exceptionally light or heavy. Thus in the Satipo region in 1973 the first rains came early (in September) and were followed by an extraordinarily heavy rainy season. The effect of the irregular weather on the crops of that year was disastrous. The coffee harvest, the mainstay of the local economy, was the poorest in recent history. The heavy rains prevented the coffee plants from flowering and developing properly, a process that should occur in the latter part of the dry season. Since coffee production and other agricultural activities in the high jungle are oriented to the normal cycle of seasons, unexpected shifts in this cycle are damaging and potentially devastating.

All of the other environmental variables discussed thus far— soil quality, erosion, altitude—also affect agricultural pro-

Table 3. Average monthly rainfall in Satipo, 1953–60 (in millimeters)

Month	Average precipitation
January	259
February	255
March	239
April	173
May	124
June	79
July	92
August	59
September	107
October	255
November	179
December	263
Annual average	2,084

SOURCE: ONERN (1962:35).

ductivity, but these factors are consistent and predictable, whereas rainfall is variable and unpredictable. These elements of certainty and uncertainty play separate and equally vital roles in the establishment of ecological relationships. The adaptation of jungle settlers to their environment consists first in knowing and adjusting to the constant elements in their surroundings, and second in developing strategies for survival during and after periods of abnormal climatic conditions. High jungle ecology is based on this twofold adaptive process. As we shall see, different populations have had different degrees of success in adapting to the ceja de montaña environment.

The Aboriginal Campa Ecosystem

The Campas or Asháninkas are one of the largest of the more than fifty native Indian groups of the Peruvian jungle. They inhabit a vast area of the central selva, including the basins and watersheds of the Apurimac, Ene, Perené, Satipo, Tambo, Upper Ucayali, and Pichis rivers. Estimates of the present Campa population range from 30,000 (Denevan 1972:62) to 45,000 (Varese 1972:11), but no accurate census figures are available. The Campas do not form a tribe, nor do they have any social or political groupings larger than local clusters of from one to six or seven conjugal families. They are best identified by a series of distinctive cultural attributes, a common language (a variant of the Arawak linguistic stock), and a term of self-designation, Asháninka, meaning "our people" or "ourselves." These features together distinguish the Campas from neighboring ethnolinguistic groups—the Machiguengas, Piros, Conibos, Cashibos, and Amueshas.

Except for a few remote settlements, all Campas now live in contact with colonist society and are incorporated in varying degrees into the national market economy. As a result, their aboriginal patterns of social and economic organization have been altered substantially. The effects of colonization on the Campas will be considered in a later chapter; here our concern is with the ecology of the native inhabitants of the high jungle before the opening of the region as a frontier zone. The following description of the aboriginal ecosystem is derived from older Campa informants now living in colonized areas who recalled and related to me how their people lived in precontact times.

Traditionally the Campas maintained a subsistence economy based on hunting, fishing, gathering, and the cultivation of a small number of crops. The population was both widely dispersed and highly mobile, a demographic pattern well suited to the exploitation of the natural resources of the region. The men hunted with bows and arrows, working alone or in small groups at night. Although success varied from season to season and from year to year, hunting was a constant activity that provided an essential part of the Campas' food supply. Fishing, in the form of large, organized fish poisonings, was practiced during the dry season. A group of families would join together to construct a dam, closing off a section of a stream where the fish would be trapped. A special poison called *cube* or *barbasco* was then put in the water to stun the fish, causing them to float to the surface. This was a highly effective technique that yielded large quantities of food at certain times of the year. The seasonal gathering of wild nuts, roots, and edible plants by the women was another Campa practice that, like hunting and fishing, played a vital part in the annual subsistence cycle. In general, the Campas seem to have achieved an ecological balance whereby a wide variety of environmental resources were consumed but were never so far depleted that they could not be regenerated.

The intermittent or seasonal nature of hunting, fishing, and gathering meant that food was plentiful at certain times and scarce at others. The Campas offset this irregularity in their food supply by cultivating *yuca* or sweet manioc (*Manihot utillisma*), a crop that could be harvested throughout the year. The advantage of cultivating yuca, a starchy tuber, was that once it reached maturity it could be harvested as needed and did not have to be consumed immediately to prevent spoilage. Fish and game, in contrast, spoiled within two days and could not be stored or preserved for future use. Yuca was harvested as early as eight months or as late as two years after planting; it was simply allowed to grow until needed. The storage potential of manioc and the unique adaptability of this crop to nutrient-deficient tropical soils (Morán 1976, 1979) contributed significantly to the adaptive success of the Campa population. Small-scale horticulture supplied the foodstuffs that filled the gaps between hunting, fishing, and gathering expeditions.

The Campas were highly skilled in the slash-and-burn and long-forest-fallow techniques of tropical horticulture. Although they possessed only a primitive technology consisting of stone axes and a few other tools, Campa men rapidly cleared small areas of jungle land for cultivation. Normally, garden sites were selected and cleared during the early part of the dry season. Platforms were built halfway up each large tree, where the diameter of the trunk is much smaller than at the base. The Campa men then felled the tree at this point, aiming it so that other trees would be toppled like dominoes. The felled trees and other vegetation were allowed to dry for several weeks before they were burned. A "good burn" was essential, because it was primarily the ashes that fertilized the new garden. Often several burnings were necessary to prepare the land properly for cultivation.

Amid the stubble and the scorched remains of scattered tree trunks, the Campas planted their crops. Although yuca was the principal crop, corn, beans, and peanuts were also cultivated, as were cotton and cube, the plant from which fish poison was obtained. The favored pattern was to mix these crops throughout the garden so that their particular nutrient requirements would be evenly distributed. Once planted, the garden was never weeded or reworked; the jungle was allowed to grow back and to take over the plot completely after all crops had been harvested. A new plot was cleared and planted long before the old garden stopped producing, so that a smooth transition and a stable food supply were ensured. A typical garden produced for a maximum of two years, after which it was abandoned and left in fallow for from eight to ten years or more. These short cultivation cycles and the long periods of fallow ensured the preservation of the rain-forest environment and the renewal of resources for later use.

The ecosystem described above must be understood within the context of a widely dispersed and highly mobile population. The basic units of Campa socioeconomic organization were local clusters of from one to as many as six or seven nuclear families united under a single headman (a respected elder male). Because of the social norm of uxorilocal residence, the local group often consisted of a man and his wife, their daughters, and their daughters' husbands and children. The various families of a local group usually did not form a village, but resided in a series of huts spaced from fifty to one hundred yards or more apart and connected by jungle trails. A Campa expression says that the members of a local group lived within "shouting distance" of each other. The members of a local group also cultivated a common garden and hunted and fished together. Tasks were delegated according to a well-defined division of labor (along age and sex lines) that structured the subsistence cycle on which all depended.

The local groups were scattered throughout Campa territory, with at least half a day's walk separating one settlement from its nearest neighbor. This population dispersal was essential to the Campas' mode of interaction with their environment. They preferred to live close to their supplies of game and fish, and since these resources became scarce as population density increased, local groups tended to divide and disperse once a maximum size (approximately forty to fifty people) was reached. A balance between population and resources was maintained by the even distribution of each across the high jungle terrain. Large, concentrated settlements were unknown and would have been completely inconsistent with the Campa view of ecology.

Just as there were no large settlements, neither were there any stable or permanent ones. The Campas were a highly mobile people who seldom lived in a single place for more than three or four years at a time. Many factors could lead to a change in residence, only some of which are directly ecological. A steadily diminishing yield in hunting and fishing activities would cause a local group to search for a new settlement site with more plentiful resources. When a new residence was found, gardens were begun in that area; the actual move usually occurred after these gardens entered into production. Another environmental factor that often caused a local group to abandon its territory was malaria. At the lower elevations of the ceja de montaña, malaria was a serious problem that could greatly weaken a population long exposed to its attacks. The Campas frequently moved to higher altitudes (above 3,000 feet) for limited periods to escape and recuperate from the effects of malaria. The mosquitoes that carried malaria did not exist at these higher elevations. There seems to have been a general tendency to migrate back and forth between malarious and nonmalarious zones.

Sociocultural as well as ecological factors caused Campa groups to resettle from time to time. In Campa culture a kind of taboo fell on the hut and the entire settlement in which a person had died. Thus local groups normally abandoned and burned their homes after the death of one of their members. In some cases a very sick person would be taken away to die in a remote spot where he or she would not contaminate the settlement. Usually, however, a death within the local group was followed by collective migration to a new area. Factional disputes within the local group also brought about resettlement; the hostile segments separated and moved to different regions. The Campas say that irreconcilable personality differences and unequal contributions to the communal work load were two major causes of conflict and group division. Undoubtedly, environmental and sociocultural factors often coincided in group decisions to migrate. If a death occurred at a time when the local group was suffering heavily from malaria, the group would honor both sociocultural and environmental principles by abandoning its settlement for a site at a higher altitude.

The overall impression one gains of the Campas in their aboriginal condition is that there was a close congruity or adaptive fit between sociocultural and ecological systems, a pattern that had been worked out over thousands of years in the high jungle environment. Campa sociocultural organization reflects a fundamental understanding of the need for balance between population and environment in the tropical forest. Perhaps one exaggerates this harmony when looking backward from the modern perspective of the havoc wrought on the high jungle environment (and on the Campas) by colonization. Nevertheless, the aboriginal ecosystem seems to have been remarkably successful in simultaneously using and preserving environmental resources in an economy of subsistence.

The Colonist Ecosystem

Pioneer settlement of the Satipo region began in the late 1920s, when a group of Franciscan missionaries opened a trail from the monastery of Santa Rosa de Ocopa, in the central highlands, to the missionary station of Puerto Ocopa, in the ceja de montaña. The Franciscans, who had been violently expelled from Campa territory in the famous Juan Santos Atahualpa revolt of 1743 (Lehnertz 1972, Varese 1973), hoped that colonization would help them to reestablish a base of operations among the hostile Indians. The first pioneer families were recruited in Lima and brought to the Franciscan monastery, where they began the six-day walk to the newly founded colony of Satipo. By 1930 more than two hundred families had settled in Satipo and plans were being made to widen the existing trail into an all-weather road that would further open the region for colonization. The full history of the colony will be discussed in a later chapter; my purpose here is to explain the ecological transformation that took place as colonization progressed.

In contrast to the nomadic Campas, the new inhabitants of the high jungle settled permanently on plots of land that they owned. According to Peruvian law, all jungle lands belonged to the state (the national government) but could be claimed by individuals and purchased for a small fee. In 1928 the Peruvian government established a land office in Satipo to receive *denun-*

cios (land claims) and to issue titles. Thus the principle of private landownership was introduced at the earliest stage of colonization. This principle proved to be a primary determinant of the emerging ecological order of frontier society.

As settlers arrived, they began to populate the area surrounding the small town of Satipo, the administrative and commercial center of the region. Each new group of immigrants extended the frontier by settling beyond the previous limits of the colony, in areas where free or unclaimed land could be found. Trails were built to the earliest settlement sites and then extended by later groups of colonists who claimed land beyond those sites. Each colonist family lived on its own property, where the family members constructed a house and cleared land for cultivation. No towns or nucleated settlements were formed by the farmers. Rather, a pattern evolved in which the farms or *chacras* of the colonist families were spread out along a line of communication—a trail, a primitive road, or a river—with houses spaced at least two hundred yards apart. This lineal settlement pattern developed spontaneously as a mechanism of frontier expansion and continues to the present day.

The lineal pattern stands in sharp contrast to the radial settlement scheme characteristic of farming communities in highland Peru and in most peasant societies. In a radial settlement, households are clustered in villages and agricultural lands surround the community in a broad circle. Farmers live in town and travel to and from their fields each day. In a lineal settlement, households are scattered along the routes of communication and each farm family lives and works on a single plot of land. The population is highly dispersed (though sequentially arranged) and communities are vaguely defined.[3] The distinctive forms of the lineal and radial settlements can be seen in Figure 3.

[3]A different form of dispersed settlement is found in the Peruvian *altiplano* (high plains above 12,000 feet in elevation), where herders are widely scattered in order to make efficient use of the available pastureland. Houses (which in this transhumant culture are often only temporary shelters) are dispersed in scattershot fashion. Communication in the altiplano occurs across open terrain and is not confined to a few well-traveled routes (as is the case in the montaña).

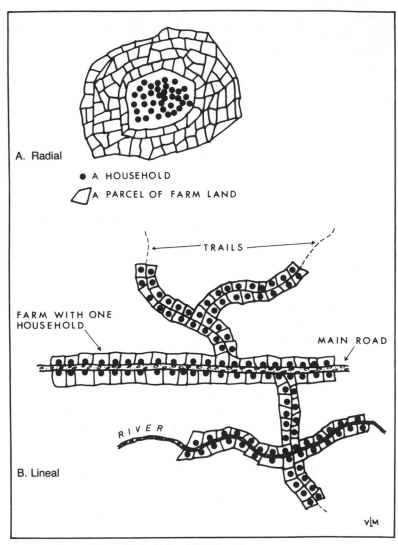

Figure 3. Radial and lineal settlement patterns.

60

Like the private ownership of land, the lineal arrangement of homesteads formed part of the new ecology of frontier society. This new ecology was basically one of permanent settlement and intensive exploitation of the environment. In contrast to the Campas, the colonists sought to alter the environment in order to build a stable farming economy oriented to market demands. New crops were introduced, as were new techniques of cultivation which have often damaged the environment. The colonists have depleted soil and other natural resources with little regard for their replenishment or restoration. An overall strategy of development and resource use has been lacking, a condition that is more true of the Satipo colony today than at any other time in its history. Nevertheless, the colonist ecosystem has certain patterns and consistencies that deserve careful examination.

Colonists exploit the environment by means of two different systems of agriculture. The first is the standard slash-and-burn, shifting cultivation system practiced in tropical forest environments throughout the world. Corn, rice, beans, yuca, peanuts, and a few vegetables are produced by this method. The second is a system of permanent cultivation of tree crops (coffee or fruit) that require special planting and maintenance techniques. Nearly all jungle settlers practice both kinds of farming and can cite the advantages and disadvantages of each. They can also discuss the environmental changes that take place as a result of each farming method. An analysis of the interaction between population and environment via these two agricultural systems reveals the major ecological problems of colonization.

The colonist version of slash-and-burn cultivation is similar in some of its general features to the Campa version. In the middle of the dry season an area of jungle land is selected as a garden site and then cleared. The cut trees and undergrowth are left to dry for several weeks in the hot sun before they are burned. The ashes that remain after burning mix with the soil and improve the garden's fertility. Crops are then planted and left to grow with little or no further cultivation. Weeds, vines, and shrubs take over the garden within a year or two, but by that time the crops have been harvested and the plot has been abandoned. In order to maintain a stable food supply, a new garden site is selected, cleared, burned, and planted before the old plot is deserted. Old garden sites are often reused, but only after a period of fallow during which the soil regains some of its lost nutrients.

In certain other respects the colonist slash-and-burn system differs greatly from Campa practice. Most important, the colonist system is not associated with a shifting or migratory settlement pattern. Colonists live permanently on the land they own and do not move when one garden is abandoned and a new one begun. To the extent possible, colonists rotate garden sites within their property in order to allow for periods of fallow between cultivations. Ideally, colonists will have at any one time only part of their land under cultivation and the greater part in fallow. Unfortunately, this ideal is seldom achieved for lack of sufficient amounts of land to permit optimal garden rotation.

In fact, most colonists cannot afford to rest their land for more than two or three years between cultivations. Under the Campa slash-and-burn system, as we have seen, land was allowed to lie fallow for from eight to ten years or more. The shorter fallow period allowed by colonists means that the *purma* or secondary jungle growth never regains a forest-like condition before it is cut and burned to prepare for another planting. This short fallow cycle places an excessive drain on soil resources that results in steadily decreasing agricultural productivity. Although colonists realize the advantages of the long fallow cycle, they do not have enough land to maintain such a system effectively.

It is impossible to calculate exactly how much land a colonist family would need in order to practice the long-forest-fallow system. The amount would vary according to the type of land (pampa, falda, or ladera), the crops to be grown (corn, for example, depletes soil minerals more rapidly than yuca), the size of the family, and other factors. Depending on these variables, as little as thirty or as much as one hundred hectares of land would be required for an average family farm. For reasons to be considered later in a discussion of land tenure, a majority of Satipo's colonists own less than thirty hectares and therefore cannot balance their immediate subsistence needs with the long periods of fallow required for maximum agricultural yield. Thus in many parts of the Satipo region one observes a general downward spiral in which short periods of fallow cause lower productivity, which creates greater food scarcity, which leads to the replanting of land after even shorter periods of fallow. In this vicious ecological cycle both the human and the environmental elements suffer.

The short-fallow slash-and-burn system may eventually so weaken the soil that the original rain-forest vegetation can no longer be regenerated. Farmlands that are abandoned after being totally depleted are usually covered by tall grasses and shrubs rather than by a regrowth of the natural forest. This process is occurring in only a few parts of the Satipo area today, but undoubtedly it will become a more serious problem as colonization advances. The long-range environmental impact of the growth of savannah grass at the expense of forests is as yet unknown. But it is almost certain that such factors as the weather, including the all-important seasonal rainfall pattern, will be affected.

The other system of agriculture practiced by colonists, the permanent cultivation of tree crops, has also altered the high jungle environment, adding to the complex ecological problems of colonization. All of the major commercial or cash crops of the Satipo region—coffee, bananas, papayas, citrus fruits, avocados, and cacao—are grown under the permanent cultivation system. This method of agriculture begins much as the slash-and-burn system; an area of jungle land is selected and then cleared and burned to prepare for planting. But the tree crops that are planted (unlike corn, beans, and yuca) have long, successive maturation cycles and develop into stable groves or orchards. These orchards are reworked and weeded regularly and are not abandoned after harvest or allowed to lie fallow. The first harvest comes as early as nine months (in the case of bananas) or as late as four years (in the case of coffee) after planting. Subsequent harvests may occur annually (coffee and avocados), semiannually (citrus fruits and cacao), or perennially (bananas and papayas).

The most important of the cash crops grown under the permanent cultivation system is coffee. One of the distinct advantages of coffee is that it produces well on the mountain slopes (the ladera zone), where other crops grow poorly if at all. In fact, the term "coffee soil" is used by colonists to refer to the reddish, highly acidic, low-fertility soil of the steeper mountain slopes. Coffee is also the only crop that provides a defense against the serious problem of erosion in the ladera zone. Since coffee must receive minimal sunlight, the fields are covered with shade trees, which serve not only to block the sun with their leaves and branches but also to impede erosion with their deep roots. Thus, owing in part to its unique adaptability to the adverse conditions of the mountain-slope environment, coffee has become the primary crop of the permanent cultivation system.

The yearly round of farming activities in the high jungle is closely oriented to the production cycle of coffee. The work year begins in May or June, when the coffee trees are cleaned of all berries remaining from the previous harvest and then pruned. Pruning improves production by making the coffee tree sprout new branches each year. Immediately after pruning the entire coffee grove is weeded, the first of three weedings spaced four months apart. By July or August, the height of the dry season, the coffee trees are ready for the application of fertilizer and insecticide. Since coffee groves are never fallowed, artificial fertilizer must be added yearly to replenish soil nutrients. Urea is the fertilizer most commonly used. Insecticide is equally necessary in coffee production, since insect pests, especially a variety called *la broca,* can severely damage the crop. Once treated with insecticide, the coffee trees are left to bud and flower, a process that normally takes place from August to October. By November small green berries have formed; they will grow and ripen during the central part of the rainy season.

The harvest begins in late February or early March, when the first berries reach maturity and are ready to be picked. The initial phase of the harvest is called *la rebusca* and involves the gathering of the few scattered berries that ripen early. By middle or late March the first full maturation stage is reached and as much as half of the coffee crop ripens at once. During this phase, called *primera mano,* the colonist must hire outside laborers to assist in the urgent task of picking the red berries before they become overripe and fall off the trees. The second and third maturation stages, *segunda mano* and *tercera mano* respectively, occur later (in April and May) and also require intense efforts to harvest the ripe berries before they are lost. In June the harvest concludes with the *raspa,* or final collection of all remaining red and green berries.

Throughout the harvest the coffee must be processed as it is picked. Almost as much work is involved in the various stages of coffee processing as in the harvest itself. The berries must first be soaked in a water tank, then hulled, washed, and finally dried for three days in the sun. Consequently, each coffee grower needs a wooden or concrete water tank, a small hulling machine, and a few sheets of plastic or a concrete platform on which to dry the coffee. The size and complexity of the processing plant depend on the amount of coffee produced. Usually the family members process the berries themselves and hire migrant laborers to do the actual harvesting.

This annual production cycle of coffee sets the basic rhythm of farm life in Satipo. During periods of intense activity (such as the harvest), colonists devote all of their time to the coffee crop. In the slack periods of the coffee cycle colonists generally cultivate other crops for subsistence and for sale. As we have seen, some of these latter crops (such as corn, beans, and manioc) are grown under the short-fallow slash-and-burn system. But others are grown, like coffee, by permanent cultivation techniques.

The primary difference between coffee and the other crops of the permanent cultivation system is that only coffee will produce on the steeper mountain slopes (which represent 70 percent of the total surface area). The other permanent crops—bananas, papayas, citrus fruits, avocados, cacao—must be planted in the valley bottoms and on the lower slopes (the pampa and falda zones). Only the best farmland can sustain the high nutrient requirements of these crops. And even on the best farmland, the building and maintenance of stable fruit groves or orchards is a complex, problem-ridden undertaking.

Typically, fruit trees yield good harvests for the first few years after they enter production. But soon thereafter production levels begin to drop sharply as soil minerals are depleted and as plant diseases spread. By the third year colonists must begin regular fertilization and fumigation of their fruit trees if they hope to maintain previous yields.

The case of bananas, the most important of the fruit tree crops, illustrates this problem. Banana trees produce their first cluster of fruit approximately nine months after planting and yield two clusters per year from then on. Soon after the second year of production, however, the banana trees begin to yield fruit in increasingly smaller clusters. This decrease in productivity is due to soil exhaustion and to the effects of several plant diseases. At this point the colonist must decide either to abandon the banana grove or to invest in the fertilizer and insecticide necessary to maintain a satisfactory level of production. Usually the latter course of action is taken, since the costs of starting a new banana crop would be greater than the expense of preserving an old one. The life of a banana grove may be extended from six to ten years by constant fertilization and fumigation.

The same basic pattern of development holds for the other fruit trees of the permanent cultivation system. The major problems of soil exhaustion and disease begin in the second or third year of production and grow steadily worse unless remedial measures are taken. In many cases solutions are found, but in others the remedy is either unknown or too expensive. For example, a common disease that attacks citrus and avocado trees, called *la tristeza* (literally, "the sadness"), attacks in the third or fourth year of production and causes the tree to lose all of its leaves, turn barren, and die. This disease is poorly understood and as yet no remedy has been found. Scattered throughout the Satipo region today are dozens of once productive citrus groves that were ruined by la tristeza.

Other diseases, some as severe as la tristeza, compound the problems of growing fruit crops under the permanent cultivation system. Even coffee, which was relatively free of disease as recently as ten years ago, is now plagued by several kinds of fungus and insect pests. The humid, frost-free environment of the high jungle is ideal for the spread of these crop diseases. Furthermore, as fruit groves develop and exhaust soil resources, the trees become weaker and more susceptible to disease. So serious is the problem that colonists often lose as much as 50 percent of each year's harvest to various crop diseases.

It should be clear by now that the permanent cultivation system is poorly adapted to the high jungle environment. The development of stable or intensive agriculture is made exceedingly difficult by the rapid growth of weeds, soil exhaustion, and crop diseases. Significantly, these same problems are avoided under the shifting slash-and-burn system, in which short cycles of cultivation allow crops to be harvested before weeds, soil depletion, and diseases set in. Moreover, the fallowing of land, a standard phase of slash-and-burn practice, restores nutrients to the soil and eliminates the need for artificial fertilization, a major expense of the permanent cultivation system. On the whole and given the constraints of the high jungle environment, the slash-and-burn method is undoubtedly a more viable agricultural system than permanent cultivation.

As we have seen, however, the success of the slash-and-burn system depends on the resting or fallowing of land between cultivations. If the periods of fallow are too short, not only is the agricultural yield diminished, but also an ecological imbalance is created which leads to general environmental deterioration. Such is the case with the colonists' form of slash-and-burn cultivation; two or three years of fallow are not sufficient to regenerate the land's exhausted resources or to restore environmental equilibrium. The problem is essentially one of wastefulness and mismanagement on a large scale; there is no comprehensive plan for coordinating population settlement with resource distribution. As a result, the colonists' landholdings are currently too small to permit proper rotation of gardens and adequate periods of fallow.

Nevertheless, the slash-and-burn system can be an effective method of tropical agriculture when a few basic rules of environmental preservation are followed, a conclusion supported by scientific research in the area of rain-forest ecology. Once considered a primitive or incipient farming technique, swidden agriculture is now seen by the scientific community as an ingenious adaptation to the fragile rain-forest environment (e.g., Meggers 1971, Geertz 1963a, Lathrap 1970). According to Geertz (1963a:16), "in ecological terms, the most distinctive positive characteristic of swidden agriculture ... is that it is integrated into and, when genuinely adaptive, maintains the pre-existing natural ecosystem into which it is projected, rather than creating and sustaining one organized along novel lines and displaying novel dynamics." It is generally believed that slash-and-burn activities, if properly administered, can sustain moderate agricultural yields without harming the environment or permanently depleting the natural resource base. The key to this equilibrium is, of course, the fallow cycle. Ecologists warn that if population density exceeds the carrying capacity of the land, old plots are recultivated too soon and an irreversible process of environmental deterioration begins.

The question, then, is at what level of human exploitation environmental degradation sets in. Although the problems of population density and the carrying capacity of the tropical forest have been much discussed by anthropologists, precise figures are difficult to obtain. A few formulas have been devised for calculating carrying capacity (e.g., Carneiro 1956, Conklin 1959). These formulas incorporate such factors as the necessary fallow period, the amount of land needed to feed one person, and the total amount of available land. Robert Carneiro applies his formula to the Kuikuru Indians of central Brazil and shows that the home territory of this tribe could actually support a population more than ten times its present size without damaging the environment (Carneiro 1956:232). In general, the aboriginal tropical forest peoples of South America, including the Campas, seem to have maintained such low population densities that only a fraction of the potential carrying capacity of their land was realized.

In theory, then, colonization of the Satipo region could have been carried out without disrupting the Campa subsistence cycle and without exceeding the carrying capacity of the land. In fact, colonists destroyed the Campa ecosystem and grossly exceeded the carrying capacity of the land by introducing cash crops. The market orientation of the colonists, together with their wasteful and inept farming methods, largely accounts for the environmental deterioration evident in the Satipo region today. The population of the tropical forest has not merely increased as a result of colonization; there has been a profound change in the patterns of land use and a redefinition of the goals of human activity. To understand Satipo's rapidly changing ecology it is necessary to comprehend not only the demography but also the ideology of frontier expansion.

Colonists overcultivate their land for a variety of reasons. Because of the scarcity of land that is accessible by road, and hence suitable for cash crops, most settlers are unable to acquire the minimum amount of land needed to practice a stable form of swidden cultivation. As stated earlier, this minimum amount ranges from thirty hectares of good land to one hundred hectares of poor land. In addition, many colonists are simply indifferent to the problem of agricultural proficiency. The exigencies of day-to-day survival supersede the need for long-term planning and efficient resource use. Finally, the colonists of Satipo are not unlike the frontier settlers of other nations and other eras in that they view the land and its resources as plunder to be exploited. Their carelessness comes from a conviction that new forests always remain to be conquered. Thus, until the natural resources of El Dorado are exhausted, the process of colonization seems destined to pursue its present reckless course.

This gloomy prediction is not based solely on the evidence from Satipo. Reports from other colonization zones in Peru (Wesche 1971, Martínez 1969, CENCIRA 1973) and Brazil (Davis 1977, Sioli 1973, Goodland and Irwin 1975) indicate that similar ecological problems arise whenever the rain forest is tampered with. One of the oldest colonization zones in the Amazon rain forest, the Bragantina area, east of Belém in Brazil, provides an excellent example of the long-term effects of uncontrolled slash-and-burn agriculture. This area was colonized between 1883 and 1908 (Davis 1977:142) and has been cultivated continuously by the short-fallow method since that time. During this period the farmers have destroyed the forest and converted the Bragantina zone into what one observer has called a "ghost landscape." As a result of this devastation, "today, the Bragantina is covered by a monotonous expanse of unproductive secondary growth, lateritic sandstone, and rock. The soils in this region can no longer hold water, and droughts are much longer than they were in the past. With one of the largest populations in the state of Pará, the Bragantina is now considered to be a 'semi-desert,' a region whose lands have diminished yearly and whose soils have ceased to produce" (Davis 1977:143).

Reports of similar ecological disasters in other parts of the South American tropical forest are growing in number (Denevan 1973, MacNeil 1972). Some ecologists confidently predict that if present trends continue, the Amazon rain forest will have ceased to exist by the end of this century. It will have been replaced, according to Denevan (1973:130), by grassland and scrub savannah, with some secondary forest growth. At this point in the process of environmental deterioration it will no longer be possible to regenerate a mature rain forest. The "green desert" of scrub growth and savannah will become, in effect, a stable ecosystem. This outcome is virtually ensured unless tight controls are placed soon on the settlement and exploitation of the rain forest.

At various times and in various ways the South American nations with tropical forest territories have attempted to control or direct the colonization process and to implement a rational program of rain-forest development. The Peruvian government has recently sponsored at least three controlled colonization projects, none of which was adequately financed or effectively managed (Wesche 1971). Brazil in the early 1970s undertook a much more ambitious program of rational settlement in which planned communities were established at specified intervals along newly opened highways. This scheme, which sought to create thousands of small but efficient family farms, was abandoned in 1975 in favor of a colonization program that simply awards enormous tracts of undeveloped jungle land to large agribusiness enterprises and multinational corporations (Davis 1977, Wood and Schmink 1978). The Brazilian minister of planning argued in 1975 that "the necessity to avoid a predatory occupation, with a consequent process of deforestation, and to promote the maintenance of ecological equilibrium, leads us to invite large enterprises to assume the task of developing the [Amazon] region" (cited in Wood and Schmink 1978:18–19).

The agribusiness and multinational firms have proven, however, to be as indifferent as peasant frontiersmen to the question of ecological stability. Vast tracts of virgin forest have been damaged or destroyed by commercial timber operations. Even greater damage has been done by cattle ranchers who use chemical herbicides rather than traditional slash-and-burn methods to clear lands and establish pastures (Davis 1977:147). Virtually unregulated by the Brazilian government, the foreign and domestic companies that have obtained land concessions in the Amazon basin are rapidly destabilizing an ecosystem whose demise would have worldwide climatic repercussions.

From an ecological point of view, Peru would be unwise to adopt the Brazilian policy of favoring capitalist enterprises over

family farms. This strategy would only accelerate the deforestation process and bring the Peruvian montaña dangerously close
to the ecological point of no return. Scientists have consistently
held to the view that the key to an ecologically sound development policy for the Amazon basin will be found not among the
modern concepts of corporate planning, but among the indigenous concepts of land and resource management. Though
Satipo's farmers are reluctant to admit it (for reasons that will
become clear in later chapters), they have repeatedly tapped the
Campas' vast knowledge of the rain forest in learning to cope
with their new environment. The problem, as we have seen, is
that the ideologies of frontier expansion and native subsistence
are fundamentally opposed. A resolution of the conflict at this
level, without which the colonization effort is doomed, remains a
remote possibility unless and until the point of no return is
reached.

3

Microcosm and Macrocosm

We have seen that the changing ecology of Satipo is part of a continuing response by colonists to market fluctuations. As the farmers receive information from Lima and abroad concerning the present and future prices of their crops, they make production decisions that invariably affect the environment. The patterns of land use and agricultural production in Satipo are largely determined by external market considerations. Local ecological relationships are encompassed by and integrated with an economic system of national and international dimensions.

Consider, for example, the effect of a sharp increase in the international market price of coffee on the ecology of crop production in Satipo. As rising prices create a rush to clear and plant more land in coffee, colonists ignore the established standards or conventions in the cultivation of that crop. As noted earlier, coffee is normally grown on the steeper mountain slopes, where it produces best in terms of quality and quantity. But when market conditions are favorable, colonists plant coffee on the flat valley bottoms (pampas) and on the lower slopes (faldas) as well. These areas, which represent the region's best farmland, are usually reserved for the cultivation of subsistence crops. During a boom period in the coffee industry, however, cash cropping almost entirely replaces subsistence farming as the region slides toward a monocrop economy. During the worldwide coffee boom of the 1950s, Satipo's agricultural system was transformed in precisely this manner.

Another result of what colonists refer to as the *fiebre del café* (coffee fever) of the 1950s was a fundamental change in the patterns of landownership in Satipo. Before the coffee boom, small family farms rarely exceeding fifty hectares were the basic units of agricultural production. But when coffee prices began to soar, wealthy investors from the coast of Peru became interested in the Satipo region for the first time and began to buy and accumulate lands for the purpose of developing coffee plantations or estates. Landholdings of from 100 to 1,000 hectares became common as large tracts of virgin land were purchased from the government and as some small farms were absorbed into the growing estates. An elite of prominent coffee growers formed and soon came to monopolize the region's farmland and to dominate the social and economic life of the Satipo community.

The international coffee boom of the 1950s obviously had a profound impact on local patterns of land tenure and land use. Other examples of the transforming effects of larger, outside forces on the Satipo colony could be cited. The point to be made here is that in the study of this small, remote frontier settlement the question of context is crucial. Thus the parameters of our investigation must be broad enough to encompass the vast network of ties that extend from the little community to such distant centers as the North American and European coffee markets. Any less comprehensive system of analysis would be inadequate to the task of explaining the complex processes of change and development in a frontier microcosm. In this chapter the interlocking of macrosystem and microsystem will be examined from a historical perspective, beginning with the earliest attempts at exploration and settlement and proceeding to the present day.

Early History of the Eastern Frontier

No sooner had the Spaniards completed their conquest of the Inca state and divided the spoils of victory than their attention turned to the vast, unknown jungles lying east of the Andes. In this region, legend proclaimed, a golden civilization called El Dorado could be found. Numerous expeditions set out to find the land of unbounded wealth but all ended in disaster. The debilitating heat, the bothersome insects and diseases, and the hostile Indian groups of the jungle turned back even the most determined explorers. Nothing, however, seemed to tarnish the myth of a land of untold wealth hidden in the depths of the eastern rain forests. For roughly three hundred years, from the mid-sixteenth to the mid-nineteenth century, successive expeditions of fortune seekers tried in vain to locate the elusive El Dorado.

The only other activity of note during this period is the work of Catholic missionaries among the indigenous peoples of the jungle. The Jesuit and Franciscan orders founded their first jungle missions in the early seventeenth century and continued to build new bases of operations as they established contact with various Indian groups. The Campa Indians, who lived in the vicinity of present-day Satipo, were first contacted by the Franciscans in 1635. From the very beginning, however, the Campas were hostile to missionary activity. In fact, during the seventeenth and early eighteenth centuries mission stations were burned and razed by the Campas as fast as the Franciscans could construct them (Alan K. Craig 1972:130).

Although the Franciscans did manage to gain a foothold in Campa territory during the 1730s, they were expelled once again in a violent uprising in 1743. Several inconclusive studies of this rebellion (e.g., Lehnertz 1972, Varese 1973) indicate that it was led by a mestizo named Juan Santos Atahualpa, who claimed to be a direct descendant of the last Inca ruler and whose mission was to liberate the Indian race and to reconstitute the Inca Empire. The millennial movement led by Juan Santos united the Campas with other lowland Indian groups in a successful campaign to destroy all Hispanic influence in the central montaña. The Franciscans were driven completely out of this part of the Peruvian jungle and did not return for more than a hundred years (Lehnertz 1972:123). From the mid-eighteenth to the mid-nineteenth century little contact occurred between the indigenous peoples of the central high jungle and Peruvian national society.

This long period of isolation was broken finally and definitively in the late nineteenth century when the rubber boom, the first in a long series of extractive boom-and-bust industries, swept across the Amazon region. The tapping of wild rubber trees in the upper Amazon basin began in the early 1860s and reached its height in the years between 1895 and 1912. Rubber was crucial to the development of heavy industry in the United States and Europe at the turn of the century and the Amazon basin contained the world's only supply of this vital raw material. When the seeds of Amazonian rubber trees were smuggled out of Brazil and used to start rubber plantations in Southeast Asia, however, the end of the boom era was ensured. As Asian rubber began to flood the international market after 1913, the previously inflated price of this raw material dropped precipitously and the gathering of rubber in the Amazon region became uneconomical.

The rise and fall of the rubber industry had a profound impact on the Campa Indians of the central montaña, as it did on all indigenous groups of the Peruvian jungle. One might think that the Campas should have been less affected than other groups by the rubber boom, since most of their territory lay in the high jungle or montaña while the rubber trees grew only in the lower elevations of the selva baja. But it was the Campas' labor, not their land, that the rubber tappers wanted. Native workers were badly needed by the various companies that had obtained large concessions of jungle land from the Peruvian government for the purpose of rubber extraction. Company owners used any means necessary to obtain native laborers, often conducting armed raids into Campa territory to capture and enslave the Indians.

A favorite tactic of the rubber companies in organizing slave raids was to take advantage of the traditional rivalries and enmities among the various Indian groups. Thus the companies would give rifles and ammunition to the Conibos, a group that had a long history of hostilities with the Campas, and then demand repayment in Campa slaves. Similarly, the Campas were furnished with arms to be paid for with Conibo slaves. Furthermore, factions within Campa society itself were manipulated by the rubber companies into attacking and capturing slaves from each other. This practice, which is discussed at length by Varese (1973:242–50), continued unabated throughout the rubber boom. Even today the Campas of Satipo relate the histories of several particularly fierce Campa chiefs who trafficked in the slavery of their own people.

Most of the captured Indians who were taken to the rubber-gathering camps of the low jungle never returned. The punishing work of rubber collection, along with numerous diseases and a constant food shortage, proved fatal to a majority of the workers. Many more Indian slaves died while attempting to escape from their armed overseers. Varese (1973:247) estimates that in the major centers of rubber production, such as the Putumayo River basin, about 80 percent of the indigenous population were wiped out. Although accurate figures are impossible to obtain, it appears that the Campa population was reduced by nearly half during the rubber boom. Had a fortuitous shift in the world market not caused the collapse of the Peruvian rubber industry, the Campas might well have been exterminated.

The rubber boom also marked the return of missionaries to the Peruvian jungle after an absence of more than a century. The Franciscans reentered the central montaña and Campa territory on the coattails, as it were, of the rubber companies. A comfortable and mutually beneficial relationship developed between the Franciscans and the rubber companies. The conversion of souls apparently was facilitated by the oppressive conditions of the rubber camps. Padre Sala, a Franciscan priest who traveled through the central montaña in 1896 and reported on the progress of the newly established missions in that area, declared: "Once the rubber tapper has subjugated the ferocious Indian at gunpoint, it is the opportune time for the missionary priest to enter and immediately offer him [the Indian] the services and consolations of our Holy Religion.... By means of terror and moderate punishment, they [the Indians] will be obliged to seek the piety of the missionary priest, and he, in turn, will be able to exercise his divine ministries upon those unhappy creatures" (quoted in Varese 1973:248–49; my translation).

Given this philosophy of salvation, it is not surprising that when the rubber industry collapsed, the Franciscans sought other means of preserving the subjugation of the indigenous population. Permanent colonization and settlement of the jungle by "civilized" Peruvians offered the best means to that end. Padre Sala himself suggested this course of action at the close of the nineteenth century: "If their [the Indians'] lands are colonized, they will be surrounded and absorbed, and thus obliged by force, if not by shame, to follow the customs of civilized peoples" (quoted in Varese 1973:249; my translation).

Such was the spirit in which the Franciscans began to promote the colonization of the central montaña. Several Franciscan expeditions set out to survey the various parts of this immense region and to select sites for future colonization projects. Thus in 1912 an expedition led by Monseñor Francisco Irazola journeyed up the Perené and Pangá rivers to the Satipo Valley. There they discovered a Campa settlement on a high plain on the left bank of the Satipo River. They immediately decided that this was an ideal locale in which to establish a center of colonization. Plans for the opening of the Satipo region to selected colonists were drawn up by Monseñor Irazola and taken to Lima for what he hoped would be government approval and support. In 1919 the Peruvian government passed a resolution that declared that all lands of Satipo and Río Negro (an adjacent valley) belonged to the state and that an "orderly colonization" would be carried out by the state in this area. Under these inauspicious conditions, the Satipo colony was officially born.

The Colonization and Settlement of Satipo

Long before Satipo was officially declared a colonization zone, a small number of pioneers had moved into the region to cultivate coca, a plant whose leaves are chewed by peasants of the sierra and the montaña for the purpose of alleviating hunger, thirst, pain, and fatigue.[1] The coca trade probably dates back to Inca and pre-Inca times (William Isbell 1968). Murra (1972) has documented the existence of four sixteenth-century trade networks that included coca as an important item of exchange. The available archaeological and ethnohistorical evidence indicates that for centuries small groups of highland settlers penetrated the montaña for the purpose of cultivating coca and introducing it into the vast trade networks that supplied widely dispersed populations with the products of diverse ecological zones. In its modern form the coca trade is carried out largely by highland peasants who migrate seasonally to the montaña in search of employment. These migrant laborers usually bring with them a sack of potatoes or other highland produce to exchange for coca (Burchard 1974). Though coca plays only a minor role in contemporary frontier agriculture, the settlement of the montaña

---

[1]Recent research indicates that coca leaves, though they contain the alkaloid cocaine, are a mild stimulant and are not, as was once believed, strongly addictive (Hanna 1976, Picón-Reátegui 1976). Moreover, there is growing evidence that coca chewing is an important adjunct of the high-carbohydrate diet of the Andean peasantry. Coca aids in the absorption of carbohydrates and prevents problems of carbohydrate metabolism (Burchard 1977). Vitamins A, B, and C are also derived from coca chewing, as are several alkaloids that reduce the production of red blood cells and thereby provide relief from the symptoms of a chronic form of high-altitude sickness known as polycythemia (Fuchs 1978).

by *cocaleros* (coca cultivators and traders) represents the earliest form of colonization.

It was the cocaleros who opened the first trails joining the highland and jungle regions of central Peru. The coca trade of central Peru was an established, prosperous enterprise in the early 1900s. In 1924, according to one informant who arrived in Satipo during that year, there were approximately thirty coca farms in the upper part of the valley and a constant flow of Quechua traders transported goods to and from the frontier zone.

The first state-sponsored colonists did not arrive in Satipo until 1926. The government of President Augusto Leguía had recruited these colonists in Lima, assuring them that if they agreed to settle in Satipo, they would receive an allotment of jungle land and would be provided with tools and food rations for the first few years. Most of the recruits were small farmers and craftsmen from the coast of Peru who were attracted by the vast supply of virgin lands in the montaña. None of the government settlers had ever seen the jungle, however, or had any notion of the hardships they would face. They were misled by the promoters of the colonization project, who described the Satipo region as a veritable El Dorado, a land of unlimited opportunity for the ambitious, hard-working farmer.

The enlisted colonists were assembled at the Franciscan monastery of Santa Rosa de Ocopa in the central highlands. From there they departed on foot for the newly founded government colony at Satipo, a journey of at least six days. To reach Satipo the colonists had to cross three separate mountain ridges at altitudes of 15,000 feet or more before finally descending into the montaña. Many migrants died en route from exhaustion and the extreme cold of the Andean nights; upon arriving in the jungle, others succumbed to the unaccustomed heat and tropical diseases (such as malaria). Though there was talk of building a motor road to facilitate transport to and from the frontier zone, this project was not to be completed for many years. The colonists who were fortunate enough to reach Satipo had little hope of turning back, since the return trip of roughly eleven days (all uphill) would have been impossible in their condition.

Between 1926 and 1929 some two hundred families settled in Satipo as government colonists. For a token fee each family received thirty hectares of choice jungle land along the flat plains of the Satipo and Río Negro valleys. The promised tools and food rations, however, proved to be inadequate. The colonists were forced to rely on their own resources from the very beginning, living by hunting and gathering in the jungle until their gardens began to produce. Even today the few remaining colonists from this era speak of the *gran engaño* (great deceit) of the Peruvian government and relate the various methods that the pioneers employed to survive during the colony's early years.

The overthrow of President Leguía (a strong advocate of frontier settlement) by General Luis Sánchez Cerro in 1930 marked the end of the government colonization program in Satipo. The small amount of aid that the colony had received up to that point was immediately cut off. Government plans for the expansion of the colony and for the construction of a road were canceled. The tenuous hopes that Satipo's settlers had held for the future of the colony were lost as it became clear that they would be completely abandoned by the Peruvian government. At least half of the pioneers deserted the colony under these dire conditions, leaving their houses and farms and returning to their original homelands. By 1932, according to a census taken by the designated head or chief of the colony,[2] only 121 families remained in Satipo.

The dismal situation of the colony did not improve until 1939, when a new government under the leadership of President Manuel Prado appropriated funds for the construction of a road to Satipo. Departing from the highland town of Concepción, the road crews advanced steadily and completed their work in 1941.

[2]The chief of the colony at this time was Teodoro Noriega, one of the region's first settlers. Noriega still lives in Satipo today, and much of my historical sketch of the colony's formative years is based on information he provided in several extensive interviews.

Once the road was opened, it was no longer necessary to recruit colonists for Satipo; new settlers arrived on their own account, attracted by the cheap lands and by the commercial opportunities of the frontier zone. The volume of land claims presented at the government land office increased rapidly after 1940 as the frontier expanded well beyond the original limits of the colony. Both agriculture and lumbering became profitable once the market centers of the highlands and coast became accessible by road.

Along with the boom in land sales and the expansion of the frontier in the early 1940s came an inevitable confrontation between the pioneers and the native Campas. Before that time, the Campas had simply retreated farther into the jungle to avoid conflicts with the settlers. With the new wave of immigrants, however, this strategy became increasingly difficult and unrealistic. As an alternative a few Campas resorted to open warfare, attacking and burning colonist farms and houses. But the majority soon came to accept the colonists' presence and sought to establish some form of peaceful coexistence with them.

The colonists, in turn, were eager to develop friendly relations with the Campas in order to exploit their labor potential. Normally, an agreement was reached by which the Campas were allowed to remain on land that a colonist had purchased as long as they were employed by that settler. According to the oral agreements that were made, the natives would receive some amount of merchandise (shotguns, machetes, metal pots and pans, mirrors, beads) in return for clearing and burning a designated area of land. Thus, for example, a group of twenty Campa men might agree to clear and burn ten hectares of land (about two months' work) in exchange for a shotgun and two machetes. Payment was never made in cash; utilitarian goods or trinkets were used to pay for the Campas' labor services. This system clearly worked to the colonists' advantage. The Campas were always underpaid and were easily deceived by colonists who decided not to deliver all of the goods they had promised. Such fraudulent practices were tolerated and even defended by local authorities, most of whom were landowners who committed these very abuses themselves.

The present generation of Campas explain that during that period of early frontier expansion they did not know how to defend themselves, did not fully realize that their lands and livelihood were being taken away, did not understand the ways of "civilization." The Campas' determination and ability to resist the colonists' invasion were further broken by a series of epidemic diseases (most damaging were measles, whooping cough, and tuberculosis) which greatly reduced the native population in both strength and numbers. Some natives once again chose to flee farther into the interior in order to escape the ravages of these diseases and to avoid the constant abuses of colonist society. Most Campas, however (including many of their influential leaders or headmen), favored accommodation with the colonists and commitment to a new, "civilized" way of life.[3]

Without the assistance of the Campas, the development of frontier civilization would have been impossible. Campa labor was cheap and also highly skilled in the techniques of slash-and-burn agriculture. The natives could clear an area of jungle land in half the time required by recent settlers, who were unaccustomed to this kind of work. In addition, the colonists learned from the Campas how to build jungle houses, how to plant crops, how to fish and hunt, and so on. Finally, the discovery in the United States of the industrial value of a plant that the Campas used as a fish poison led to the commercial cultivation of that plant by Satipo's colonists, an activity that sustained the frontier economy for more than twenty years.

The root of the barbasco or cube plant, from which the Campas obtained their fish poison, began to be cultivated commercially in Satipo about 1935. A few years earlier scientists in the United States had discovered that a valuable chemical called rotenone could be extracted from the barbasco root and used in

---

[3]The ideology of civilization and its use in day-to-day relations between the colonists and natives of Satipo are discussed in Chapter 5.

the production of insecticides. The price of barbasco on the international market began to soar in 1940, just as the road to Satipo was being completed. The lucrative market and the new route of access to it combined to stimulate Satipo's colonists to plant as much land as possible in barbasco. The colony's first boom crop also attracted new immigrants and boosted land sales throughout the early and middle 1940s. By 1947 Satipo was a small but prosperous community, exporting barbasco and a few lesser products such as lumber and coca in ever increasing quantities. The population of the colony had reached 5,000 (Ortiz 1961:317) and the prospects for continued growth and development were excellent.

The good fortune of the colony was suddenly reversed in November 1947, however, when a devastating earthquake struck the central high jungle region of Peru. The landslides produced by the earthquake buried the road to Satipo along its entire length, leaving the colony totally isolated from the market centers that were its livelihood. Colonist homes and chacras (cultivated fields) located along the road were also severely damaged. Virtually everything that the settlers had managed to build over a twenty-year period was destroyed in a few minutes.

When the full extent of the damage to the road had been assessed, the colonists realized that a major reconstruction project was needed and that only the national government would be capable of sponsoring such an undertaking. Representatives of the colony went directly to the Peruvian president, General Manuel Odría, to ask for his support in rebuilding the road. But General Odría was unsympathetic to the colonists' plight and refused to allocate funds for the project. This rejection was only the beginning of what was to become a frustrating thirteen-year campaign to obtain government funds for the reopening of the road to Satipo.

When it became clear that the road would not be immediately reconstructed, a group of colonists joined together and built an airstrip. An irregular air service to Satipo from San Ramón (the nearest jungle town connected by road to the coast) began in 1949. Although this system of transport was inadequate, it provided a means by which basic supplies (food staples, tools, medicines) could be brought in and the barbasco harvest taken out. But the further development of the colony could not be sustained by this tenuous air link. During the rainy season, months would pass when not a single plane was able to reach Satipo. A sense of isolation and despair grew in the colony and many settlers decided to leave, abandoning their farms and returning to their respective homelands.

The colonists who remained in Satipo survived by a combination of subsistence farming and the cultivation of barbasco for cash income. The high cost of air transport eliminated the market potential of all crops except barbasco and of course reduced the profits from the barbasco trade as well. Under these conditions a meager existence was the most that a colonist could hope for. As the years passed without any progress on the road reconstruction project, it appeared that the colony might have to be deserted altogether.

In fact, the death of Satipo seemed inevitable in 1953, when the world market price of barbasco suddenly fell by more than 50 percent. In that year an artificial substitute for rotenone, the chemical insecticide that was extracted from the barbasco root, was invented in the United States. The demand for barbasco by the industrialized nations decreased as rapidly as it had risen and the price dropped accordingly. Soon the selling price did not even cover the air-freight expenses incurred in bringing the product to market. Large fields of barbasco, representing substantial investments by Satipo's farmers, were simply abandoned. As fate would have it, however, a new boom crop emerged just as the barbasco industry began to falter, infusing new life in a moribund frontier community.

The Coffee Fever

During and shortly after the Korean War a worldwide scarcity of coffee drove prices sharply upward on the North American and European coffee markets (see Table 4). In Peru, as in most tropical and subtropical nations of Africa, Asia, and Latin

Table 4. Annual average prices of Peruvian coffee on the New York market, 1947–72 (in cents per pound)

Year	Average price	Year	Average price
1947	$0.27	1960	$0.34
1948	0.27	1961	0.31
1949	0.28	1962	0.30
1950	0.46	1963	0.30
1951	0.51	1964	0.42
1952	0.47	1965	0.39
1953	0.52	1966	0.38
1954	0.70	1967	0.40
1955	0.53	1968	0.40
1956	0.63	1969	0.41
1957	0.53	1970	0.53
1958	0.44	1971	0.45
1959	0.37	1972	0.50

SOURCE: Pan American Coffee Bureau (1966–72); statistics provided by U.S. Department of Commerce.

America, there was an immediate rush for lands suitable for coffee production. Virtually overnight the coffee boom radically transformed many small rural communities and frontier zones of the underdeveloped world. One such profoundly affected community was the Satipo colony.

Whereas the barbasco trade had never been lucrative enough to attract wealthy investors to Satipo, the coffee boom was a different matter. As the news reached Peru of the tremendous profits being reaped by Central American and Brazilian coffee growers, many commercial farmers began to acquire lands in the ceja de montaña for the purpose of forming coffee estates. Satipo, with its ideal climate for coffee cultivation and its abundance of cheap land, attracted a large number of new settlers. The lack of a road to the colony presented no serious obstacle, since the coffee could easily be taken out by plane. Thus began what is still referred to as the coffee fever, a phenomenon that redirected the course of frontier development and whose long-term effects can be seen in the complex problems of the Satipo community today.

The new colonists, convinced that El Dorado awaited them in

the montaña, purchased large tracts (from 100 to 1,000 hectares) of land sight unseen at government offices in Lima. Many were led to believe that roads or mule trails leading to their lands already existed or were under construction. But upon arriving in Satipo the settlers frequently discovered that their lands lay far from the established routes of communication and that the director of the local government land office could give them only vague instructions as to how to reach their "farms." Yet despite these setbacks few settlers lost hope, and in a short time new trails were cut and a spirit of optimism and prosperity came to prevail in the colony.

The opening in 1953 of a branch office of the Banco de Fomento Agropecuario further aided Satipo's economic recovery. Previously the state bank had maintained a strict policy of denying credit to Satipo's colonists. But the coffee fever seized financiers and farmers alike and suddenly millions of soles became available for the development of coffee plantations. The loan program introduced by the state bank supported all of Satipo's major coffee growers in their ambitious undertakings. The high initial costs of developing a coffee plantation made independent financing virtually impossible. Furthermore, since coffee trees mature slowly and produce their first full harvest in the fourth year after planting, the growers needed long-term credit of the sort that only a large bank could supply.

Thus it was primarily the credit system of the state bank that launched Satipo into the boom phase of coffee production. From the perspective of present conditions in the colony, however, one can see that this loan program has been and continues to be a dismal failure. Nothing seems to arouse the colonists' feelings of anger, bitterness, and frustration more than a discussion of the policies and practices of the state bank. If there is one point of unanimity among colonists, it is that the failings of the state bank are largely responsible for the depression and stagnation in which the Satipo community is presently mired. A close examination of the state bank's loan program reveals how this institution has come to be so universally despised.

When the first long-term loans for coffee cultivation were granted in 1953, two types of borrowing privileges were established. The first was designed for small-scale agriculture and allowed the colonist to borrow up to S/.50,000 (about $2,000) over a 4-year period. The second type of borrowing privilege was for large-scale agriculture and set no ceiling on the amount of money that a colonist could receive. Although the latter status was clearly the most favored one, no formal rules were announced to determine which individuals would qualify for such loans. Rather, it became common practice for preferred lending status to be accorded as the result of a deal, usually involving graft or influence peddling of some kind, arranged between the more prominent members of the new group of settlers and bank officials.

Without contacts or influence both at the local branch office and at the headquarters of the state bank in Lima (where all loans had to be approved), a farmer could not obtain preferred lending status. The new colonists who came to Satipo from the coast usually had such influential contacts, and consequently received the most generous loans. The older (and more experienced) colonists were fortunate to obtain credit as small-scale farmers; many were unable to borrow money at all. This fact caused great resentment and ill feeling toward the bank by a majority of Satipo's settlers. They realized that the large-scale coffee growers were being placed by the state bank at a distinct advantage over the small farmers of the region. The figures presented in Table 5 reveal the nature of this advantage. The large-scale farmers were granted nearly 80 percent of the total supply of bank credit even though they represented only one-third of the borrowing population. The other two-thirds of the borrowers, the small-scale coffee growers, received a mere 20 percent of the long-term credit provided by the state bank. A comparison of the average amounts of each type of loan further emphasizes the imbalance in the distribution of bank funds. Those colonists who had been designated small-scale farmers received an average of S/.27,221 each. The select group of

Table 5. Characteristics of loans granted by the Satipo branch of the Banco de Fomento Agropecuario to small-scale and large-scale farmers, 1953–60

Loan characteristics	Small-scale agriculture	Large-scale agriculture
A. Number of loans	309	173
B. Number of hectares worked with loans	1,522	2,984
C. Total value of loans	S/.8,411,400	S/.28,006,640
D. Average amount allotted per loan (C/A)	S/.27,221	S/.161,888
E. Average amount allotted per hectare (C/B)	S/.5,527	S/.9,386

Source: Data provided by ONERN (1962:143).

large-scale growers, in contrast, were allotted an average of S/.161,888 per person, with some loans exceeding S/.0.5 million.

The most significant statistic, however, is the different amounts allotted to the small and large coffee growers for each hectare of cultivated land. The costs to the farmer of establishing one hectare of coffee and preserving it until the first harvest are shown in Table 6. The total 4-year cost of approximately S/.9,033 per hectare (which includes the standard 12 percent annual interest charged by the bank) applied equally to all farmers. Yet the state bank maintained a policy of granting the large-scale growers nearly 70 percent more than the small farmers for each hectare of coffee planted. Thus the large growers, who received S/.9,386 per hectare (see Table 5), were able to meet (and slightly exceed) their costs of production while the small growers fell far short with only S/.5,527.

In effect, the small farmers were forced to reduce their expenses in such vital areas as the weeding of the grove and the application of insecticides, with the result that the normal development of the coffee trees was impaired and subsequent harvests were diminished. The large growers, with more borrowed money to invest in the development of their coffee crop, invariably obtained a much higher yield per hectare than the small farmers. In many other respects, too, the small growers were

Table 6. Approximate costs of establishing and maintaining one hectare of coffee from planting to first harvest, Satipo, 1950s

Year and item	Cost
First year	
Tools	S/.200
Clearing and burning of terrain	1,150
Planting	500
	S/.1,850
12% interest on average capital base	111
Total cost at end of first year	S/.1,961
Second year	
Debt carried over from first year	1,961
Three annual weedings	1,400
Purchase and application of fungicides	425
	S/.3,786
12% interest on average capital base	344
Total cost at end of second year	S/.4,130
Third year	
Debt carried over from second year	4,130
Three annual weedings	1,050
Purchase and application of fungicides	606
	S/.5,786
12% interest on average capital base	595
Total cost at end of third year	S/.6,381
Fourth year	
Debt carried over from third year	6,381
Three annual weedings	1,050
Purchase and application of fungicides	730
	S/.8,161
12% interest on average capital base	872
Total cost at end of fourth year	S/.9,033

SOURCE: Data provided by ONERN (1962:annex 4).

placed at a distinct disadvantage. The bureaucratic procedures required for approval of a loan were far more complex and time-consuming for the small farmer than for the influential large grower. And the state bank maintained a definite schedule of payments to the large-scale farmers but distributed funds to the small growers at irregular intervals, so that money was often unavailable to them when they needed it to complete vital tasks connected with the annual growth cycle of coffee. Finally, the state bank closely supervised and controlled the use of bank money by small farmers but rarely required any accounting by the major borrowers, so that large sums of agricultural credit were frequently put to unauthorized uses.

Obviously, the problems of the small-scale farmers were manifold and virtually insurmountable. In contrast, the privileged group of colonists, who were supported generously, if not excessively, by the state bank, had ample opportunities to profit from the coffee boom. While it is not surprising, then, that the small growers failed in their farming ventures and defaulted on their loans, it is somewhat puzzling that the large estate owners were equally unsuccessful. To be sure, in the long run it was the "bust" or rapid decline in the world market price of coffee after 1959 (see Table 4) that ruined Satipo's farmers, large and small. But even before the bust many of the large plantations had failed and gone bankrupt. It seems that part of the problem lay in the fact that many of the large growers spent little time in Satipo, continuing to enjoy the comfortable life of the coast while entrusting their farms to administrators, most of whom were salaried employees who were given no incentive (such as a percentage of the crop) to increase production. Other members of the local elite simply found that they could not produce as much coffee per hectare as they had anticipated and so abandoned their marginally profitable plantations and left the colony. Still others, taking advantage of the lack of loan supervision, maintained phantom farms in the montaña while investing their agricultural credit in more profitable and less risky business endeavors on the coast.

In short, through its lending policies the state bank planted the seeds of an agricultural system that could not flower. By granting almost 80 percent of its credit reserves to men who had come to Satipo as speculators or opportunists, the state bank carelessly squandered resources that might have been put to good use by the more qualified, experienced colonists of the region. Moreover, by fostering a monocrop system rather than attempting to diversify the frontier economy, the bank only wor-

Table 7. Principal crops produced under
the credit program of the Banco de Fomento
Agropecuario of Satipo, 1953–60

Crop or product	Percentage of total credit fund allotted
Coffee	86.0%
Oranges	5.2
Bananas	1.6
Pineapples	0.2
Cattle	7.0
All products	100.0%

SOURCE: Data provided by ONERN (1962:144).

sened the devastating impact of the market bust, which could
have been foreseen even at the height of the coffee fever. But by
1959, on the eve of the plunge in coffee prices that was to continue throughout the 1960s, Satipo was firmly entrenched in a
one-crop pattern. The figures presented in Table 7 reveal the extent to which the state bank encouraged dependence on coffee.

These figures reflect the policy of the state bank rather than
the interests of the colonist population. Many settlers claim that
in the late 1950s they became concerned about their overdepen-
dence on coffee and attempted to persuade bank officials to
provide more credit for the cultivation of tropical fruits, corn,
rice, and other crops. The colonists' hopes for greater crop diversification had been lifted by the resumption of efforts to re-
build the road to Satipo, a project that was completed in 1959.
The reopening of the road made possible the commercial production of a large number of crops that could not have been
marketed previously because of the high costs of air transport.
Despite the colonists' pleas, however, the state bank refused to
alter its basic policy and continued to make only token grants of
credit for crops other than coffee. Thus when the inevitable bust
in the international coffee market began, the Satipo colony was
caught in a hopeless position, committed by long-term credit
arrangements to a single crop that no longer yielded a profit.

Economic Depression and Agrarian Reform

The depression in the world coffee market, which lasted throughout the 1960s, had far-reaching consequences for the social and economic organization of the Satipo colony. The plantation system was shattered and the pieces that remained were picked up and distributed among a new wave of immigrants in a process that the colonists have come to refer to as "agrarian reform." The new settlers came primarily from the impoverished and overpopulated sierra west of Satipo, and they eagerly took over the abandoned and bankrupt coffee estates. But before proceeding to an explanation of the profound changes that have taken place in Satipo as a result of the fall in coffee prices and this spontaneous "agrarian reform," it is necessary to consider briefly the system of labor relations that evolved during the period of rapid growth in coffee production. This background should serve to illuminate a rather confusing series of later events.

The labor required for the development of the coffee industry in Satipo was of various kinds and came from various sources. First, workers were needed to clear and burn the jungle site that had been selected for the future coffee grove. Second, full-time laborers were sought to plant the seedlings and the accompanying shade trees and to perform the annual chores that would bring the grove to maturity over a four-year period. These men, usually called *mejoreros,* or improvers, were paid a certain amount per hectare of coffee cultivated. Third, temporary laborers were needed in large numbers for the annual coffee harvest. The harvesters, who were employed for from one to three months, were paid according to the quantity of coffee they gathered. As each worker brought in his day's harvest, the berries were measured in five-gallon cans and the worker was paid a set amount for each canful.

The first category of workers, those who cleared and burned the forest to prepare for planting, was composed primarily of Campa Indians. The Campas generally were hired under a verbal contract by which they agreed to clear a designated area of land in exchange for a given amount of merchandise (a system similar to that described earlier). In addition, the patrón often assisted the Campas in obtaining an area of land close to his farm where they could settle permanently. It was clearly in the colonist's best interest to have a group of Campas residing nearby, forming a pool of cheap and highly skilled labor that could be drawn on when they were needed. Thus a colonist would often donate land to the Campas or would assist them in securing a grant of land from the government office in Satipo. This action resulted in the formation of what are currently called "native reserves," small Campa communities scattered throughout the colonized zones. At one time the Indians of each of these now-independent settlements were bound in a kind of patron-client relationship to one of Satipo's prominent coffee growers.

The second class of workers, the mejoreros, was made up largely of peasants who had migrated from their native communities in the highlands to the montaña during the coffee fever. Most of these settlers had come to Satipo in the hope of finding land and, with credit from the state bank, starting their own farms. But because of the land monopoly of the coffee estates and the numerous problems connected with the state bank's loan program, many aspiring colonists did not find land or credit and were forced to seek employment from the minority who did. The mejoreros thus became the principal labor force behind the development of the coffee industry; it was they that planted and cultivated the coffee groves until the trees had reached maturity and produced their first harvest.

At harvesttime a third type of laborer was needed—the transient or seasonal farmhand who could be hired for the duration of the harvest and then released. Only a few of these workers came from the Satipo community itself; most were recruited from small highland Indian villages and brought to the montaña under an arrangement known as the *enganche*. The enganche system was basically quite simple. The landowner or, more often, his representative (the enganchador) went each year in

January or February to the highland districts closest to Satipo—Comas, Andamarca, Andahuaylas, Ayacucho—to engage from as few as ten to as many as one hundred peasants for the coffee harvest that would begin in March. The recruits were given enough money to pay for their transportation to and from the montaña as well as an advance on the wages they would earn there. The *enganchados* (as the contracted laborers were called) agreed to work for as long as three months, during which time they would receive their meals as well as their earnings for each five-gallon can of coffee beans they picked.

The success of the enganche system derived in part from its excellent timing. That is, the coffee harvest in the montaña took place between the planting and harvest seasons in the sierra, a period when the highland Indians were free to leave their communities and seek outside employment to supplement their annual incomes. Thus the peasants could migrate to Satipo after sowing their small subsistence plots in December and return to harvest them by May, earning in the meantime enough extra money to make it through the year. Another reason for the success of the enganche system was the relatively high wages paid by the coffee growers in the montaña. In 1960, for example, a common farmhand in the sierra earned about S/.5 per day while a coffee harvester was paid from S/.15 to S/.25 daily (depending on the amount of coffee beans gathered) plus meals. In short, the enganche system provided an opportunity for Indians from some of the most remote and impoverished areas of the Andean highlands to explore a new land, the montaña, and to earn some badly needed cash in the process. During the coffee fever thousands of highland peasants traveled to and from the Satipo region each year.

Mainly as a result of the experience gained by the peasant enganchados, news of the montaña and of the opportunities that existed there spread throughout the highland provinces closest to Satipo. Each year returning migrants brought back fresh information about the frontier zone—about the crops, the weather, the people—which stirred the interest of those who sought to escape from the hopeless poverty of the sierra. The reopening of the road to Satipo in 1960 greatly facilitated access to the colony and brought about even more interaction and communication between sierra and montaña. In subsequent years peasants from the highlands came to Satipo to look not only for seasonal employment but also for land of their own on which to settle and establish a farm. This new tide of immigrants grew steadily throughout the 1960s and continues to the present day.

Kinship networks played an important role in the resettlement process. An established colonist would provide food and shelter for his newly arrived relatives and would initiate their education in the techniques of montaña agriculture. To "have family" in the montaña was almost a necessary condition for resettlement since few highland immigrants came with sufficient resources to support themselves while they established their own farms. In this respect Satipo is part of a national pattern of population mobility. Héctor Martínez (1969) reports that kinship links encourage and enable peasants to leave the desolate altiplano of Puno and migrate to the recently colonized Tambopata Valley, in the southern Peruvian montaña. The same phenomenon has been observed in the mass migration of highland peasants to Lima. Paul Doughty (1970), Susan Bloom Lobo (1976), and others have described the numerous ways in which kinship bonds facilitate the transition from rural to urban residence. Migrants to the city and the frontier have adopted, at least in this regard, a common strategy of survival.

By montaña standards, the colonists from the sierra had modest ambitions. They hoped to build family farms on from twenty to fifty hectares of land and to raise subsistence crops and a cash crop (such as coffee) on a small scale. In the highlands they had been *minifundistas*, peasant farmers scratching out a bare living from a few scattered plots of poor land totaling no more than one or two hectares. To them, twenty to fifty hectares was an immense landholding, more than they had ever imagined possible in their native communities where the "richest" family owned perhaps as much as five hectares.

But while there was no land scarcity in the montaña, other serious problems tended to thwart the modest ambitions of the new settlers. The colony in the early 1960s was reeling from the effects of the coffee bust, and the shaky credit structure erected by the state bank was near collapse. Furthermore, the ownership of the land in the region was in a state of confusion. During the height of the coffee fever much land had been bought by speculators, not for immediate use but for resale at a later date. This land could not be claimed by the peasant immigrants because it was already owned, even though the owners often lived on the coast and did not cultivate any part of their terrain. Another large portion of the region's land was held by a few remaining coffee growers who cultivated only a fraction of their estates, allowing the rest of their property to lie idle. Finally, many thousands of hectares that were abandoned by their bankrupt owners had been taken over by the state bank and could not be claimed by new colonists until the old debts were somehow settled.

Thus the land-hungry peasants who migrated to Satipo in the 1960s found themselves in a rather strange predicament. First of all, along the region's major roads and trails large areas of choice terrain lay abandoned and uncultivated. A survey of landholdings in Satipo in 1960 (ONERN 1962:131–35) shows that of 155,000 hectares that were either legally owned or officially claimed (pending issuance of title), only 5,800 or less than 4 percent were actually under cultivation. Second, the region's only unclaimed lands were in extremely remote (and thus highly undesirable) areas located at least three days' walk from the town of Satipo. Consequently, the new immigrants were placed in the absurd position of having to bypass large areas of abandoned farmland in order to reach the distant and isolated corners of the region where they could find plots of unclaimed land on which to settle.

Although a few colonists ventured into these outlying areas, the majority sought, by a variety of means, to acquire the unused lands closer to the colony's center. In this regard the settlers had to distinguish between abandoned lands that "owed" to the state bank (*terrenos que debieron al banco*)[4] and other unused lands that did not. The takeover of unused lands that had never been cultivated with a loan from the bank was far easier than the takeover of bankrupt and indebted estates. In the former case, which was unfortunately not the most common one, small groups of peasant immigrants invaded the land and divided it among themselves, justifying their action by saying that they had carried out agrarian reform, a policy that the Peruvian government had formally advocated but never implemented. In the case of abandoned lands that the bank held as collateral, however, the law required any new occupants to repay the previous owner's loan (with interest) over a period of several years. A bankrupt estate was usually divided into small plots that were awarded to new colonists, each of whom agreed to pay off a part of the total debt. This general process of splitting up large estates and their debts to create small farms is also referred to by the colonists of Satipo as agrarian reform.

It is important to point out that the impetus and direction of the agrarian reform movement have come from below, from the peasant immigrants who encountered a highly problematic situation and devised their own solution to it. The intervention of government agencies in the redistribution of lands came only after the basic agrarian reform was a fait accompli. Typically, once a group of peasants had invaded and taken over a piece of abandoned terrain, they announced their action to local authorities and asked for recognition as legal owners of the land. In no case were such groups forcefully ejected from the land they had occupied. Of course, when state bank officials learned that an abandoned estate had been invaded, they immediately notified the new settlers of their obligation to repay the previous

---

[4]When colonists speak of lands that "owe" to the state bank, they refer to lands offered as collateral for loans that were subsequently foreclosed. By default, these lands became the property of the state bank, which could then resell them. The sum of any and all uncollected debts and accumulated interest associated with a particular piece of land constituted the selling price of that land.

owner's debt. The peasants were generally willing to accept this obligation, since along with it came official approval of their action and acknowledgment of their ownership of the land.

What, then, has been the outcome of the agrarian reform process? What have the new colonists been able to do with the land once it has become theirs? Such questions, to be considered in the chapters that follow, can be answered only tentatively, since the process is still unfolding. Nevertheless, certain ominous patterns have emerged which indicate that the land reform that was expected to be the catalyst of a thorough social and economic transformation has turned out to be only a step, and a small one at that, in the right direction. In effect, the removal of one barrier to rural development has revealed the existence of a series of other barriers, some of which are even more forbidding than the first. And the peasants have learned that, unlike the first barrier, subsequent barriers cannot be removed by sheer force, but must be dismantled by the coordinated effort of many diverse groups and agencies.

At the national level an undoing of the old order by means of agrarian reform is now virtually complete. But the shaping of a new order, prosperous as well as just, has turned out to be a far more formidable task than was once believed. Postreform Peru has only begun to discover the depth and complexity of its social and economic underdevelopment. The manifold problems of the reformed agrarian communities indicate how long and arduous the road to takeoff will be. Satipo shares many of these basic problems and represents the plight of thousands of rural communities throughout Peru. In other respects the frontier is unique, a product of a peculiar history and a highly volatile mixture of native and diverse immigrant groups. A brief overview of Peru's experiment with agrarian reform should illustrate some of the similarities and differences between Satipo and other recently transformed rural communities.

The issue of land reform in Peru has a long and bitter history. Ever since the Spanish conquistadors carved their vast estates out of the Inca domain, Indian communities have struggled to regain the land they lost. In the first centuries after the Spanish conquest of 1532, Indian rebellions took the form of millenarian uprisings that sought to banish the Spaniards and to restore the Inca state. One of the last great revolts of this kind was led by Tupac Amaru in 1780. Although the Indians eventually relinquished their hope of restoring Inca sovereignty, the quest for land reform continued throughout the nineteenth and early twentieth centuries. The 1920s and 1930s were decades of unusually frequent and fervent protests that were brutally repressed. Although much legislation addressing the Indians' grievances has been passed since the turn of the century (Davies 1974), in the early 1960s latifundios or large estates still encompassed over 75 percent of the cultivable land in the sierra (Handelman 1975:26). Major changes in Peru's land-tenure system have occurred only in the last twenty years.

The origin of the modern land reform movement in Peru lies in a wave of peasant land invasions that followed the election of Fernando Belaúnde as president in 1963. Agrarian reform had been one of Belaúnde's major campaign promises, and his election precipitated a series of illegal land seizures by peasants who believed that their unauthorized actions would later be ratified by law. According to one reliable source (CIDA 1966), some 350 to 450 communities and 300,000 peasants from all parts of Peru were involved in the land occupations. Many of these peasant communities claimed that they were only recovering lands that had been stolen from them by rich and powerful landlords. Since Belaúnde had promised to expropriate and redistribute the lands of the large estates, the peasants felt that they were entitled to lay claim to their ancestral properties in anticipation of the impending agrarian reform legislation (Strasma 1976:298).

In some regions of Peru, particularly in the southern departments of Cuzco, Puno, and Ayacucho, the land invasions were severely repressed by police and national guard forces. Bloodshed and violence prevailed in the South from 1963 until the peasant revolt was crushed in 1965. The landlords of southern Peru formed their own "defense leagues" and convinced Belaúnde that the revolt was inspired by communists and, if not repressed, could lead to a revolutionary situation (Handelman 1975:123). In the central highlands the government took a far more conciliatory stance toward the peasant land seizures. One reason for this difference is that the property invasions in Pasco and Junín were led not by leftists but by leaders of the politically moderate APRA and Acción Popular parties (Handelman 1975:122). Moreover, landlord resistance was minimal in the central zone. With few exceptions, the peasants were able to keep the land they occupied.

The agrarian reform movement in Satipo emerged during this period of nationwide ferment. Most of Satipo's peasant immigrants came from the central highlands and thus knew of the successful land invasions carried out in that zone. The land occupations in Satipo closely resembled those of the central sierra both in the tactics used and in the response elicited from government authorities. Like their central highland counterparts, the peasants of Satipo took the law in their own hands and, by abstaining from radical politics, succeeded in convincing the government that their claims were modest and amply justified.

At the same time that Satipo was undergoing profound changes, the southern montaña province of La Convención was also in upheaval. Because of the more radical nature of the land reform movement in La Convención, this province became the focus of national and international attention and the subject of much social-scientific research (e.g., Hobsbawm 1969, Wesley W. Craig 1967, Fioravanti 1974). La Convención Valley, like Satipo, was dominated by coffee estates, many of which were owned by absentee landlords and all of which relied on a labor force of peasants recruited from the neighboring highlands. The insurrection against the landlords of La Convención, however, took a form much different from that of Satipo.

As early as 1952 the peasants attached to various coffee estates of La Convención Valley had formed unions (Handelman

1975:73). In 1958 eight of these unions joined together to form the Provincial Peasant Federation of La Convención, an organization that coordinated the first valley-wide strike against the landlords. Shortly after this strike Hugo Blanco, a young agronomist with ties to the Trotskyist movement, arrived in La Convención with the intention of developing the unrest into "a more ideological and militant movement that would eventually serve as a model for rural revolt in the highlands" (Handelman 1975:174). Over the next two years Blanco persuaded the peasants to radicalize their demands and to form armed defense militias. Under Blanco's leadership the peasant revolt in La Convención, which had begun as a modest quest for land reform, acquired a revolutionary ideology and a military capability.

In Satipo the land reform movement consisted of nothing more than simple invasions of mostly abandoned property by loosely organized groups of peasants. Unions, federations, and strikes were all unknown in Satipo. There is no history of a labor movement in the central montaña nor is there a history of significant opposition to peasant land seizures. No leaders from outside Satipo figured in the land occupations and the movement was attached to no larger political scheme. The concept of armed militias was equally foreign to the colonists of Satipo.

The spontaneous, disorganized land grabbing that occurred in Satipo is probably more characteristic of the land reform activity in Peru's frontier zones during the tumultuous mid-1960s than is the organized movement in La Convención. The combination of factors that led to the radicalization of the peasants of La Convención apparently did not exist elsewhere (Hobsbawm 1969). Although armed revolutionary guerrilla units operated in other parts of the montaña, including the Satipo Valley (as we shall see in Chapter 4), these cadres were composed almost exclusively of student militants from the coast and they failed to win the support of the local population (Béjar 1970). In most of the montaña the peasants' quest for land was realized without significant leadership or organization. Moreover, for most peasants the possession of land was an end in itself and not the first step in a larger revolutionary program.

The next major phase in the Peruvian agrarian struggle was marked by a shift from peasant-initiated to government-initiated reform under the military regime that replaced Belaúnde in 1968. The government of President Juan Velasco Alvarado rewrote the agrarian reform laws of Peru in order to limit the amount of land that an individual could own to 150 hectares of irrigated land on the coast or its agricultural equivalent in other ecological zones (Strasma 1976:301). The Velasco regime also sought to stimulate the formation of agrarian cooperatives and collective systems of production. Unlike previous legislation, the new laws were as much concerned with the postreform structure of Peruvian agrarian society as with the process of expropriation itself. In addition, the military leaders made it clear that the land occupations of the past would no longer be tolerated and that, in effect, agrarian reform would now be planned and directed from above.

To demonstrate its commitment to change, the Velasco government expropriated eight of the nation's largest coastal sugar plantations within hours after issuing its land reform decree in June 1969. Under previous agrarian reform laws, these modern agribusinesses had been exempted from expropriation. In the early 1970s the remnants of the estate system in the highlands came under attack. The military government set up "agrarian reform zones" in the highlands and systematically allocated all former estate lands to groups of peasants organized into cooperatives. The desire and the ability of the Velasco regime to introduce sweeping changes in the Peruvian countryside was clearly demonstrated by 1975, the target date for the completion of the redistribution phase of the agrarian reform program.

The cooperatives that formed the backbone of the new farming system were basically of two kinds: Agrarian Production Cooperatives (Cooperativas Agrarias de Producción, or CAP) and Agrarian Societies of Social Interest (Sociedades Agrícolas de

Interés Social, or SAIS). The production cooperative was a concept designed to convert the modern and efficient coastal sugar plantations into equally modern and efficient enterprises owned and managed by the workers themselves. By maintaining economies of scale in production, marketing, finance, and administration, the sugar cooperatives were expected to equal or exceed the performance of the private sugar estates (Long 1977:172). The SAIS concept, in contrast, was developed in response to the more complex situation in the highlands, where various sectors of the peasantry were at odds over the distribution of former estate lands. Large administrative entities, or SAIS, were created to integrate the *colonos,* or former servants of the estates, with the *comuneros,* or members of freeholding peasant communities. In theory both the CAP and the SAIS were autonomous, self-managing enterprises. In fact the military regime appointed all high-level administrators and constantly meddled in the affairs of the cooperatives.

The Velasco government never established a clear policy for the formation of agrarian cooperatives in the montaña. In Satipo and in other colonization zones, cooperatives for the marketing of coffee already existed. These cooperatives were local creations, and their sole purpose was to collect the coffee produced by local growers and to sell it for the best price that could be obtained from the export companies in Lima. Rather than attempt to impose the CAP or SAIS model, neither of which was suited to the social and economic conditions of the frontier, the military regime sought to expand the role of the coffee cooperatives and to place them under government supervision and control.

The extension of government control over the theoretically self-managing cooperatives became a troublesome issue in the montaña and in the nation as a whole. Throughout Peru the price of land reform was the acceptance of a new form of paternalism in which the state filled the role vacated by the landlords. Neither the colonists of Satipo nor the peasants of the highlands and the coast were willing to pay that price. As a result,

Velasco's land reform movement, rather than ushering in a period of growth and development in Peruvian agriculture, produced a stalemate between an authoritarian government and an insubordinate peasantry. This impasse has not yet been resolved, either in Satipo or elsewhere in Peru.

The political and economic stalemate in the Peruvian agrarian sector is symbolized by the heavy burden of debt that the peasants are forced to carry. As we saw in connection with Satipo's spontaneous agrarian reform, most of the coffee estates invaded by the peasants were "indebted" to the state bank because the former landlords had failed to cancel their farm-development loans. The peasants who occupied a bankrupt estate and divided it into small farms were required to divide the debt into equal portions and assume responsibility for repayment. A similar fate befell the beneficiaries of land reform in the highland and coastal zones. Here the new laws decreed that the former landlords would be compensated (in the form of government bonds) for the loss of their property. The peasants, or more precisely the recently formed peasant cooperatives, were required to reimburse the government over a twenty-five-year period for the total value of the expropriated property. According to Norman Long (1977:174), the repayment and servicing of these debts often account for as much as 50 percent of a cooperative's gross income in any one year. Thus the agrarian debt is borne individually in the montaña and collectively in the highlands and on the coast.

The result, however, is much the same. Income that might be used for farm improvements is earmarked for the financing of debts. Both the colonists of Satipo and the highland and coastal cooperatives have vigorously protested this drain on their resources. They point out the contradictions of a land reform program that, in their view, punishes the peasants as much as or more than the landlords. The fact that the government has not yielded on this issue is perhaps explained by politics more than by simple economics. As long as the peasants of Peru are individually or collectively beholden to the state, the government can amply justify its intervention in local affairs. In his study of the central highlands, Long (1977:177) concludes that the agrarian debt gives the government an excuse to intervene in the management of the cooperatives. In Satipo individual debts give state bank officials the right to inspect colonists' farms and to examine the administrative records of the cooperative. Thus a new mode of political and economic domination has emerged in Peru. Satipo, like thousands of rural communities throughout the nation, must now cope with the infinitely more complex problems of the postreform era.

The Contemporary Setting

When the historical background and the larger context of frontier expansion are established, modern conditions in the Satipo colony can at least be brought into partial focus. It has been the purpose of this chapter to lay that background and context with an eye toward understanding the current phase of frontier development. In some cases, the legacy of the past is directly responsible for modern conditions, as in the continuing conflicts over debts to the state bank incurred in the era of coffee fever and transferred or handed down (without ever being repaid) to the present. In other cases, as the cliché has it, history seems simply to repeat itself, always in a new form or guise. Thus the current rapid growth of the lumber industry in Satipo can be seen in the context of a long series of boom-and-bust economic cycles dating back to the rubber boom of the late nineteenth century. As the dominant leitmotiv of Peruvian frontier history, the boom-and-bust cycle symbolizes the aimless and ultimately futile search for El Dorado in the eastern jungles. The Satipo colony, past and present, has been a victim, a willing victim in some instances, of these ephemeral boom industries.

Having laid the background, then, we can proceed to an examination of contemporary frontier society and its agonizing quest for development. The following case study of a community of forty-four colonist families reveals most of the basic elements or themes in the ongoing process of colonization. At the same time it is a study of a unique group of individuals whose beliefs and actions defy facile conclusions or interpretations. Thus, as we have used the past to illuminate the present, so we shall use the particular to illuminate the general, carefully guarding against the dangers of oversimplification and distortion that lie in either analytic path.

4

The Community of Pérez Godoy

My first visit to the colonist settlement of Pérez Godoy, located in a narrow canyon about five kilometers from the town of Satipo, was on a rainy morning in January 1974. At that time of year, the height of the montaña's rainy season, the narrow dirt roads leading to settled areas turn into ankle-deep mud. In climbing up the canyon to reach the first colonist farms I had slipped several times, adding a new layer of mud to my clothes with each fall. Exhausted, I stopped at one point along the road to rest and perhaps to reconsider my whole purpose in being there.

Shortly, a colonist who had seen me from his house on a hill above the road came to ask me if I would like to stop in and rest for a while. By the time we reached his house I was out of breath again and hardly prepared for my first anthropological interview. Instead, he talked about several things that were on his mind and I simply listened.

He explained that he was, like me, new to the area, having left his native community in the Andean highlands three years ago to look for land and a better life in the montaña. Since coming to the jungle, however, he had experienced many disappointments and frustrations. He had purchased a twenty-hectare farm from another colonist only to find out later that the land belonged to the state bank by default of the previous owner on the repayment of a loan. Forced to accept responsibility for the old debt, the new settler worked in his coffee groves from dawn to dusk each day just to make enough money to feed his family and to pay the bank. He had been forced to abandon his plans to build a good house, to expand his farm by planting new citrus and coffee groves, to buy a sewing machine for his wife so that his children might have decent clothing. The tasks of day-to-day subsistence consumed all of his time and energy. These hardships were compounded by extreme isolation and loneliness. There was little feeling of community, he said, among the colonists of Pérez Godoy, and there were many disputes and animosities between neighbors. The school where the settlers of Pérez Godoy sent their children was run-down and yet the parents were unwilling to cooperate in fixing it. The quality of instruction at the school was so poor that his oldest son, who had just finished the fifth grade, could not read and could barely sign his name. The attraction of the montaña, he concluded, had been an *engaño* (deceit), and his only hope was eventually to find a way out.

Over the course of a year, as my study of the Pérez Godoy settlement progressed, this rather desultory account of one man's experiences and observations became part of a larger script having many characters, a succession of acts, and a few basic themes at once simple and complex. In this chapter I hope to present that script as a coherent whole, as the intelligible sum of a set of often confusing and contradictory parts. In ordering the data, however, I have tried not to impose a sense of stability or continuity on a community that remains very much in flux. The community of Pérez Godoy, like Peruvian frontier society generally, does not lend itself to the construction of a tidy ethnography in which social, economic, religious, and political life are shown to be neatly interwoven. Inevitably, many loose ends remain in the study of an erratic, faltering process such as colonization. These loose ends are, in one sense, a testimony to the accuracy of one's understanding of a transitional, disequilibrated society.

Act One: The Takeover of an Abandoned Estate

Among the forty-four families that make up the settlement of Pérez Godoy are several men who consider themselves the founding fathers and the local historians, as it were, of the community. When I expressed an interest in how the settlement was formed and how it had changed or evolved through the years, these men were more than willing to relate their respective versions of that story. Not surprisingly, each version emphasized the prominence of the narrator's role in the events described. What follows is a synthesis of local history that stresses the common elements in the various accounts I was offered.

In 1963 the Satipo colony was undergoing a series of important, if somewhat ambiguous, changes. The road to the colony, destroyed in the earthquake of 1947, had been recently reopened, facilitating commerce with the highlands and the coast and stimulating a new wave of migration to the frontier. Just at that time, however, the price of coffee had begun to fall on the international market, foreshadowing the decline and eventual collapse of the local economy. Thus a rather strange combination of boom and depression prevailed in Satipo. In this atmosphere of uncertainty the Pérez Godoy community was founded.

Nearly all of the original twenty-eight colonists of Pérez Godoy came to Satipo soon after the reopening of the road in 1961. They were peasants from various towns and provinces of the central highlands who had left the poverty of their native communities in the hope of claiming a parcel of good farmland in the montaña. As we saw in Chapter 3, however, these peasant immigrants found that the only free or unclaimed lands were located at a great distance (at least three days' walk) from the center of the colony. The settlers' chances for survival, much less for successful commercial farming, in these remote zones were virtually nil. At the same time large tracts of land that had been claimed and purchased by wealthy speculators at the height of the coffee fever now lay abandoned and uncultivated. As the price of coffee fell, the amount of abandoned farmland increased. The choice location of this land along the region's major roads and trails made it the most desirable from the standpoint of the new settlers seeking homesteads. But since they had no money with which to purchase the unused land from its legal owners, the only way the peasants could acquire it was through illegal occupations or "invasions."

The Pérez Godoy settlement was formed in precisely this manner. Most of the twenty-eight immigrants who joined together in a kind of club called the Institución Pérez Godoy had been in Satipo for over a year, working as farm laborers or in other odd jobs while continuing to search for their own piece of land. In the course of a few organizational meetings, the members decided to take over an area of land of approximately one thousand hectares which was owned in absentia by a merchant of Chinese descent named Chang. The abandoned terrain was located in a steep canyon formed by the Timari River, only five kilometers from the town of Satipo and accessible by a road that passed along the foot of the canyon. Chang had never farmed the land or, more important, borrowed money from the state bank in order to make improvements on his property. There were thus no outstanding debts to the state bank for which the invading peasants could be held accountable. Foreseeing no major obstacles to their proposed action, the families occupied Chang's property in early 1963 and immediately began to make jungle clearings in which to build their houses and plant their crops. The settlement was named after the incumbent president of Peru, Ricardo Pérez Godoy, and a delegation was sent to Lima to proclaim the land seizure and to ask for official sanction.

The colonists argued that the land no longer belonged to Chang because he had violated the terms of the Jungle Lands Law, under which the original title had been issued. This law called for the landowner to bring at least 30 percent of his property under cultivation within five years after purchase, and to increase that percentage in each subsequent year. As of 1963, ten years after the government had sold slightly more than one thousand hectares to Chang, the entire estate remained uncultivated. Yet, the government itself initiated no action against either Chang or the many other land speculators of Satipo who had similarly failed to comply with the law. The officials responsible for revoking land titles could normally be dissuaded from their task with small bribes or favors. In the end the peasant settlers of Satipo pursued their own style of law enforcement via the invasion and mass settlement of abandoned, unused lands.

It is important to remember that the peasants sought to legitimate their action by citing the established legal code. They used no revolutionary rhetoric or even implied any criticism of the structure of political-judicial authority. They perceived the occupation of an abandoned estate as an act of justice consistent with (if not dictated by) existing laws related to the sale and use of Peruvian jungle lands. The naming of the settlement after the president of Peru and the request for his paternalistic sanction of the invasion further underscored the colonists' desire to play by the rules. Moreover, the issue of land occupation was never attached to a larger program for social or economic change. The goal of the colonists of Pérez Godoy was simple and quite specific: the attainment of a plot of land for each family. By their statements and actions the peasants made it clear that they had no grander ambitions.

In Chapter 3 I stated that the agrarian reform movement in Satipo (of which Pérez Godoy is typical) took place during a period of nationwide ferment. I pointed out similarities between the peasant land invasions of the montaña and those of the central and southern sierra. I should note that similarities also exist between events in Satipo and developments on the Peruvian coast.

In their motives, objectives, and tactics, the colonists of Satipo displayed the same blend of tenacity and moderation that was

shown by the migrants who invaded uninhabited lands surrounding the capital city of Lima. The urban land invasions of
the 1960s and 1970s (as described by Isbell 1978, Mangin 1970,
Collier 1976, and others) were motivated by a scarcity of low-cost
housing for the thousands of highland peasants who were mi-
grating to Lima. Like the colonists of Pérez Godoy, the urban
squatters were interested only in acquiring a piece of land on
which to settle. Their illegal land occupations were not acts of
defiance and were not tied to leftist political campaigns. On the
contrary, the urban land invasions were carried out in a spirit of
patriotism and political neutrality. Peruvian flags were prominently displayed in the new squatter settlements, most of which
had been founded on major national holidays and named after
past presidents of Peru or their wives (Mangin 1970:50). Although there is no direct link between the land invasions of the
coast and those of the montaña, the colonists of Satipo were
definitely influenced by the urban squatter movement.

One basic difference between the squatter settlements of the
coast and those of the montaña is that the colonists, unlike their
urban counterparts, encountered little or no opposition from
landlords, the police, or the Guardia Civil. Whereas eviction was
common in the first stage of an organized land seizure in Lima
(Isbell 1978:183), government authorities in Satipo did not oppose the occupation of abandoned terrain by landless peasants.
In fact, the colonists of Pérez Godoy gained government support
for their action. Although the bureaucratic machinery required
nearly eight years to process and approve their claims, the Peruvian president granted de facto recognition of the settlement
soon after the invasion occurred.

Ironically, at the same time that the squatters were obtaining
rights to abandoned land through established legal channels, a
small guerrilla movement was afoot in certain isolated parts of
the Satipo region. The guerrillas, primarily leftist students and
workers from the coast, had assumed that the colonists would be
sympathetic to their cause. With the jungle's ideal conditions for
guerrilla warfare and with the support of the local population,

the revolutionaries thought that their movement would spread rapidly.[1] But in fact, far from supporting the revolutionary cause, the colonists aided government troops in locating the guerrillas and often joined in attacks against them. One of the leaders of the Pérez Godoy settlement told me that he had been approached in 1963 by a small band of guerrillas who offered military backing of the recent land invasion. The colonist led the guerrillas to believe that he wanted their assistance while secretly reporting their location to the army commander in Satipo. According to this colonist, the government forces subsequently set up an ambush in which all of the guerrillas were killed.

It is clear, then, that the settlers of Pérez Godoy were guided by a conservative ideology whose goals were immediate and practical. The more radical, long-term solutions offered by the revolutionaries were seen as jeopardizing rather than enhancing recent gains. Accordingly, the colonists collaborated in ridding frontier society of a guerrilla movement that threatened to interfere with the tasks of developing the newly won land. Having secured at last a piece of land to call their own, the peasants were eager to begin the farming ventures of which they had long dreamed.

The colonists first agreed to divide the occupied land equally among themselves. Each of the twenty-eight member families received thirty hectares while a separate area of approximately one hundred hectares was set aside as communal property. Here the future school and municipal council buildings would be erected. In addition, the colonists agreed that on one day of each week a community work session (*faena*) would be held, and that each family would be required to participate. By this means various projects that concerned and benefited all of the settlers would be carried out. As a familiar, traditional form of coopera-

---

[1] An excellent account of the aims and tactics of the guerrilla forces that operated in the Peruvian montaña from 1962 to 1965 is found in Béjar (1970). A chronology and a bibliography of the guerrilla movement have been prepared by Leon Campbell (1973).

tion in Andean society, the faena adapted well to the exigencies of frontier life.

For example, a road had to be built from the base to the upper reaches of the Timari canyon, where the last farms of the Pérez Godoy settlement are located. All of the colonists needed this road in order to market their coffee and other farm produce. Under the *cooperación popular* (popular cooperation) program of the Belaúnde government (1964–68), the colonists of Pérez Godoy were able to borrow a bulldozer to use in the road-construction project. The community members shared the gasoline and other operating costs of the bulldozer and supplied additional labor at their weekly faenas. Within a year after the land invasion, a crude but serviceable road had been cut along the riverbank leading to the upper end of the canyon. The faena method is still employed at present when repairs and maintenance work are needed to keep the road open.

But the faena system was and is used only for special communal projects; farming and other routine tasks are carried out by individual colonist families working alone. Since the earliest days of the Pérez Godoy settlement, husband, wife, and children have formed the basic social unit of production. In clearing the land, building a house, and cultivating the crops, each nuclear family relied on its own resources. The self-sufficient family farm was the ideal toward which the colonists' efforts were directed. In the twelve years of the colony's existence, certain problems and crises have tended to accentuate this highly individualistic ideology. Undoubtedly the most prominent of these crises was the reorganization of the colony by government agencies, a process that began in 1966 and resulted in a series of conflicts that deeply divided the Pérez Godoy community.

Act Two: Government Intervention

As the colonists describe it, one day approximately three years after the petition for government sanction of the land invasion had been submitted a group of surveyors and engineers appeared at Pérez Godoy, saying that they had been sent to survey the canyon, to measure the farms, and to establish clear boundaries between them. This would be the first step, they explained, in the process of granting the squatters legal titles to their land. Naturally, the officials were welcomed as the long-awaited adjudicators of the colonists' claims. Moreover, the colonists hoped that the exact measurement of their parcels by a neutral party would put an end to the numerous boundary disputes that had begun to emerge in the colony. They assumed that the government would essentially ratify the existing distribution of lands while resolving the minor disputes over borders evenhandedly.

In fact, the action taken by the surveyors was of a very different sort. The parcels of land that the colonists had allotted themselves were deemed too large. Most families had placed between five and ten of their thirty hectares under active cultivation, reserving the remainder for future use. The government surveyors decided to take this temporarily idle land and grant it to peasants from outside the community. In all, sixty-four individual family parcels were created where only twenty-eight had existed before. As a result, the average size of the colonist landholding in Pérez Godoy was reduced from thirty to about fourteen hectares.

The protests of the community's twenty-eight original members were of no avail. When word spread through the Satipo region that the government was reassigning land parcels in Pérez Godoy, claimants appeared who had never even seen the settlement. Many of these newcomers were accommodated with land allotments equal in size to those granted to the founding families. This policy produced great resentment among the latter group of settlers, especially since it was their land that was being given to the recent arrivals. If the older colonists wished to receive legal titles to their farms, however, they had to accept the conditions laid down by the government. Nearly all of the old settlers had to give up most of the virgin land that they had set aside for future expansion or rotational use (under the shifting cultivation system).

Since the addition of the thirty-six new families, the Pérez Godoy colony has been plagued by an ever growing list of problems. In describing the changes that have taken place, colonists most often mention the adverse effects of the government-imposed reorganization on community spirit and the faena system. The new settlers entered the colony after the road had already been built and after the provisional school and municipal council buildings had been completed. All of these public works carried out by the founding families were used by the new colonists even though they had contributed nothing to them. Furthermore, many newcomers refused to recognize their obligation to participate in future faena projects. There was a lack of consensus on the rights and duties of each settler who resided in the reorganized Pérez Godoy colony. Under these conditions the faenas became more and more difficult to organize and the previous community structure, rather than absorbing the additional families, simply collapsed. Even though the old and new settlers shared certain interests—the maintenance of the road, the improvement of the local school, and so on—the bitterness that had carried over from the days of the colony's reorganization was too great to be overcome.

A second major problem was the weakening of the family farm unit. The parcels granted by the government ranged from nine to twenty-four hectares, with the average landholding consisting of about fourteen hectares. This substantial reduction in the size of family farm units (from an original thirty hectares) undermined their viability. The soil of the Timari canyon, which was of poor quality to begin with, was rapidly depleted by intensive cultivation. The parcel given to each colonist by the government was too small to permit any form of land management (such as periodic fallowing) that would preserve or restore the soil's fertility. There was virtually nothing that the colonists could do to prevent the steady deterioration of their farmland. As the harvests began to decrease year by year, many colonists of Pérez Godoy were forced either to abandon their farms or to seek some kind of outside employment to supplement their diminishing incomes. The achievement of a self-sufficient family farm, a difficult feat at best, became an impossibility in the wake of the changes brought about by government reorganization of the Pérez Godoy colony.

By 1968, only two years after the resettlement, almost a third of the sixty-four families had given up and moved away. Those who left usually sold their land to new colonists or to remaining settlers who wished to acquire a second parcel. These transactions between colonists were not recognized by the government and were considered illegal. Nevertheless, the pattern of high turnover among the settlers and the privately arranged transfers of land continue to the present day. Some parcels have changed hands four or five times in the brief period since they were first assigned by the government.

For this and other reasons, nearly all of the original contracts under which the sixty-four families received their land are no longer valid. Some of the contracts were annulled almost immediately when the colonists refused to pay certain fees for the issuance of their land titles. The settlers who failed to pay these fees reverted to the status of squatters (now on state land). Other contracts were invalidated when the colonists sold their land or rented it (through a sharecropping arrangement) to another person. The terms of the contract stated clearly that the grantee and his family were required to live on their land and to cultivate it themselves. But the colonists generally did not follow these rules, which they saw as unfair and unrealistic in light of actual conditions in the colony. In fact, I was told in the government land office in Satipo that all of the settlers of Pérez Godoy had violated their contracts and therefore could not claim legal titles to their property.

Government officials in Satipo also blame the colonists for the general climate of stagnation and depression that prevails in Pérez Godoy. The colonists, in turn, are equally insistent that the changes introduced by the government have brought about the present crisis. Wherever the blame may lie, it is clear that the expectations of both the colonists and the government have not been realized. The spirit of optimism and high ambition that characterized the founding of the colony is nowhere evident today.

Act Three: The Deepening Economic Crisis

The narrow dirt road intersecting the region's main highway bears no sign or other indication that this is the entrance to Pérez Godoy. Only a school and few scattered houses, visible from the highway, call one's attention to this otherwise secluded settlement. Entering by the side road one comes first to a little store and bar owned by Máximo Capcha. This is virtually the only place where colonists are likely to gather informally, usually to discuss mutual problems and concerns over a few glasses of beer. Máximo and his wife, Yolanda, are well liked by the community and through them it is possible to meet nearly all of the settlers of Pérez Godoy.

To reach the colonist homesteads one follows the winding road that passes in front of the Capcha store and continues up the Timari canyon for about three kilometers before coming to an abrupt halt at the face of a cliff. On either side of the road, spaced approximately one hundred meters apart, are the colonists' dwellings. They range in size and complexity from two-story wooden houses with corrugated tin roofs to small Campa-style huts. Since coffee is the primary, and in many cases the only, crop produced by the settlers of Pérez Godoy, an area next to each house is reserved for the hulling, washing, and drying of coffee beans. Whether these processing plants are simple or elaborate depends on the amount of coffee produced at any given farm. The cultivated fields or chacras lie on the hill slope behind the house and coffee-processing complex. A network of footpaths extends from the house site up to the various parts of the chacra, where colonists spend most of the daylight hours. If you approach a colonist's home by day, you will usually encounter a woman or small child who explains that the rest of the family has been working in the chacra since dawn and will not return until sunset. The colonists say that one person must stay at home during the day to guard against the theft of household possessions.

The Pérez Godoy settlement is made up of small, independent family farms producing a few subsistence crops but relying primarily on the cash income derived from coffee cultivation. It should be pointed out first of all that the essentially monocrop system found in Pérez Godoy was not designed by the farmers. If the colonists could choose in this matter, they would definitely opt for a pattern of crop diversification over the present form of coffee dependency. But the colonists have never had this option. As we have seen, one factor that has profoundly influenced local agricultural planning is government policy. If it were not for government intervention, the farms would be larger and thus the cultivation patterns would be different. Another decisive factor in the emergence of the monocrop system is the environment. The steep slopes and the reddish, highly acidic soil of the Timari canyon are unsuited to virtually all crops except coffee. As we saw in Chapter 2, the development of agriculture in the quebradas or narrow canyons of the ceja de montaña is severely hindered by low soil fertility and high susceptibility to erosion. The settlers of Pérez Godoy who have attempted to plant bananas, citrus trees, corn, and a variety of other crops on the canyon slopes have had uniformly negative results. Only on the lowest gradients next to the riverbed can colonists sow small plots of yuca and corn and a few scattered banana trees. This area of relatively fertile land represents a mere 3 percent of the total surface area in the Timari canyon and it cannot produce enough basic subsistence crops to meet each family's needs. In Pérez Godoy no family provides more than 25 percent of its own food supply from garden plots and for the majority of settlers the figure is closer to 10 percent.

In effect, the colonists have no choice but to tie their fate to the vagaries of the coffee industry. Though the days of Satipo's coffee fever are long past, the monoculture system staggers onward. This once profitable crop grown on large estates now forms the backbone of an imperiled peasant economy. In Pérez

Godoy, a vicious circle of undercapitalization, poor cultivation techniques, ever decreasing harvests, diminishing profits, and a lack of reinvestment and proper maintenance has reduced the coffee industry to something less than a subsistence enterprise.

To analyze the depressed state of coffee farming in Pérez Godoy it is best to begin with a discussion of the agricultural credit system. Basically, the settlers have access to two sources of credit: the Banco de Fomento Agropecuario and the private coffee buyers of Satipo. Of the thirty-seven colonist families interviewed in the course of my study of Pérez Godoy,[2] twenty stated that they financed the annual round of activities connected with the production cycle of coffee with loans from the state bank. They borrow money at a 12 percent annual rate of interest under the condition that at the end of the harvest season they will deliver all of their coffee to the local farmers' cooperative, where the amount owed to the bank will be discounted before they are paid. The bank allows each borrower a certain amount of money per hectare of coffee cultivated. For example, a colonist with 4 hectares of coffee in 1974 received S/.7,000 per hectare or S/.28,000 in all. The colonist may borrow year after year in this manner as long as the debt is canceled with each harvest. It is now a bank policy that one year's loan must be completely paid off before any money can be granted for the following year.

A second source of credit is the coffee merchants of Satipo, who "advance" or lend money under the *habilitado* system. An independent coffee buyer or *habilitador* advances a colonist (the habilitado) small amounts of cash during the year to be repaid when the harvested crop is delivered to the creditor. Ostensibly, no interest is charged on the money borrowed under this arrangement, but borrowers must agree to sell all of their coffee to the merchant/creditor at a price designated by him. The habilitador makes his profit by paying his debtors 15 to 20 per-

---

[2] At present a total of forty-four families make up the community of Pérez Godoy. Of these families, six reside only part of the year in the colony and were unavailable for interviews at the time of my research. One couple refused to be interviewed or to cooperate with my study in any way.

cent less than the actual market value of their coffee. In 1974, for example, the farmers' cooperative of Satipo was paying S/.1,800 per quintal (100-pound sack) of coffee while the habilitadores were paying S/.1,500.

Only ten of the thirty-seven families interviewed in Pérez Godoy received money under the habilitado system. These ten were unanimous in their dissatisfaction with this kind of credit arrangement. They were not free, they complained, to sell their coffee for the best price. Furthermore, the merchant/creditors were said to be unscrupulous and miserly, always cheating the farmers in the weighing of the coffee and in the calculation of its value. Often, my informants claimed, they cannot bring in enough coffee to cancel their debts to the habilitador and are thus forced to repeat the cycle of indebtedness for another year. If this process continues for several years in succession, as it frequently does, a colonist is unlikely ever to get out of debt.

The colonists who obtain credit from the state bank are in a somewhat different, though to their minds equally hopeless, position. The high rate of interest charged by the bank is a target of constant complaint. In addition, the settlers resent the fact that the bank sends inspectors two or three times a year to each borrower's farm, charging the colonist S/.500 per visit. Although the inspectors are supposed to evaluate the progress of the coffee crop and give technical advice, they seldom perform this service. The colonists say that when the inspectors visit Pérez Godoy, they travel only as far as Máximo Capcha's bar, where they order a round of beers and send a few children as messengers to summon the bank's clients from their homes. The officials expect the farmers to present themselves at the bar and provide the information necessary to complete the inspection forms.[3] This abuse is tolerated because the colonists fear that if they registered a protest, they might lose their credit altogether.

---

[3]On two separate occasions I saw inspectors from the state bank working at Pérez Godoy. The first occasion served to confirm the account detailed above. On the second occasion, however, I encountered two officials with a jeep visiting a colonist farm located midway up the canyon. Upon inquiring, I was told that

There is no clear consensus in the Pérez Godoy community as to which credit system—the state bank's or the coffee merchants'—is worse. Either way, it seems, the colonists soon find themselves working from sunup to sundown just to break even with their creditors. Moreover, neither system provides the colonists with enough credit to make the kinds of investment in labor, tools, fertilizer, and insecticide that would guarantee a high yield per hectare. As the costs of coffee production have risen in recent years, the cash shortage has become particularly acute. My informants in Pérez Godoy said that it now (as of 1974) costs between S/.11,000 and S/.13,000 per year to maintain one hectare of coffee in good condition. Yet the bank lends only S/.7,000 per hectare and the habilitadores allow even less. Consequently, the farmers are forced to skimp on the care and improvement of their coffee groves, a practice that inevitably results in diminishing harvests.

The cutback in expenditures has brought about a sharp reduction in the number of migrant wage laborers employed to supplement the basic nuclear-family work force. The colonists of Pérez Godoy say that the routine tasks involved in maintaining a coffee grove require far more labor than the family unit alone can furnish. But in the last few years, according to the farmers, the number of landless peasants seeking work has declined. The lessening supply of migrant farm laborers has served to raise the wages they can command, making their services almost unaffordable from the colonists' point of view. Ironically, the settlers contend that the agrarian reform is to blame for this problem, since it "has given a piece of land to everyone," leaving no sizable landless work force to seek part-time employment at subsistence wages. Although the colonists are aware that their own status as landowners was made possible by the social changes of which they now complain, their more immediate and practical con-

---

when the bank can furnish the inspectors with a jeep, they will generally make farm-to-farm visits. But when they are without transportation, as they generally are, the officials do not even attempt to carry out their assigned duties.

cerns overshadow these considerations. The fact that the settlers cannot hire as many farm laborers as they need places the entire coffee industry in jeopardy.

The shortage of labor is felt year-round in Pérez Godoy. The annual cycle of activities—weeding, pruning, fertilizing, fumigating, and so on—strains and often exceeds the labor capacity of each colonist family. It is at harvesttime, however, that the labor potential of the individual family is most inadequate. When the coffee berries ripen, they must be picked by hand within a very short time or they will turn black and fall off the trees. The colonists say that when there is a good harvest, they need four or five workers for each hectare of coffee grove. Since the average grove in Pérez Godoy consists of about four hectares, a farmer ideally should employ from sixteen to twenty workers to bring in the harvest.

But even though migrant laborers do come from the adjacent highlands to find temporary work in the montaña, they do not come in sufficient numbers to meet the colonists' needs. When I interviewed colonists during the harvest season, they invariably complained about being short-handed. The farmers told me that they regularly lost as much as one-third of their crop for want of harvesters. In their opinion, the blame for the farm-labor shortage is shared by the agrarian reform and the growing lumber industry of Satipo. Quite simply, a seasonal migrant can make about 50 percent more as a lumberjack than he can as a day laborer on a colonist's farm. At the time of my study, the settlers of Pérez Godoy were paying S/.50 (about $1) as a daily wage while the lumber dealers and sawmill owners of the area were offering S/.100. Even during the harvest, when farmworkers are paid according to the amount of coffee they gather (and so can earn as much as S/.100 or more a day), colonists have a difficult time competing with the lumber industry for the few available wage laborers.

Just as the price of labor has climbed beyond the colonists' reach, so also has an inflationary spiral affected the prices of tools, fertilizers, and insecticides. Some of these basic items have doubled or tripled in price in the last two years as a result of import restrictions that have greatly reduced supplies. The most essential tool of the colonists' trade, the machete, quintupled in price between 1968 and 1974 as a result of new national import policies barely understood by the settlers and of course entirely beyond their control. For the same reason, the fertilizer urea and the insecticide BHC, both necessary for the maintenance of a healthy coffee grove, have become scarce and, when available, extremely expensive. But as the farmers point out, while inflation has driven up the costs of production, the market price of coffee has increased hardly at all.

Inflation has an added dimension for the colonists of Pérez Godoy. As we saw earlier, the land in Pérez Godoy is too poor to support the cultivation of subsistence crops and thus the farmers are forced to buy their foodstuffs in town with the cash earned from coffee cultivation. The prices of basic foodstuffs have risen sharply in recent years relative to the incomes derived from coffee farming. The colonists assert that agrarian reform has caused a decline in production in all sectors of Peruvian agriculture, forcing a steady rise in the prices of such increasingly scarce foods as rice, beans, potatoes, sugar, and bread. Whatever its cause may be, constant inflation in the costs of essential foodstuffs is a painful fact with which the settlers of Pérez Godoy must live.

The rising costs of coffee cultivation and family subsistence threaten to paralyze the local system of production. The colonists' inability to invest in the preservation of their coffee groves has already resulted in smaller harvests. In the early years of the Pérez Godoy colony, the coffee groves generally yielded from ten to fifteen quintals per hectare. In 1974 the farmers I interviewed were obtaining only from two to five quintals from each hectare. Though weather conditions had been particularly bad that year, the severe drop in productivity reflects a general trend both in Pérez Godoy and in the Satipo region as a whole. Colonists pointed out the decreasing use of pesticide (owing to its excessively high cost) as a particularly important cause of the overall decline in production. In Pérez Godoy the spread of coffee-tree diseases has been rampant in recent years, contributing heavily to the crisis in productivity that is now apparent at every farm.

Among the settlers of Pérez Godoy there has been a twofold reaction to this crisis. A large number of colonists have abandoned their parcels and left the community altogether. Of the sixty-four colonists who received land allotments from the government in 1966, only twenty-one remained in 1974. The other twenty-three families who currently reside in Pérez Godoy have arrived in the years since the government reorganization of the colony, taking over land that was offered for sale or simply abandoned by the original owners. The rate of turnover in the colony is now higher than at any earlier time in its brief history. Over the course of the single year in which I observed developments in Pérez Godoy, four families left the community and many others expressed to me their desire or intention to move out in the near future.

Other settlers, reacting differently to the economic crisis, have devised strategies for supplementing their incomes from coffee cultivation with part-time work or small business ventures outside of the farm. Many of these colonists have also acquired second parcels of land from departing neighbors or from other community members. I found no family, however, not even among the eleven that now own two parcels of land, that supports itself entirely from coffee production. Out of necessity all settler families in Pérez Godoy seek some kind of income from a source other than their own farms.

Many colonists, for example, work part of the year in the lumber industry. They either earn a daily wage or are paid according to the number of board feet of timber that they can cut and deliver to a sawmill. Other settlers find temporary employment on various farms located throughout the Satipo region (though generally not in the Pérez Godoy colony itself). Still others move from their farms to a site near the main highway and establish a small business of some sort. Máximo Capcha, the owner of the store and bar that mark the entrance to Pérez Godoy, is one example of this trend. He and his wife still maintain a coffee grove and a farmhouse farther up the canyon, but their primary interest now lies in their business establishment. Two other small stores, both owned by colonists of Pérez Godoy, have recently been built beside the main highway. Finally, one member of the community has opened a little gas station on the outskirts of the town of Satipo, saying that if he has any success he will buy a good piece of land ("better than the one the government gave me") and will start a cattle ranch.

While these assorted strategies do contribute to the day-to-day survival of the community, they obviously do not offer a solution to the deepening economic crisis in Pérez Godoy. The ever higher rate of abandonment seems to furnish ample evidence in support of this claim. Moreover, as the colonists take their own labor away from the coffee groves and spend it on subsidiary activities, the problem of decreasing productivity per unit of land becomes more severe. Colonists would say that this predicament is both lamentable and inevitable. It is a fundamental irony of colonization that whereas a family's farm demands all of its members' time and energy, it cannot in turn provide for all of their subsistence needs.

Act Four: The Deepening Social Crisis

To the extent that a community exists among the settlers of present-day Pérez Godoy, it is organized around the local schoolhouse. A parents' association functions to promote and carry out improvements in school facilities. Membership and participation in this organization are obligatory for all colonists whose children attend the school. The government assists the educational development of rural communities only by providing teachers; the construction and provisioning of a schoolhouse as well as the purchase of books and other supplies are considered parental responsibilities. Accordingly, in each canyon or other zone of colonist settlement one finds a parents' association such as that of Pérez Godoy. While these associations have as their primary reason for being a common concern for the children's education, they may also serve to bring colonists together in order to make local road repairs or elect a delegate to the assembly of the farmers' cooperative in Satipo. Any problem that affects the whole community will usually be discussed and dealt with through the structure of the parents' association.

The problem with the parents' association of Pérez Godoy is that it is poorly organized, lacking in leadership, and generally ineffectual. The colonists themselves are the first to acknowledge these shortcomings. They attribute the community's problems to the selfish interests of its members, all of whom are afraid that excessive demands will be made on their time and money by communal work projects. Whenever the subject of holding a faena came up during my study, accusations were made that certain people never contributed to or participated in such functions and that this lack of cooperation explained in part the backwardness and poverty found in Pérez Godoy. When I asked the accused why they chose not to support the parents' association, they usually said that they had disagreements with other families in the colony, and that in any case, they planned to leave their farms and move elsewhere in the near future. No one, for that matter, seemed to hold much hope for the development of Pérez Godoy, an attitude that made all of the settlers somewhat reluctant to invest their energies in any major community improvements.

During the year in which I studied Pérez Godoy, only three faenas or communal work sessions were held, and all of them were poorly attended. One faena that I observed was particularly revealing of the problems that plague the community. On this occasion a meeting of the parents' association had been called for two purposes: to discuss the need for another teacher at the school and to organize a work crew to repair the road. The first order of business was to collect every community member's signature on a petition requesting the national government to send an additional schoolteacher to Pérez Godoy. The petition explained that there were 120 students at the school and only two teachers. This situation had grown intolerable, the colonists argued, from the standpoint of both the teachers, who were overworked, and the children, who were learning nothing. But while the colonists agreed that the petition should be hand-delivered to the Ministry of Education in Lima by a delegation of colonists from Pérez Godoy, they could not agree on who should go and how the trip should be financed. A number of settlers, including some of those whose children attended the school, were unwilling to contribute money to send a delegation to Lima. One man became furious at those who refused to cooperate, saying that they were "stupid peasants" and that their children would be the same for lack of a decent education. Several bitter exchanges took place before the group decided to send the petition by mail to Lima, knowing full well that presented in this form, the petition stood no chance of even being read.

The second objective of the meeting—the organization of a faena for road repairs—provoked even greater dissension among the colonists. It was then the height of the rainy season and the heavy logging trucks that entered the colony to take lumber from certain farms had left huge ruts in the muddy road, making it almost impassable. The majority of colonists had no lumber to sell and were thus resentful of the damage done to their road by the logging trucks. The five or six families who did have timber to sell claimed that the road belonged to everyone and that they, as members of the community, had the right to use it. This latter group was unwilling, however, to accept sole responsibility for the road repairs made necessary by their logging activities. The colonists who had no part in the lumber business protested and asserted that they would set up a blockade at the entrance to the colony if the loggers did not soon agree to fix the road. What began as a discussion of the need for road repairs soon degenerated into an angry exchange of accusations and expressions of mutual contempt. The meeting broke up with no agreement having been reached as to who would serve in the faena or when it would be held.

What was most striking about this dispute was the apparent absence of any rules or common understandings regarding the rights and obligations of each settler vis-à-vis the community. The atmosphere at the meeting was one of genuine confusion and anomie. There was no consensus as to how a dispute should be resolved or even as to what rules debate and discussion should follow. Many colonists told me that in their native communities in the highlands "things were very different." There the elected officials of a village determined specific solutions to all contested matters, thus avoiding the kind of agonizing chaos that prevailed in Pérez Godoy. The settlers could not explain exactly why such a system of government had never been developed in the montaña but said that it had something to do with the different ethnic and provincial origins of the settlers and the inability of immigrants of diverse backgrounds to understand each other.

Often colonists told me that people from different towns and provinces in the sierra have different customs, distinct ways of acting and speaking that serve to set them apart. They also said that they frequently do not get along with colonists who come from towns or districts other than their own. An array of ethnic stereotypes—the lazy *andamarquino* (person from Andamarca), the rebellious and pugnacious *huancaino* (person from Huancayo), the sly and deceptive *jaujino* (person from Jauja)—are employed by the colonists in defining what are perceived to be basically antagonistic social groups. In a context of confrontation, as in the meeting at the schoolhouse, these stereotypes are often invoked to explain the behavior of particular individuals. Thus one man charged that the people who refused to donate money to send a delegation to Lima were typical of the "lazy, backward peasants who come to the montaña from Andamarca." Many of the colonists thus accused were indeed from Andamarca, and they received the insult with bitter indignation. Before the meeting was over, many more ethnic slurs had been exchanged and several old divisions within the Pérez Godoy community had been deepened.

The diverse ethnic origins of the settlers clearly establish, then, certain basic lines of cleavage in the colony. These social divisions are complicated by a variety of other factors. We have already seen how a fundamental split developed between the twenty-eight founding families of Pérez Godoy and the thirty-six families who were resettled there by the Peruvian government. This division, a product of the colony's reorganization crisis, continues to the present day. I often heard members of the founding group speak in disparaging terms of the "opportunists" and "land grabbers" who entered the colony with government backing. In the ten years since the reorganization scheme was carried out there has never been a full rapprochement between these two factions, even though the intensity of the conflict has gradually subsided. Rather, colonists tend to trace the contemporary problems of Pérez Godoy back to the reorganization, saying that this event precipitated a steady decline in community spirit. The reorganized colony has become, in effect, a loosely articulated series of peasant homesteads, a social whole by virtue of juxtaposition rather than mutual self-conception.

Land boundaries are another important source of conflict in this frontier settlement. Although the measurement of the colonists' parcels by government surveyors was supposed to have eliminated all questions concerning property boundaries, in reality these questions were never resolved. In the colony today it is common to find neighbors who do not speak to each other because of a long-standing disagreement over the boundary between their two farms. Several colonists claim to have been "invaded" (a term they use frequently) by ambitious and unscrupulous neighbors. One man, asserting that another settler had made a clearing and planted crops on disputed terrain, proceeded to pull up the seedlings and to destroy the chacra of his adversary. The latter, I was told, retaliated by stealing several of the first man's chickens. Such vendettas may continue for years, with obvious consequences for the functioning of the community as an integrated whole.

A final obstacle to the development of Pérez Godoy as a community is the high rate of abandonment and turnover among the colonists. Many of the early leaders of the colony have now moved away, transferring their farms to new settlers, many of whom have themselves abandoned the farms after a few years of unrewarded toil. This lack of stability is often cited by the colonists as an impediment to the development of community solidarity and spirit. They say that new colonists arrive and expect to make use of such public works as the road and the school without accepting the responsibilities that accompany those privileges. The newcomers generally do not understand or appreciate the community effort required to build and maintain those public facilities. Open conflicts occasionally arise between the older and newer residents of the colony over precisely this problem.

In addition, colonists who are considering the possibility of leaving Pérez Godoy are usually reluctant to contribute their time and effort to community development projects. Several colonists told me that they no longer attended the faenas because they would soon be moving out of the community in search of a better living and working environment. It simply made no sense from their point of view to establish roots in a settlement that held so little promise and which they hoped to leave in the near future. By this strategy, the less one has invested in community improvements, the less reason there is to stay in Pérez Godoy when other opportunities present themselves.

From the evidence here presented it should be obvious that the lines of division in the social fabric of Pérez Godoy are multiple and complex. The fragmentation of the community is so complete as to cast doubt on the existence of any level of social organization higher than that of the family homestead. The absence of a communal ideology is as painfully apparent to the actors in this society as it is to the outside observer. Most colonists express their awareness of this ideological vacuum by contrasting the patterning of social life in their native highland communities with the disorder of a frontier settlement. It is hard, they say, to live among virtual strangers, not to share the expectations, values, and beliefs of one's neighbors, not to enjoy a cause larger than one's own. This profound feeling of isolation and loneliness emerges repeatedly in the colonists' personal accounts of their experiences in the montaña.

Pérez Godoy in Perspective

The themes of individualism and social fragmentation are inconsistent with the classic anthropological model of Andean culture and society. Although a few researchers have reported high levels of conflict and aggression among the villagers they studied (Bolton 1972, Dew 1969), the literature on Andean populations is dominated by the themes of communalism, social solidarity, reciprocity, and interdependence. In particular, ethnographic studies of highland Indian communities (e.g., Stein 1961, Doughty 1968, Alberti and Mayer 1974, Billie Jean Isbell 1978) and migrant associations in Lima (e.g., Doughty 1970, Mangin 1959, Matos Mar 1966) have documented numerous forms of cooperation and mutual aid among the nation's poor. Undoubtedly the communalism of Andean populations has been overstated and idealized. But the fact that such frontier settlements as Pérez Godoy deviate radically from the familiar pattern requires explanation.

The religious holidays and ceremonies that define and express communal relations in the Andes are not observed or performed in Pérez Godoy. There is no community church, although some of the settlers occasionally attend mass in the town of Satipo. The baptisms, weddings, and funerals of community members are also held at the Catholic church in Satipo. Absent are the religious brotherhoods or *cofradías* and the hierarchy of religious officials that play such prominent roles in the affairs of highland Indian villages. The colonists of Pérez Godoy and of other frontier communities have attempted to organize themselves without the familiar supporting institutions of folk Catholicism.

We have seen that in the brief period between the formation of the Pérez Godoy colony and its reorganization by the Peruvian government, a moderately successful faena or collective labor system was established. The faena, a secular institution that is a cornerstone of communal life in the highlands, was recreated among the twenty-eight founding families of Pérez Godoy. They completed a major communal task—the construction of a three-kilometer road from the base to the upper reaches of the Timari canyon—and they successfully lobbied for official sanction of the land invasion that they had jointly planned and carried out. For a short while a version of the much-celebrated spirit of Andean communalism and reciprocity prevailed in Pérez Godoy.

The government's reorganization of the colony dealt a crippling blow to the emerging community structure. With ample justification one could accuse the government of knowingly or unknowingly upsetting the fragile balance of common interests that had held the community together. Even in the highlands and on the coast of Peru, where communal organizations are noted for their strength and longevity, recent government programs have created friction and conflict among community members. Pierre van den Berghe and George Primov (1977), for example, have shown that the government is creating internal tensions in the indigenous communities of southern Peru. These tensions are the result of what van den Berghe and Primov term a "naive" attempt to impose an alien form of cooperative organization on the peasants. Similarly, in a study of communalism among the urban poor in Peru, Susan Bloom Lobo (1976) found that the government caused dismay and disorder in attempting to reorganize an irregular squatter settlement into uniform city-block units. Lobo states that communal solidarity in Lima is based on the bonds of kinship and common regional origin. In the case she studied, the government tried to form a new and different basis of communal organization, an effort that ended in failure.

It seems that the spirit of cooperation has been dampened wherever the central authorities have played a significant role in community formation or reformation. The belated participation of the state in Satipo's spontaneous agrarian reform has affected the local population in much the same way that recent government programs have affected rural and urban communities throughout Peru. If the purportedly strong and stable communities of the highlands and the coast have been crippled by misguided government policies, then it is not surprising that the fledgling communal structure of Pérez Godoy simply collapsed under the weight of reform. In short, it appears that the classic model of Andean society is increasingly out of step with changing social, economic, and political conditions. The thesis that communalism is somehow ingrained in the Andean peasantry, a misleading implication at best, has been undermined by the forces of change.

In emphasizing the role of external forces in dissolving communal bonds, one must take care not to ignore or overlook internal divisions. The vexing issue of ethnic heterogeneity must figure prominently in any explanation of Satipo's flaccid social structure.[4] Stated simply, colonists find it extremely difficult to establish relations of trust and mutual support with members of ethnic groups other than their own. In Pérez Godoy, as in all of the colonist communities of the Satipo region, one finds a mixture of immigrants from various districts and provinces of the central highlands. But each highlander is accustomed to living and working only with the people of his or her native region. The colonists have discovered that it is not easy to form new communities out of the old communal molds. Thus the counter-

---

[4]The diverse provincial origins of the highland immigrants represent only one of several major sources of internal division, as we shall see in Chapter 5.

part of the solidary, ethnically homogeneous highland community is the disorganized, ethnically heterogeneous montaña settlement.

Although ethnic diversity and social fragmentation appear to go hand in hand, the organizational success of highlanders who have moved to Lima provides evidence to the contrary. Students of the urbanization process in Peru assert that regional associations rekindle the spirit of communalism in the ethnically heterogeneous capital city. These urban mutual-aid societies create and maintain social contacts among immigrants from the same highland region. According to Paul Doughty (1970:32), the regional associations or clubs "sponsor activities which permit social continuity not only during the stressful initial period of adjustment to life in the metropolis but for a lifetime." By means of the regional club, highland communities are to a certain degree reconstituted in the city. Doughty (1970:45) concludes that "the regional clubs not only constitute important communities of social interaction for a large proportion of the migrants, but they also represent actual extensions of the rural society and culture of which the migrants voluntarily continue to be a part."

These organizations (which, it should be noted, preserve rather than dissolve ethnic boundaries) do not exist in Satipo. One does notice a certain camaraderie among individuals who have immigrated to Satipo from the same highland region. A colonist refers to persons from his native community or province as his *paisanos* (literally "countrymen"). Men and women associate more often with their paisanos than with persons of other ethnic backgrounds. The settlers say that they prefer to socialize with their paisanos because there is more trust and understanding in these relationships. One need not be afraid or reluctant, they say, to ask a favor or seek advice from one's paisanos. Settlers rely primarily on their paisanos for relief from the isolation, boredom, and loneliness of frontier life.

Nevertheless, the montaña offers no formal or institutional expression of paisano solidarity similar to the regional associations of Lima. The absence of such clubs is perhaps explained by Fred Jongkind's (1974) theory that the regional association is an inherently *urban* institution rather than, as Doughty (1970) argues, a manifestation of rural life in the city. Jongkind's study of the regional clubs of Lima led him to conclude that

> the regional club is essentially elitist, composed of well-adjusted and successful migrants. That they have united in regional associations is not a result of feelings of solidarity with the *copaisanos* [sic] of the homeland or in Lima, but is probably more a result of prestige motivations. The regional association offers the successful migrant the opportunity to measure his success against the standards of the "old world" and to have it recognized by his *copaisanos* in Lima and in the homeland. [Jongkind 1974:481]

If the regional association is, as Jongkind claims, an essentially urban institution composed of upwardly mobile immigrants, then it certainly would not flourish in a place like Satipo, which is not urban and which now offers no channels for upward mobility. If, on the other hand, the regional club is merely a manifestation of highland culture among city dwellers, then one would expect to find a similar manifestation among the colonists of Satipo, who, like their urban counterparts, identify strongly with their places of origin. The fact that regional associations have never been established in Satipo lends support to Jongkind's thesis.

Thus, for reasons outlined above, the much-admired and oft-extolled forms of Andean communal organization have not been successfully transplanted from the highlands to the montaña. As the case of Pérez Godoy illustrates, the question of how to submerge differences and disagreements within a larger framework of common interests and concerns remains unanswered. The informal networks of kinsmen and paisanos are important in day-to-day survival but they do not answer the need for a community-wide mechanism of social integration. Until such a mechanism is developed, the problems and complaints of the colonists will not receive attention at the national level. Their weak collective voice cannot be heard above the voices of more effectively organized sectors of the Peruvian population.

5

Ethnicity and
Social Consciousness

While I believe that the principal barrier to the development of Satipo lies in the nature of national market integration, it is not my intention to suggest or imply that if this barrier were removed the colony would soon be launched into the takeoff phase of economic growth. I would not for a moment offer yet another panacea to a nation that too often has had its complex developmental task reduced to simple formulas. Peru is not perched on the threshold of development; the road ahead is long and arduous. There are as many imponderable elements in the nation-building process as there are clear-cut problems with obvious solutions. As our attention shifts from the economic to the social aspects of development, it becomes increasingly difficult to diagnose the ills of a particular country and to suggest how they might be remedied.

Among the imponderables of development, ideology stands out as a particularly important problem. In such a country as Peru, where racial, ethnic, linguistic, and economic factors divide and redivide the population, the quest for development and the search for a national identity and consciousness are necessar-

138

ily intertwined. Economic growth is, in fact, the end product of a social process in which the organization of production is reshaped by new ideological commitments. The power of ideology to stimulate an economy is infinitely greater than the power of simple capital investments. Development begins with the redefinition of crucial social relationships and values, a process that generates new opportunities and increases work incentives.

In Peru, however, the national plan and purpose are as yet undefined. The "revolutionary" government of the armed forces was not successful in promoting its eclectic ideology of development and was forced by mounting popular dissent to return the country to civilian rule. None of the political parties now contending for power has yet devised a developmental strategy that the others can support. A retreat to the past, to the days before agrarian reform and the nationalization of the country's basic industries, is clearly out of the question. To forge ahead without a new model of national integration is equally impossible. For now and the foreseeable future, the Peruvian people are likely to flounder in the transitional phase of development, to plunge deeper into moral confusion and social disorganization. Peru has all the signs of becoming what Clifford Geertz (1965:152) has termed a "permanently transitional" society in which "both tradition and modernity seem to be receding at an increasing rate, leaving only the relics of the first and the simulacre of the second."

The problems of Peruvian frontier society graphically illustrate this lack of ideological direction and commitment. The Satipo colony is without innovative leadership, without an all-embracing normative code, without even a partial or tentative framework for collective action. It is not for want of effort or initiative, however, that the colonists of Satipo are disunited. The formation of the farmers' cooperative and a few lesser associational interest groups are proof enough of the settlers' willingness to work for the common good. What is missing is a model or design for the colony's future that would submerge numerous internal (primarily ethnic) divisions within a larger

ideology of cooperation and social solidarity. In the absence of
such a model, great strife and discord will continue to plague the
cooperative and other colonist organizations. The settlers recognize and freely admit that their divisiveness hinders the development of Satipo and favors those who would profit from the
social and geographic isolation of the pioneer family. And yet,
the colonists contend, there are differences in background, belief, language, and custom that are difficult if not impossible to
overcome. "We are different peoples," the colonists often say,
"and we don't understand each other."

The purpose of this chapter is to examine the ethnic composition of a frontier settlement, to define the various categories of
people who inhabit the montaña, and to reveal the mechanisms
by which ethnic boundaries are maintained. Guiding our venture into the complex realm of sociocultural analysis will be the
actors' own criteria for recognizing and distinguishing status
categories. Purely observational or objective differences, those
that strike the anthropologist as significant, are of little value in
explaining the patterns of social action. These patterns, by definition, reflect the actors' perceptions of the social system and of
their place within it. Consequently, if our task is to explain behavior and its normative basis, then we seek to understand (in
the sense of *verstehen*) the criteria by which colonists judge each
other and assign social identities.

Several kinds of data contribute to the general study of status
differences. One body of data consists of the overt diacritic elements that actors employ in labeling or assigning social identities. These are the attributes of status, and they include such
diverse features as style of dress, type of house construction, and
patterns of eating and drinking behavior. A distinctive trait or
cluster of traits may denote a particular status and thus serve to
distinguish one group from another. For example, a man who
enters the town of Satipo wearing facial paint and carrying a bow
and arrow is readily identified by the townspeople as a Campa.
Only the Campas paint designs on their faces and only the Cam-

pas hunt with bows and arrows. The diacritic features associated with a particular status do not, however, correspond exactly to the boundaries of that status group. While any man who wears facial paint is labeled a Campa, some men who never paint their faces are assigned Campa status nonetheless. Thus, although diacritic traits are among the most salient forms of social identification, they represent only one criterion of status assessment.

Another criterion has less to do with overt signals than with the subjective value orientations held by or attributed to people of different ethnic backgrounds. Colonists believe that standards of morality vary from group to group and that one's thinking and behavior are consistent with one's ethnic affiliation. For instance, colonists who have immigrated to Satipo from the sierra carry with them the reputation of their provincial homelands. Thus settlers from Huancayo are expected to act in a manner consistent with their ethnic origins (in this case to be rebellious and pugnacious). Similarly, colonists from Andamarca bear the social stereotype of their fellow andamarquinos, that of conservative, dull, and somewhat lazy peasants. These are not self-characterizations but rather images projected on certain status categories by persons outside of those categories. Colonists do not tend to see their own ethnic group as other groups see it. In any case, value orientations, professed or imputed, define status categories and demarcate ethnic boundaries.

A final source of data on the status system lies in the study of face-to-face interaction among persons of different social categories. Patterned interaction, even more than diacritic markers and basic value orientations, reveals the boundaries between status groups. The anthropologist both observes interaction between individuals of different status and questions informants about the kinds of behavior that would be expected in various hypothetical social situations. More subtle than diacritic signals and gross ethnic stereotypes, the patterns of face-to-face interaction yield important insights into the meaning of status distinctions in the realm of daily life.

The emphasis placed here on interaction is significant in that it constitutes an implied criticism of the "plural society" approach to ethnic problems. Scholars of the pluralist school, founded by J. S. Furnivall (1948) and M. G. Smith (1965), believe that an ethnically heterogeneous society is not one society but many. Each ethnic group is seen as a semiautonomous community with well-defined boundaries, a distinctive institutional structure, and a spirit of self-reliance. An ethnically diverse nation is seen as a crude amalgam of discrete, self-contained segments (variously labeled subcultures, castes, segregated collectivities and ethnic enclaves). The pluralists contend that interaction among these segments is minimal and is confined to the marketplace and the political arena. As defined by van den Berghe (1970:14), "plural societies are those that are segmented into two or more groups that have distinct and duplicatory sets of institutions, except in the political and economic spheres where the institutions are shared." In all other spheres of social activity the component groups coexist as a medley of incongruous elements.

In Peru, as in the countries of Africa, Asia, and the Caribbean, anthropologists have invoked the plural-society model to account for internal social divisions and the seeming lack of national integration. Allan Holmberg, one of the most influential analysts of Peruvian social problems, writes: "Peru is a nation of relatively unintegrated plural societies. The Quechua and Aymara Indians, for example, are but two instances of fragmented social communities, separated from each other and from the nation as a whole by geographic, linguistic, and cultural differences" (1960:67).

José Matos Mar, a distinguished Peruvian anthropologist, reaches a similar conclusion:

> Peruvian national society appears divided into geographic, economic, social, and cultural islands, giving the impression of an articulated archipelago, one that is weak in communication. . . . In these conditions the diffusion of scientific and technical progress is limited. . . . A juxtaposition of social, economic, political, and mental structures prevails in various ways in the heart of the

nation, often without relation, without connection, without dissemination, and without causation. [Matos Mar 1969:41–42; my translation]

Along with many other critics (see Frank 1967:123–42; Stavenhagen 1973), I believe that the plural-society view is inaccurate and misleading. The number of relationships between individuals of different segments is far greater than the model suggests. The notion of sharp and pervasive cleavage, of systematic dissociation of isolated collectivities, distorts the realities of social process in Peru. Put to the empirical test, the pluralist thesis is overwhelmed by contradictory evidence. No amount of patching, revision, or reformulation would allow this model to overcome its empirical and conceptual inadequacies.

The claim I wish to make is that the ethnic elements of Peruvian society are indeed mixed, that the problem lies not in a lack of integration but in the present *mode* of integration (the basis of which is extreme inequality). I hope to substantiate this claim in my analysis of frontier society. The question that I began with in the field was whether or not the system of ethnic relations in a mixed community such as Satipo provided the sort of social environment in which development could occur. Knowing that developed and developing nations (such as Japan, the United States, and India) share no single social or cultural framework, I did not want simply to judge local patterns in terms of some preconceived, generalized model. The problem of development, history has shown, varies from nation to nation and from region to region. At the same time, I felt that it was incorrect to assume that all sociocultural settings are equally disposed, given the right combination of external stimuli, toward sustained growth and development. Without a system of coordinated, persistent, and productive social relations, how could a community effectively respond to expanding opportunities? Thus I wanted to study the network of social relations on the frontier and to evaluate this network as a potential grid for the organization of productive forces.

As I mentioned earlier, I found the frontier colony of Satipo to be greatly divided and virtually devoid of creative social adaptations. I hasten to add that my informants fully agreed with this conclusion. "We are not one," they often said, "and we do not understand each other." How, then, are these people divided and what exactly is this lack of understanding of which they speak?

In listening to colonists describe their social surroundings, I realized that there were divisions and divisions within divisions. At the broadest level settlers recognize three status categories: uncivilized people (*gente no civilizada*), civilized people (*gente civilizada*), and cultured people (*gente de cultura*). The first category includes most of the region's Campa population and refers especially to those natives who preserve numerous aboriginal customs and traditions. The second group, *los civilizados*, is highly diverse, including a few Campas and nearly all of Satipo's immigrant population. Finally, cultured status is reserved for a very small number of well-educated and sophisticated local citizens, nearly all of whom live in the town of Satipo and hold important posts in local business and government. There are fewer than fifty people in this category.

The concepts of civilization and culture are the cornerstones, as it were, of local ideology. My informants tended to define civilization by contrasting it with the aboriginal Campa way of life. Civilization is associated with the conquest of the jungle region and its native inhabitants by various immigrant groups. There is an overtone of Christianity in the notion of civilization, but more important is the idea that a group of wandering hunters and gatherers was displaced by people who established permanent agricultural settlements and who built roads, schools, and a town. Culture, in the minds of Peruvian frontiersmen, is a major step above civilization. A cultured person is a businessman or an educated woman of means or a trained professional (such as a lawyer, a doctor, or an engineer) whose knowledge and expertise in matters of great importance distinguish him or her from mere civilized folk. To be cultured is to be well read and articulate, to use words and concepts that most people do not understand. Culture is identified not with frontier conquest and expansion, but with the rather stilted life-style of a transplanted metropolitan elite.

Many other status categories are of course subsumed within the tripartite (uncivilized, civilized, cultured) model. But as a general framework for the discussion of status differences, the model serves well. Let us proceed, then, to a more detailed analysis of Satipo's complex social character, employing this model as our basic guide.

Los Vecinos Notables: **The Cultured Elite**

One of the first public events that I attended in Satipo was a cockfight. I was invited by a friend who worked in a sawmill near town and who was an expert in all aspects of cockfighting. After we had paid our entrance fee and taken our places in the stands that surrounded the cockfighting ring, I noticed that one group in attendance seemed different from the rest. They were several dozen in number and they were seated together in one part of the stands. One could not help observing that they were better dressed, fairer skinned, and on the whole more dignified in appearance than the rest of the crowd. When the cockfights began, they made bets only among themselves and in amounts that far exceeded the paltry sums wagered by other members of the gallery.

Noting my interest in this group, my friend explained that these people were the *vecinos notables* (the notable or distinguished citizens) of Satipo. They are, he said, gente de cultura. Indeed, I already recognized several members of the group, even though I had been in Satipo only a few weeks. I knew that one man was the director of the local branch office of the state agricultural bank. Two other men whom I recognized were the mayor of Satipo and the town's only medical doctor. The remaining members of the group, I was later to learn, were men of similar stature in the community: directors of government agencies, owners of Satipo's major business establishments, and political officeholders. In the course of my research I became close friends with a few of Satipo's vecinos notables and through them I learned much about frontier society.

In Satipo, as in most provincial towns of Peru, elite status is synonymous with the ethnic terms *criollo* and *mestizo*. Much has been written about the multiple meanings of these two terms (Simmons 1965, Tschopik 1948, Patch 1967, Bourricaud 1975, van den Berghe and Primov 1977). At one level *criollo* refers to the "Peruvian-born descendants of the Spaniards" and their "upper class culture" (Simmons 1965). Criollos flaunt their Spanish ancestry and identify with the aristocratic culture of Lima, Arequipa, and a few other coastal cities (van den Berghe 1974:21). Criollo culture is, according to François Bourricaud (1975:353), an "ossified" version of the taste, manners, and lifestyle of the Spanish colonial elite.

Although the term *mestizo* suggests mixed ancestry rather than pure Iberian descent, this racial distinction is of minor significance. More important is the fact that criollo or mestizo identity implies distance from and disdain for the Indian component of Peruvian society. Criollos and mestizos are superior to the Indians in education, wealth, fluency in Spanish, and professional skills. Although racial criteria are also employed in distinguishing the criollos and mestizos from the Indians, economic and sociocultural criteria are cited more often. When van den Berghe and Primov (1977:134) asked their informants in the Cuzco region to distinguish a mestizo from an *indio,* they found that sociocultural factors were mentioned twice as often as racial factors.

At another level *criollo* has a very different meaning from the one outlined above. In its popular contemporary use, *criollismo* is associated with certain modes of thought and behavior characteristic of the lower and middle classes of Lima. Richard Patch (1967) and Ozzie Simmons (1965) state that modern urban criollos are those people who, regardless of their backgrounds or origins, have adopted the patterns of dress, speech, and general behavior associated with upward mobility in the capital city.

Thus Indian immigrants from the highlands, as they become acclimatized to the city and as they consciously or unconsciously discard the signs or traits of Indianness, are said to become *acriollados*. By this definition a criollo may be of Japanese, Chinese, black, or Indian descent as long as he is thoroughly "Peruvianized" and incorporated into the popular culture of Lima (Patch 1967:21).

Of the two meanings of *criollo* discussed thus far, the first meaning is much closer to the sense in which this term is used in the town and province of Satipo. Outside of Lima, as a rule, criollo or mestizo identity is a mark of upper-class status. Simmons (1965:527) affirms that in the provinces criollos are members of the local upper class who "enhance their status in the rural community by imitation of the way of life of the capital, and for them this means orientation to *criollismo,* which they regard as the acme of 'urban sophistication.'" Thus for our present purposes the terms *criollo* and *mestizo* will be understood to imply either national or local elite status.

Criollos and mestizos dominate the economic, cultural, and political life of the Peruvian nation. The symbol and the substance of criollo and mestizo dominance is the capital city of Lima. As Simmons writes (1965:521), "Lima has been traditionally considered, by both its own inhabitants and those of the provinces, as the source and the pulse of *criollismo.*" To have access to power, wealth, and status, criollos find it highly advantageous to live and work in the capital city. It is for this reason that the criollos and mestizos of Satipo tend to feel isolated from the mainstream of national life, and consequently dissatisfied with their role in the colonization effort. Most of the vecinos notables of Satipo would abandon the colony at a moment's notice if an opportunity arose to move to Lima.

Thus many of the vecinos notables are living in Satipo out of necessity rather than by choice. This is particularly true of those who have come to direct the branch offices of various government agencies. These middle-echelon bureaucrats are, in effect, serving time in a remote province in the hope of being rewarded at a later date with a job assignment in Lima or elsewhere on the coast. As a group the vecinos notables show little affection for the montaña; in their minds Satipo is a boring, backward, and insignificant jungle town. Only business brings them to Satipo and only business compels them to stay.

So distasteful is the jungle to the local elite that a man will often leave his wife and children on the coast rather than subject them to the rigors of montaña life. At least half of the prominent citizens of Satipo are men who live alone, supporting families whom they visit on holidays or during brief vacations. One of the primary reasons for maintaining separate residences is that it allows the vecinos notables to send their children to the nation's best schools, all of which are located in urban areas. Elite parents would never enroll their children in one of Satipo's primary or secondary schools. In Peru only the best students from the best schools have a chance of gaining entrance to a university; a graduate of Satipo's inferior school system could never compete with graduates of urban institutions, public or private. In general, the prominent citizens fear that their children would not have a proper education and upbringing in Satipo, a fear that prompts them to sustain the dual-residence pattern for as long as necessary. In a sense, by establishing roots in Satipo the elite would lose, ipso facto, their cultured status. The education and training that endow a person with culture are not available in the montaña. By maintaining a strong foothold outside of the Satipo community, the elite preserve their superior position within the local status hierarchy.

In view of their disdain for frontier society, it is ironic that the vecinos notables control most of the crucial positions in the economic and political structure of the colony. They are the directors of local branch banks and government agencies. They own the region's major sawmills as well as retail stores and other commercial establishments. They hold the highest positions on the staff of the farmers' cooperative. In the political life of the community the distinguished citizens exercise a similar monopoly. The provincial governor, the mayor, and all twenty members of the Provincial Council of Satipo belong to the cultured elite. Even in Velasco's "revolutionary" era, local political appointees were selected almost exclusively from the ranks of the vecinos notables. High office is the privilege of persons of high social status.

Only a few of Satipo's prominent citizens own large amounts of land. During the coffee fever of the 1950s, vast landholdings were the basis of elite power and prestige. But by now nearly all of the original vecinos notables are gone and their estates have been divided into a multitude of peasant family farms. Of the one hundred or more patrones who came to Satipo to develop coffee estates in the 1950s, approximately ten remain (including don Pedro Sánchez, whose life history is related in Chapter 6). All of these ten survivors retain their lands but are heavily indebted to the state bank and have little hope of financial recovery. A new elite, with a new power base, has emerged in the colony. Farming is of no interest to this group of vecinos notables; they are engineers, lawyers, and businessmen who work either for the state or in private enterprise. "Since the coffee bust and the agrarian reform," an elite man once told me, "farming has become a poor man's occupation." Land, once the object of elite competition, is now the bitter inheritance of a discordant peasantry.

Since the demise of the coffee plantation economy, the elite social circle has narrowed to the town of Satipo itself. The spacious houses built in the countryside by the original vecinos notables now stand empty, a decaying testimony to an era that was over almost before it began. Today the members of the local elite seldom venture outside of town except to travel to Lima.

There are several places in town where the distinguished citizens gather. One is the Café Azul, located near the main square. In the evenings one is likely to find most of Satipo's high society congregated in this spot. It is virtually impossible to mistake this café for any other. The clientele is light-skinned (in contrast to the dark complexion of Satipo's highland immigrants) and fashionably dressed (in contrast to the threadbare clothing of most

colonists). Their drink is whiskey and not beer or rum, the popular beverages of the montaña. Their cars and pickup trucks are
parked along the street in front of the café, admired by passers-
by who could never afford such luxuries. Their conversation is
of national and international events and their tone is dour, at
once apprehensive and pessimistic. They are worried about the
Peruvian "revolution" in spite of their seemingly successful accommodation with it. Now and then a familiar beggar appears at
the entrance of the café and, after being rewarded with a piece
of bread or a few coins, backs away, nodding and bowing, into
the night.

Although they are the undisputed leaders of the Satipo colony, the vecinos notables do not enjoy wide popular support.
Beneath a surface deference bordering on servility, there is deep
resentment and ill feeling toward the elite. These underlying
sentiments are not easily detected in interactions between the
elite and the general public. The distinguished citizens are addressed by their first names preceded by *don* or *doña* (titles of
respect in Spanish). Men of elite status are frequently addressed
by a professional appellation: engineer, doctor, lawyer, judge,
mayor, or commander (in the case of a high-ranking military
officer). Colonists, particularly if they are of Indian status, bow
their heads slightly and avoid direct eye contact when speaking
to members of the elite. The prominent citizens, in turn, use first
names alone and the familiar *tu* form of address in conversations with persons of lesser status. An Indian peasant from the
highlands often is called *hijo* or *hija* (son, daughter) by members
of the elite. These patterns of face-to-face interaction clearly
demarcate the elite as a status category.

The patterns of deference and respect conceal the colonists'
true feelings. Appearances notwithstanding, there is widespread
dissatisfaction with the political and economic leadership provided by the vecinos notables. Colonists contend, for example,
that the prominent citizens use the powers of public office for
private gain. Accusations range from the embezzlement of public funds to the solicitation of bribes or favors in exchange for

government services or the use of public works projects to enhance the value of property owned by the vecinos notables.

A scandal of the latter type was brewing in Satipo at the time of my research. The mayor had decided to extend municipal water and sewer services to the eastern outskirts of town even though many central locations (some within a block of the main square) lacked such services. The Provincial Council of Satipo, composed entirely of elite men, approved the mayor's plan and allocated local government funds for its completion. Not by coincidence, the mayor owned a large piece of land on the eastern edge of town and intended to build a new house there. News of this project sparked a heated but subdued public reaction. Everyone knew that many buildings in town lacked water and sewer lines, including the municipal marketplace, the public health clinic, and the high school. Everyone (except the vecinos notables) agreed that the mayor had completely ignored the public interest and had blatantly misused the taxpayers' money. But the outrage expressed in private failed to develop into organized popular protest. The maximal expression of public discontent came in the form of anonymous leaflets distributed at various street corners. The following statements are excerpts from one such leaflet:

> It is public knowledge that the water and sewer systems in our town are a calamity. The municipal authorities do not bother to make improvements even though they know that most of the time we are consuming contaminated water filled with slime and garbage and that our sewer lines often overflow into the streets, contaminating the air with putrid odors.
> ... The Francisco Irazola High School is without the [water and sewer] services that are so essential to studious youth. The people who work in the central marketplace have such deficient services that they must stand in long lines to use the bathroom or the water faucet. The community is told that there are no funds for the installation of these badly needed facilities but we discover that there is plenty of money to extend the water and sewer systems to the lands that belong to our mayor, Juan Rázuri. One can easily guess what the mayor's motive is. In his quest for profit and illicit wealth he wants to use the people's taxes to pay for a project that improves his personal property.

... The people must stand up in order to defend their interests, to protect the rights of the community against the insane
proposals of the mayor, who manages municipal revenue as if it
were money from his own pocket.

Despite the strong and challenging language of the leaflet,
there was no organized opposition to the mayor's project. The
incident only added to the colonists' list of grievances, a list
that grows longer each day. At present there are no signs that a
confrontation is imminent, although the situation could change
at any time. The fact that the colonists are greatly divided among
themselves limits their ability to defend common interests and
concerns. No sooner is a colonist association formed than it dis-
solves in a flurry of factionalism and in-fighting. The prominent
citizens are aware of this divisiveness and they know how to take
advantage of it.

If the colonists were to overcome their differences and to
form an effective citizens' group, they would challenge the elite
on several grounds, only one of which is the abuse of power.
Another target of complaint is the elite's habit of living in semi-
exile from their coastal homelands rather than adopting the
community in which they currently reside. The colonists contend that the prominent citizens show little concern for Satipo
because they have never made it their home. They argue that
since the vecinos notables do not send their children to local
schools, they have no reason to be concerned about the quality of
education in those schools. Since the vecinos notables take their
vacations in Lima, they have no reason to lament the lack of local
recreational facilities. The same logic applies to Satipo's unpaved
streets, its inadequate water and sanitation systems, and its deficient health care services. Why should the appointed leaders
strive to improve the community if the well-being of their own
families is not at stake?

Finally, many colonists have begun to question the notion of
culture and its role in separating the prominent citizens from the
general public. Colonists often say that in their business dealings
with members of the elite, they have found the reputation of

certain cultured individuals to be undeserved. A cultured person, in the colonists' view, is supposed to have high standards of personal conduct, to be forthright and honest, to act with beneficent paternalism toward persons of lesser status. In a period that the settlers refer to rather obliquely as *el Perú de antes*,[1] the prominent citizens were for the most part good patrones who earned the respect and deference of the people by their strong leadership and worthy deeds. In contrast, many of today's vecinos notables are seen as charlatans, as impostors who seek the benefits of elite status without assuming any of its important responsibilities. The town's high-ranking government bureaucrats are often cited for this failing. In general, the leadership crisis in Satipo has called into question the ideological basis of elite power and prestige. Whether this questioning eventuates in constructive change or in greater moral confusion remains to be seen.

La Gente Civilizada: The Civilized Majority

The cultured elite represents only a fraction of Satipo's immigrant population. The great majority of settlers are, in the brusque vernacular of the frontier, merely civilized. As a status category, civilization encompasses a large, heterogeneous population. Included among the civilized are literates and illiterates, farmers and truck drivers and lumberjacks, and speakers of Spanish, Quechua, and even Campa. While they differ in many respects, the civilized are alike in their commitment to "progress" and the "conquest of the frontier" (phrases they use repeatedly). Colonists associate progress with the building of roads, schools, churches, and towns in areas that once were wilderness. The civilizados are careful to point out the differences

---

[1] This phrase, literally translated, means "the Peru of before," that is, the Peru before agrarian reform and the Velasco government. It is a phrase that establishes a background against which informants outline the changes that they perceive as having taken place in the nation as a whole since 1968. My informants used this expression with great frequency.

between themselves and the uncivilized aborigines of the Satipo region. Those people, the settlers contend, lived a nomadic hunting and gathering life that had no purpose, ambition, or direction. The strange customs and traditions of the aboriginal Campas further contributed to their backwardness. Civilization is seen as a major advance over primitive Campa society. Although the civilized are outranked by the cultured, they are ranked far above the forest natives.

Within the civilized community are divisions great and small. One way to disentangle the frayed and knotted fabric of civilization is to distinguish between greater and lesser levels of discord. The breakdown of frontier society into cultured, civilized, and uncivilized units represents the first level of conflict perceived by the settlers. The civilized category breaks down into a myriad of status distinctions based on race, language or dialect, dress, place of origin, and other defining features. In fact, it would be almost impossible to devise a status taxonomy that would comprehend all of the nuances and their meanings. What follows, then, is not a rigorous taxonomy of the civilized community, but rather an attempt to reveal certain gross and subtle status distinctions, to show on what basis they are made, and to examine their role in shaping the course of daily life.

The civilized population of Satipo is composed almost entirely of immigrants from the adjacent Andean highlands.[2] The highlanders or *serranos* are divided, at the most general level, between those who are identified as Quechua Indians and those who are seen as part of a social class that (although Indian in origin) seeks upward mobility via the establishment of a separate identity free from the constraints and stigmas of indigenous tradition. Essentially, the difference is between indios and cholos. This fundamental distinction deserves careful considera-

---

[2]Origin, in fact, serves as a rough guide to each of the three major status categories: the vecinos notables are from the coast, the civilized come from the sierra, and the uncivilized are natives of the montaña. There are some exceptions to this rule, but on the whole place of origin and social status are closely correlated.

tion in terms of both the criteria on which it is based and the way in which it structures social interaction.

The indio maintains certain patterns of dress, speech, and behavior that are associated with highland Quechua society. Among the most salient traits of Indianness are the use of Quechua in daily conversations, the wearing of traditional highland garments, and the chewing of coca. The presence of one or more of these attributes labels a person as indio rather than cholo. Normally it is a familiar cluster of diacritic elements rather than an isolated trait that serves to separate the indio from the cholo. The attributes appear in groups or they do not appear at all, a fact that simple observation readily confirms.

Cholos are not fond of the Indian population and they carefully avoid association with the symbols of Indianness described above. Thus many of my cholo informants were reluctant to admit that they knew and could speak Quechua. I observed some cholos actually feign ignorance of Quechua rather than suffer the embarrassment of speaking publicly in the language of the indios. The cholos are even more stringent in their avoidance of the coca habit, which they view as injurious as well as disgusting. In describing the indios, the cholos nearly always refer in disparaging terms to the Indians' daily use of coca. This and other symbols of Indian status are linked, in the cholo's mind, to the traditional role of the indio in Peruvian society, that of an impoverished and exploited peasant laborer. In seeking to raise their economic and social standing, the cholos have rejected the symbols of Indianness and all that these symbols represent.

The indio–cholo relationship is a stressful one in part because of the inconstancy and permeability of the line that separates them. The transition from indio to cholo status, a process that one analyst has termed *cholificación* (Bourricaud 1967), can be accomplished within an individual's lifetime or from one generation to the next. Mobility may be rapid or slow, complete or incomplete. Moreover, the indices of indio and cholo status vary from region to region and from one social context to another.

The fluid, subjective, and situational nature of this social division actually heightens awareness of its existence and creates an atmosphere of tension whenever indios and cholos interact.

The trademark of the cholos is their ability to recognize and to take advantage of even the slightest opportunity for advancement. The quintessential cholo is the petty merchant who buys and resells goods, squeezing a profit, however small, out of each transaction. But the cholo may also be a farmer, a soldier, a truck driver, a lumberjack, or a skilled craftworker. It is not a common occupation that defines the cholos but rather a common set of values, beliefs, and goals. Basically, the cholos feel that they are more ambitious, more intelligent, and more modernistic in outlook than the indios. At the very least, the cholos have lifted their sights above the day-to-day subsistence strategy pursued by the indios. On the other hand, the cholos know that their upward mobility is limited and that the competition for the scarce resources at their disposal is keen. In the end their lack of education and "culture" poses an obstacle to social mobility that not even the wily cholo can overcome. Nevertheless, the accomplishments of the cholos, given the structural constraints under which they operate, are impressive. François Bourricaud, in his perceptive analysis of the Peruvian social system (1975:355), provides some important insights in this regard:

> The *cholo* . . . occupies no fixed position or niche in the stratification system. He is fluid and elusive; you never find him where you expect him to be . . . the *cholo* is smart, he pushes, he can make money. He has learned a rudimentary way of managing which lays him open to the seductions of conspicuous consumption but gives him a considerable advantage over the Indians and traditional peasants. For this reason one finds him higher up, better placed, richer and more enterprising than his original status might seem to warrant. This ability to get on explains the negative reactions, the suspicions and aversions, directed against the *cholo*. His behavior calls into question the rigid order of old colonial society. The simple fact that, while he is neither Indian nor creole nor mestizo, he succeeds in rising demonstrates the possibilities which are open to anyone with his wits about him and which derive from what may be called the interstitial mobility of a society that is culturally very heterogeneous.

In the rural areas of Peru the cholos' gains have cost the indios much and the elite little. The cholo has become the Peruvian equivalent of the Russian kulak, an exploiter of his own kind rather than a challenger of the established order. The criollos and mestizos have ceded little power to the cholos. While opening several minor channels to mobility, particularly in the retail marketing sector, the criollos and mestizos have managed to keep the major opportunity channels firmly closed and out of the cholos' reach. The indio, in turn, is treated harshly by the emergent cholo class. In dealing with the cholos, the indios have learned that they can expect none of the paternalistic favors and concessions that were formerly granted by the patrones. From the indios' point of view, the cholo is a callous entrepreneur who refuses to be influenced by any considerations that are not strictly economic.

The indio–cholo relationship is best exemplified by the interaction between the small farmers of Satipo (mostly indios) and the independent truck drivers (mostly cholos) who buy farm produce and transport it to the capital city. In this exchange the indios are at a great disadvantage. Their farm produce, once harvested, must be sold quickly, before it spoils. The cholo truck drivers know that the indios are anxious to sell their bananas and papayas, and that they can be forced to accept an extremely low price for them. Consequently, the cholo makes the lowest possible offer whenever he finds an indio with produce to sell. If the indio hesitates or refuses, the cholo simply drives away, telling the farmer to find another buyer. Although the cholo truck drivers represent only one link in the chain of market transactions (see Chapter 7), they alone come into direct contact with the indios. For many indios, the cholos symbolize the entire marketing system and its manifold injustices.

Relations between cholos and indios are strained at best and openly antagonistic at worst. The indios tend to focus their disappointments and frustrations on the cholo merchants with whom they are forced to do business. The cholos contend, however, that they are not responsible for the indios' miserable plight. As one cholo truck driver told me, "The only way I can make a profit is by exploiting the indio worse than the *mayorista* [city merchant] exploits me." According to this cholo, the cause of the indios' present predicament lies in the awesome power of the criollo and mestizo elite. It is not the cholos who control the market economy, but rather the criollos and mestizos who work with and through their cholo agents to dominate the rural hinterland and its heavily Indian population.

As agents, however, the cholos are more intensely hated than the distant city merchants who monopolize the marketing system. This fact is not easily dismissed as "false consciousness" or as a superficial or passing phenomenon that will eventually give way to a more "realistic" class confrontation. The ideological dimensions of the indio–cholo conflict have a sobering effect on anyone who attempts to analyze the present malaise in sheer economic terms. The symbols of Indianness on the one hand and cholo modernity on the other tend to blur or obscure any underlying unity of interest. For the present, at least, the ideological struggle is foremost among the several internal struggles that confront the Peruvian nation.

By now it should be obvious that civilization, which includes both indios and cholos, is not a homogeneous social category. Nor is the indio–cholo division the only schism within the civilized community. Another source of conflict and misunderstanding lies in the diverse provincial origins of Satipo's highland immigrants. This problem has been mentioned in previous chapters, particularly with respect to the Pérez Godoy colony, but it has not yet been fully explained.

The Andean highland region of Peru has two kinds of indigenous traditions: a general tradition that was established by the spread of Inca civilization in the fifteenth century and a series of highly localized traditions that existed before Inca expansion and that have persisted in spite of the upheavals and transformations of the past five centuries. To the uninitiated observer of highland society the differences between one village or district and another do not appear to be great. One may notice, for example, that the hat and dress styles of the women in a particular town differ from those of women in another town a few miles down the road. Beyond minor differences of this sort, one might conclude, there does not seem to be any significant variation in the overall pattern of highland Quechua society. Upon closer examination, however, this initial impression proves to be entirely false and highly misleading. Indeed, as one comes to know the highlanders better, the importance of local ethnic traditions is repeatedly confirmed.

These traditions derive from the *ayllu* organizations of Inca and pre-Inca times. The ayllu was a corporate kinship group that recognized a single leader or *kuraka* and controlled certain territorial and water rights.[3] Throughout the Andean highlands, ayllus formed the core or focus of local social structure. Although hundreds of ayllus were politically integrated during the fifteenth century under the aegis of the Inca state, their separate identities and their separate properties remained intact. In fact, the consensus among students of pre-Hispanic Peru is that the autonomy and internal solidarity of each ayllu were actually reinforced by the governmental structure of the Incas.

Five centuries later, it is still common to hear highlanders refer to their native town or district in terms of its ayllu affiliation. People who leave their native community (to settle in the montaña, for example) remain strongly identified with their place of origin. In Satipo the most important point of information about a particular individual from the sierra is the person's district or province of origin (which, in turn, reveals an ayllu connection). When colonists talk about themselves or about someone they know, the individual's home town is invariably mentioned along with a description of the general characteristics of people from that area. To the settlers it is extremely important to know if someone is a huancaino, a jaujino, an andamar-

---

[3]The ayllu is a highly complex form of social organization that has been the subject of much historical and ethnographic research. Summaries of the most recent studies in the field of Andean kinship and social organization are provided in a collection of articles edited by Bolton and Mayer (1977).

quino, or whatever. When the colonists of Satipo say that "we are different peoples" and "we do not understand each other," it is usually their diverse ethnic origins that they are referring to.

The distinguishing features of each group or category are various and often quite subtle. One of the most important criteria on which ethnic differences are based is language. In the central Peruvian highlands several dialects of Quechua are spoken. Thus in an immigrant community such as Satipo the provincial origin of an Indian is revealed by the dialect of Quechua that he or she speaks. Some of the dialects, such as those of Ayacucho and Huancayo, are so different that colonists have great difficulty understanding each other. Moreover, settlers often say that they feel uncomfortable when they are with a person who, in their view, speaks a "strange" dialect of Quechua. For this reason Spanish has become the lingua franca of the frontier, the language that is used in almost all conversations except those between Quechua immigrants from the same dialect area.

Other differences include regionally distinctive forms of dress, house construction, and farming techniques. More important than any of these factors, however, is the question of values and associated personality traits. Colonists feel that each of the highland provinces has a particular social character that is derived from its ayllu tradition. It is said, for example, that the people from Huancayo (representing the Huanca ayllu) are basically hostile, unfriendly, and rebellious. The huancaino is said to be always involved in conflicts and disputes—over land, over livestock, over lovers, over practically anything. Although the huancainos acknowledge this image, they tend to portray themselves as intensely independent, strong-willed, and at times openly aggressive. This is the spirit of the Huanca people, they say, and it cannot and should not be changed.

Like the huancaino, every highlander has a reputation of some kind, whether it is the lazy and foolish andamarquino, the sly and cunning jaujino, or the miserly acobambino. These stereotypes are neither intended nor taken lightly. They are seen as real and profound divisions that could burst into open conflict at any time in a mixed community such as Satipo. In fact, one of the most bitter, and nearly violent, disputes that I observed in Satipo began with an exchange of ethnic slurs among a group of Indian settlers.

The community of Llaylla, where this confrontation occurred, is located about twenty-five kilometers south of Satipo, in an area that has been settled by small farmers of Indian peasant origin. Like the Pérez Godoy colony, Llaylla is composed of immigrants from diverse highland provinces. Andamarca, Yauyos, Ayacucho, and Andahuaylas are the areas most heavily represented. Also like Pérez Godoy, Llaylla has a parents' association that serves as the organizational focus of the thirty families that belong to the settlement. When the local school or the road is in need of maintenance or repair, a faena is called and each family is required to send one representative. This is the procedure followed by nearly all of the colonist communities of the Satipo region.

The leader of the Llaylla colony (whose official title is *teniente gobernador* or lieutenant governor) may convoke a faena whenever he believes that one is necessary. The faena that I attended was held on a Saturday (in September 1974) and was devoted to the repair of the narrow dirt road that connects the Llaylla community to the main regional highway. Shortly after dawn a member of each of the colony's thirty families was supposed to join the work gang that was assembling at the local schoolhouse. On that morning, however, twelve of the thirty laborers failed to show up. The eighteen settlers who did come to the faena felt that the work should not begin until all of the families were represented. A discussion ensued as to how to punish the families that neglected to fulfill their obligations to the community. One person suggested that the absentees be fined; another man proposed that a makeup faena be held on the following day (Sunday). It was generally agreed that the uncooperative families should not be allowed to escape their communal responsibilities.

Unable to decide exactly what course of action to take, the assembled colonists were about to disband when one person spoke up and declared that most of the missing families were from Andamarca (a highland province to the west of Satipo). All of the people from this region, he said, are backward and lazy and would never contribute to the progress of the community. This remark provoked a sharp response from a man who was a native of Andamarca and who resented this slur aimed at his homeland. A verbal free-for-all broke out in which settlers defended their own ethnic origins and insulted those of the other colonists present. The fragile unity of the Llaylla community was torn apart at the seams. Their common purpose and their common interests became lost in a maze of ethnic antipathy.[4]

Events of this kind are not unusual in Satipo. Ethnic diversity prevails in all of the region's farming communities and accounts for the basic patterns of rivalry and factionalism that emerge in these settlements. One might think that in order to avoid this problem, colonists from the same highland district or province would settle together in one part of the montaña, thereby preserving or recreating the ethnic character of their homelands. Such is not the case. Each family that migrates to Satipo settles wherever land is available; there is no consistent or controlled resettlement scheme. The result is a scattershot distribution of ethnic types rather than the enclave system that is seen, for example, in the neighborhoods of many major cities. The unity of paisanos that is such a prominent feature of immigrant organizations in Lima is not a characteristic of immigrant associations in Satipo.

---

[4]Throughout the meeting I remained in the background, quiet but not unnoticed. Several members of the community had invited me to observe the faena and they were embarrassed, to say the least, by the acrimonious exchanges that took place. The lieutenant governor in particular tried to bring order to the meeting by saying that a distinguished guest who had come to observe a community effort was being given a very negative impression of Llaylla and its people. This tactic was not successful, however, and the verbal assaults continued. When the meeting finally broke up, a few settlers sought me out to apologize for the tone of the discussion.

The only colonist associations are the residential communities that are made up of settlers who live along a particular stretch of road and send their children to a common school (Pérez Godoy and Llaylla are communities of this kind). The fact that these communities tend to be weak and divided is primarily attributable to the large number of discordant ethnic groups that are represented in each settlement. This is a conclusion with which most colonists would heartily agree. The diverse ethnic origins of Satipo's highland immigrants are a source of constant dissension and conflict within "civilized" society.

Civilization, then, is a rather complex social category. Though committed to progress and development, the civilized are impeded in that quest by more than the power of the elite. Internal divisions and factions frustrate the colonists and render them defenseless against the many injustices they suffer. At present it appears that several major ideological battles must be decided before the civilized will be ready to confront effectively the problems presented by criollo and mestizo domination of Peruvian society.

Los sin Civilización: The Campa Dilemma

Our discussion of ethnic groups and boundaries would not be complete without an analysis of the social position of Satipo's aboriginal inhabitants: the Campa natives.[5] Unlike most other instances of colonist–native contact in the South American jungles, the colonization of Satipo has led to neither the extermination nor the expulsion of the Campa people. The Campas today represent approximately 25 percent of the population in the most heavily colonized zones. In peripheral areas yet to feel the effects of intensive settlement the percentage is much higher (up

[5]The local custom is to refer to the Campas as "natives" and not as "Indians," the latter term being reserved for highlanders with strong ties to Quechua tradition. In the anthropological literature, however, the Campas are nearly always called "Indians." The distinction between *indios* and *nativos* is essential to an understanding of ethnic relations on the frontier.

to 80 percent are Campas). Of course, colonization has created major problems, some of which have threatened the Campas' very existence. But the Campas now seem to have recovered from the initial shock and disorder of pioneer invasion and are actually beginning to increase in strength and numbers. We are dealing here not with the displaced, marginal survivors of a bygone era but with an awakening national minority.

The dilemma that the Campas face in their struggle for equality and social justice is, to corrupt a famous line, to be or not to be civilized. That is the question with which several generations of Campas will have to grapple. Colonists unanimously condemn the aboriginal society as "uncivilized." Whether to accept that characterization, and in so doing to accept the burden of change, is a decision that the Campas will have to make. Let us explore a little further the ideology of civilization and its multiple uses as a tool of frontier expansion.

The concept of civilization was introduced to the montaña by the Franciscan missionaries who first contacted the Campas and who later brought the first colonists to Satipo. The goal of the Franciscans was, in the words of one nineteenth-century priest, "to liberate the tribes that live in barbarism and idolatry from their rude life and to introduce them to civilization and the Christian religion" (cited in Ortiz 1961:256). It is instructive to note exactly what the missionaries, and later the colonists, regarded as the signs or traits of barbarism and the rude life.

Among the Campas' alleged faults were their religious beliefs. The Campa religious system was and is an enigma to missionaries and colonists alike. This lack of understanding is revealed in the highly distorted and confused popular portrayal of Campa cosmology.[6] It is said that the Campas believe in numerous evil spirits, called *kamari,* and that, as a result, the natives live in constant fear of the jungle and its malevolent powers. The

---

[6]The best anthropological account of the Campa belief system is that of Gerald Weiss (1969). Here my concern is not to examine the complex world of Campa ritual and symbolism but to show how that world is described and evaluated by the pioneers of Satipo.

Campas purportedly believe in no god nor in any other benign being. Their local shamans, or *sheripiari,* are seen as eccentric wizards who effect more ills than cures. Instead of renouncing these false priests and adopting the "superior" Christian faith, the Campas have clung stubbornly to their native beliefs and practices. Characteristically, the Campas have submitted to baptism and confession only to return to their uncivilized ways immediately thereafter. Religion, then, is one area where the Campas have yet to be civilized.

Another aspect of the rude life that is often mentioned by colonists is the seminomadic existence of the aboriginal Campas. In Chapter 2 we saw that before colonization the Campa ecosystem had been based on frequent changes in settlement sites. Every two or three years the Campas would abandon their houses and gardens and move to another part of the region. This pattern of migration is seen by the colonists as crude and uncivilized. The settlers say that civilized people own their land and build permanent settlements on it. Moreover, the civilized live by agriculture and industry and not by hunting and gathering in the jungle. The Campas are said to have had no ambition, no desire for progress. As evidence of this fact the colonists cite the lack of roads, towns, and industry in the montaña before colonization. The Campas, they say, had no greater purpose in life than to hunt and fish and wander about in the forest.

Still another "barbaric" trait of the aboriginal Campas was their perpetual involvement in internecine warfare. Fierce rivalries and enmities between Campa chiefs often led to open aggression. The first missionaries and colonists of Satipo, many of whom still live in the colony today, boast of having put an end to these hostilities and of having helped the various Campa groups to live in peace and harmony with each other. Satipo's old-timers often told me that they literally stepped between groups of warring Campas and forced them to disband. While the authenticity of these accounts may be questioned, there is no doubt about the settlers' commitment to the belief that colonization imposed the norms of civilization on a group of warlike savages. An important component of the ideology of civilization is the assertion that the natives were forced by the colonists to stop their internal feuding and to settle their differences peacefully.

Finally, colonists tend to isolate certain customs and traditions of the Campas and label them "uncivilized." For example, the settlers often ridicule the elaborate designs that Campa men and women paint on their faces during periods of ritual activity. The natives' dress and bodily adornment are seen as queer and shameful. Another Campa custom on which colonists heap their scorn is the couvade. On many occasions I heard settlers describe how Campa men become weak and sickly when their wives are about to give birth. The colonists find great humor in this behavior. The practice of polygyny (common in aboriginal times) is viewed with equal disfavor by the civilized population. Whereas Campa headmen previously had three or more wives, this custom is now prohibited by law. The colonists argue that today the Campas live in a different world and that they must sooner or later conform to the ways of civilization.

The harsh treatment that the Campas receive from pioneer society is justified, therefore, in terms of the ideology of civilization. Frontier expansion has a moral as well as an economic rationale. Presumably the Campas have the option of reforming themselves and subsequently taking their place among the civilized members of society. Some colonists say that certain Campas already have made progress in this direction and are now quite close to being civilized. Campa identity, however, is an element of status that is never lost. No matter how hard individuals may strive to dissociate themselves from native tradition, colonists will always be able to detect their Campa identity (racial characteristics, if nothing else, reveal their origins). Ricardo Castro, an acculturated Campa who worked in a sawmill near town and who neither spoke nor dressed nor acted like a native, was called Campa Castro by his friends and co-workers. It is not correct, then, to say that a Campa may merge with civilized society whenever he or she chooses to accept its norms and values. At present there is virtually no way that a Campa can rise from the bottom rung of the social and economic ladder.

The Campas have no illusions about their current position within frontier society or about their prospects for future improvement. They realize that discrimination works in many overt and subtle ways to prevent assimilation. Moreover, very few Campas believe that assimilation is the answer to their problems. While the colonists, as we have seen, take a dim view of native society, the Campas have an equally low opinion of the pioneer community. In the Campas' eyes, Satipo's highland immigrants are a depraved and malicious people who would seize any opportunity to abuse them. Thus the Campas feel that they should uphold their own standards of morality and conduct and that they should pass these values on to future generations. From the Campas' viewpoint, it is neither possible nor desirable to merge with civilized society.

What, then, is the Campas' strategy for the future? How do they propose to adapt to a changing world while preserving a valued heritage? For the moment they are focusing on a few basic problems, one of which is education or, more specifically, literacy. Nearly all Campa adults are illiterate, a handicap of which they have grown acutely aware in recent years. In my research I found that often only the headman of a Campa settlement could read or sign his name. Thus in disputes over land or lumber, in dealings with the bank or the cooperative, the natives are ill prepared for the vast amounts of paperwork involved. On countless occasions the Campas have been cheated or deceived because of their inability to read or comprehend the documents they have had to sign. To correct this situation, the Campa elders have undertaken to construct and equip a school building on each native reserve. Once a building is completed, the local headman petitions the Peruvian government to send a teacher. In this way it is hoped that the abuses committed against one generation of Campas will not be repeated in the next. The Campas have an almost blind faith in the powers of education and they are doing all that they can to ensure that today's children will learn to read and write Spanish.

Another top priority of the Campas is the strengthening of the native reserve system. At present the areas of land designated as *reservas nativas* are entirely too small for the numbers of people that they accommodate. Table 8 shows the family/land ratios for the seven Campa reserves that I studied. The average landholding per family for the seven communities considered is 3.4 hectares. In contrast, the average landholding of the colonist family is roughly 20 hectares.

The Campas are literally squeezed onto lands that could not support a population half the present size. Since each reserve is surrounded by colonist farms, there is little or no room for expansion. It must be remembered that the native reserves were originally created *by colonists* who wanted to build permanent labor pools near their farms. But whereas the Campas once agreed to work for the settlers, they are no longer willing to do so. Years of mistreatment and deception have given wage labor a bitter taste for the Campas. Even though they cannot adequately feed themselves with the produce from their small garden plots, they will do anything (even suffer from hunger) rather than work for the colonists. Many times during my study I observed settlers making visits to Campa communities with the intention of hiring several part-time or full-time farm hands.

Table 8. Number of families and land area in seven native reserves, 1974

Reserve	Number of families	Land area (hectares)
Cushibiani	22	50
Santa Rosa de Panakiari	26	100
Campamento Portillo	18	100
San Pascual	18	30
Alto Sondobeni	16	60
Paureli	27	100
Yavirironi	23	70
All reserves	150	510

SOURCE: Personal census conducted in Satipo during 1974.

But in every case the offers of employment were refused. Some of the colonists later told me that their offers had been rejected because of the natives' laziness and indifference. The truth is that the Campas are no longer willing to be used and then discarded without the promised compensation.

If they are ever to become self-reliant, the Campas feel, somehow they must acquire more land. The native reserve system would be agreeable to them if only they were given enough land to live on. Ironically, in the heavily colonized zones large areas of land are currently either underworked or abandoned. Invariably these lands are part of a bankrupt estate that now belongs to the state bank and that cannot be claimed for private use unless the claimant is willing to assume responsibility for the sizable debt left by the previous owner. In numerous official petitions the natives have asked the government to grant these lands to them as compensation for the losses they suffered in the early years of pioneer settlement. The Campas would even be willing to pay for the lands on a long-term basis, provided that the selling price did not include the previous owner's debt. Thus far, however, the Campas' petitions have not emerged from the bureaucratic maze, and it is unlikely that they will be acted on in the near future. This delay is all the more painful to the Campas because their population, which had been declining, is now increasing at a rate that greatly overtaxes their land resources.

In June 1974 the "revolutionary" government of the armed forces issued a law that was supposed to enable the native peoples of the Peruvian tropical forest to expand their landholdings and to protect themselves from "all forms of exploitation." The Law of Native Communities and Agricultural Development of the Selva and Ceja de Selva decreed that the native reserves would be expanded by expropriation of privately held lands. No one in Satipo, however, colonist or native, actually believed that the government would implement this legislation in a decisive manner. Most of the Campa leaders felt that their rights were already protected under existing legislation and that the new laws were designed to recycle land claims that had already been filed years before. The Campas of Satipo were determined not to be duped by the empty promises of redundant and superfluous legislation enacted paternalistically on their behalf.

However the land issue may be resolved, it is clear that the Campas intend to remain united in their approach to this and other problems. Their strength lies in their ability to work together, a skill that the colonists have yet to develop. On the native reserves the spirit of cooperation and communal solidarity can be seen in a variety of contexts. Although farmland is individually owned, the natives nearly always work in groups, moving from field to field until all lands have been cultivated. The Campas say that they do not like to work alone (in colonist fashion) because they become bored and lonely. Thus community faenas, the bane of colonist settlements, are held often and with excellent results by the Campas. In general, there is much more social interaction and community life among the Campas than among the colonists. The social traditions of the native communities stand in sharp contrast to the disorder and anomie of Satipo's pioneer settlements.

The Campa identity crisis, in sum, seems to be resolving itself in favor of rebirth rather than assimilation. Some Campas still retreat into the jungle to escape colonization, but this problem seems to be diminishing. The paisanos, as the Campas call themselves, no longer believe that flight from the advance of civilization constitutes a wise or a realistic course of action. Nor does acculturation offer a solution to the problem of how to confront the discriminatory policies and practices of civilized society. The solution, at least for now, is to stay and to form a solid line of defense around the values and symbols of native tradition.

Unfortunately, one cannot conclude a discussion of Campa resilience on an optimistic note. While the Campas show signs of recovering from the impact of pioneer invasion, they are also being drawn into the national economy as producers of foodstuffs for the urban market. The natives already have set aside small plots of land for the cultivation of cash crops and they hope to expand these areas in the near future. But the arrangements by which farm produce from Satipo reaches the urban market are no different for natives than for colonists. The same set of exploitive market relations that afflict the colonists also afflict the Campas. And yet the vital concerns shared by these two groups are vastly overshadowed by the ethnic differences that separate them. Once again, as with cholos and indios, as with immigrants from diverse highland provinces, ethnic conflict impedes the formation of effective associational interest groups. The result is a powerless multitude of discordant voices complaining, ironically, of the very same problems.

Ethnic divisions and antagonisms create the kind of social environment in which oppressive institutions flourish. Conflict between ethnic groups is neither a cause nor an effect of poverty and stagnation; it is a medium through which the forces of economic and political domination travel with ease. With no vehicle for the expression and pursuit of class-related goals, the bulk of Satipo's inhabitants will remain where they are today: on the treadmill of day-to-day survival. As the treadmill spins, the unbridled energy and ambition that frontier families bring to their daily tasks are slowly and fruitlessly expended.

6

Seven Biographical
Portraits

Thus far I have provided only glimpses of the individual men and women who live and work under stressful
conditions in the montaña. This chapter will serve to correct
that shortcoming. An anthropological account, however discerning, of the historical and contemporary patterns of society
and culture would be vacuous without an equally discerning
portrayal of individuals and idiosyncrasies.

Informants' accounts of their life experiences are among the
most important kinds of data for anthropological analysis. In
contrast to the ordered set of facts and figures obtained in a
questionnaire, unstructured first-person narrative casts an irregular yet more diffuse light on a society and culture. Unlike
the responses given to a set of specific questions, life-history
reports are not predetermined as to shape or substance. Depending on the character and disposition of the informant, such
a report may be a detailed, chronologically ordered autobiog-
raphy or a rambling sequence of anecdotes apropos of nothing
except perhaps a vague sense of "how I ended up where I am
today." In whatever form, such accounts provide valuable in-

formation and frequently reveal certain patterns of belief or action that would have escaped the analytic grasp of an allegedly more rigorous methodology.

With the informants' testimony recorded and in hand, the anthropologist can proceed in one of two directions. He or she can glean from the material relevant bits and pieces of data, place them in an orderly arrangement, and offer them in support of a particular model of the social or cultural system. Alternatively, the anthropologist can present the material more or less as he or she receives it, overlooking (for the moment, at least) the larger design of the system and concentrating instead on individual mannerisms, idiosyncrasies, and the like. There is, after all, as much to be said for portraits as for landscapes in the study of social systems, and the anthropologist does well to exhibit both.

In this chapter my concern is with portraits—with individual variation, personal style, and a basic feeling of what it is like to be a frontier settler. I have selected from among my informants seven people who represent, as best I can determine, a cross section of Satipo's population. None is a "typical" colonist because there is simply no such thing. Rather, in their backgrounds, social and economic standings, and value orientations, they seem to cover the range of variation that I found in Peruvian frontier society. In any case, the precision with which the larger population is represented is not of primary importance here. More significant is the fact that these seven individuals became my friends. They were open and receptive to my study and gladly furnished information about their life experiences, past and present.

Pedro Sánchez

Born and raised in the department of La Libertad, in northern Peru, Pedro Sánchez came to Satipo in 1927 as one of the region's first settlers. He is now in his late sixties. In discussing the colony's past, one of his favorite diversions, don Pedro describes persons and events with remarkable clarity and detail. He is also a man of strong convictions who never hedges in the defense of a belief or opinion. Over the years, he says, innumerable wrongs and injustices have been committed against him, but he has always fought back. Don Pedro takes no small measure of pride in the fact that he has endured hardships and adversities that drove scores of other would-be settlers out of the montaña.

The earliest years of the colony were by far the worst. Don Pedro came alone to Satipo under the auspices of the short-lived government colonization program of the late 1920s. He was supposed to receive free food rations and tools from the government until his new farm began to produce, but in fact he never obtained such assistance and was forced to live "like a Campa"—that is, by hunting and gathering in the jungle—for several years. To hear the bitterness with which don Pedro describes this experience one would think that it had happened only recently rather than nearly fifty years ago. He says that the government deceived the original colonists into thinking that their basic needs would be provided for while in reality they were abandoned and left to fend for themselves.

Not long after arriving in Satipo, don Pedro contracted malaria and nearly died. During his slow convalescence he was unable to do heavy farmwork and thus fell far behind in his plans to develop the thirty hectares of land allotted to him by the government. During his first ten years in the montaña, don Pedro's primary and only goal was survival. For him as for his fellow settlers, the preservation of life itself counted as a triumph.

His first bit of good fortune came in the late 1930s, when the cultivation of barbasco as a cash crop began in Satipo. Don Pedro used his initial profits from this crop to purchase more land on which to cultivate more barbasco. He soon became the owner of two hundred hectares, one hundred of which he planted in barbasco. By all accounts his was the largest barbasco farm in the Satipo region, employing about thirty full-time laborers plus many more seasonal migrants at harvesttime. The 1940s were prosperous years and don Pedro became one of Satipo's most eminent patrones, a landowner of considerable wealth and status.

The bust in the barbasco industry caught don Pedro by surprise and left him with a once profitable farm suddenly turned worthless. His reaction was to abandon the barbasco fields and to leave the colony with the money he had managed to save during the better years. He moved to his homeland of Trujillo, on the northern coast of Peru, where he made a few business investments, none of them successful. In general, things went badly for don Pedro during the four years he spent away from the colony. Understandably, then, when news reached him that a coffee boom was under way in Satipo, he decided to return to the montaña and start anew. Fortunately, he had never sold his farm, anticipating that he might want to return there one day.

Because of his local esteem and good connections, don Pedro was able to secure a large loan from the state bank to finance the development of a coffee plantation. He began with twenty hectares of coffee and gradually increased the size of his grove to seventy-five hectares. By 1960 he was one of the largest coffee producers in the Satipo region. But when the price of coffee began to fall during the 1960s, don Pedro found himself in serious trouble. He still owed the bank more than S/.1 million and yet his earnings from the coffee crop had dwindled to almost nothing. In effect he was forced to default on the repayment of his loan in spite of constant pressure, bordering on harassment, applied by the state bank to make him meet his obligations. The bank, he says, never sympathized with the coffee growers' plight, insisting only that the loan (with interest) somehow be paid off.

Today don Pedro lives a spare but not uncomfortable farm life with his wife and three of his five children, his eldest two sons having left home to pursue university studies in Lima. His debts still hang over him, but he has resolved to ignore the occasional notices he receives from bank officials threatening legal action leading to seizure of his property. He does not believe that he will be singled out from among the hundreds of colonists who owe money to the bank and assigned some special punishment. The bank, he says, eventually will have to recognize that the debts incurred during the coffee fever and still unpaid will never be recovered.

What does concern don Pedro is the policies of the "communist" military regime that has governed Peru since 1968. Basically, he does not agree that everyone should be equal, a belief that seems to underlie all of the legislation enacted by the "revolutionary" military junta. The Indians of Peru, he asserts, need a patrón and will never get along without one. Left alone and without the guidance of a patrón, don Pedro argues, the Indian peasants from the highlands will never progress or contribute to the task of national development. They are "lazy, ignorant, and childlike," he says, "and they must be shown exactly what to do and punished if they fail to do it." One of don Pedro's favorite sayings is that to make the Indians work, the patrón must hold "their bread in one hand and a whip in the other." He contends that no less paternalistic or authoritarian system will ever work in Peru, and that the military government should acknowledge that fact instead of attempting to restructure national society along totally new and different lines.

Yet many reforms have already been introduced and don Pedro has felt their effects. "Now," he says, "you cannot get good workers because the agrarian reform has given land to the peasants and told them that they no longer need their patrón." The few laborers he does hire are completely *maleados* (turned bad or spoiled) and cannot be trusted. In recent years he has been deceived several times by peasants who came to his farm seeking employment and asking for a small advance on their wages. Once they had received the money, the peasants ran away without having worked a single day. This kind of chicanery committed against a prominent patrón of Satipo would have been inconceivable under what don Pedro refers to as the "old system." Clearly, such patrones as don Pedro no longer command the respect and deference that they were once accorded. These days, he says, even the most backward Indian is called "don," an honorific title formerly reserved for men of power and prestige. "The communists," he concludes, "are taking over and ruining all that was good in Peru."

Though it is unlikely that don Pedro's two hundred hectares will be taken over in the agrarian reform process,[1] the system of farming to which he is accustomed cannot be maintained under present conditions. The abundant and cheap labor supply represented by the impoverished Indian peasants of the highlands no longer exists. Don Pedro has reduced the size of his coffee grove to fifteen hectares and yet he is still hard put to find enough wage laborers to cultivate and harvest his crop. In the year I knew him he had no coffee harvest at all because a plant disease had so damaged his crop that it was simply not worth picking. He now makes a living primarily from the sale of bananas, citrus fruits, and corn, crops that demand less labor than coffee and yield modest profits.

Don Pedro had always hoped that upon reaching his present age he could turn over the farm to one or more of his children, giving them a good start in life. But his two oldest sons, who are studying in Lima, have expressed nothing but disdain for the montaña and have told their father that they will never return. Don Pedro's two daughters are both at home now but want to marry and move away from Satipo. Finally, his youngest son is working in the lumber business and has shown no interest in inheriting the farm. "My children are right," don Pedro admits, "when they tell me that there is no future in agriculture." The changes that are taking place in Peru "destroy a man's desire to work and to make the land produce."

The last time I saw don Pedro he showed me a letter he had

---

[1]In the course of my research in Satipo I never heard of an estate being expropriated from an owner who actually lived and worked on his or her land. Rather, the expropriation and redistribution of lands occurred only in cases similar to that of Pérez Godoy, that is, where an estate had been abandoned by its original owner and subsequently occupied by peasant invaders. Don Pedro's heavy indebtedness to the state bank further reduces the likelihood of a government takeover of his farm because of the enormous complications that would arise in the settlement of his debt.

received from a chemical company in the United States. The letter said that problems had arisen with the chemical substitute that had been invented to replace barbasco in the production of insecticides. In short, after more than twenty years since the bust in the barbasco industry, the company wanted to know if don Pedro would be interested in cultivating that crop again. To my surprise, don Pedro was indeed interested, but had reluctantly concluded that such a venture would probably be impossible nowadays. He asked me to write my countrymen a letter in my language explaining what had happened in Peru under the military regime and how things had changed. Such unjust reforms would never occur in the United States, he said, because "yours is a great and progressive nation. We Peruvians, my friend, are a very backward people."

Guillermo Vega

Guillermo Vega came to Satipo in 1958 with his parents, brothers, and sisters, a large family seeking land and a better life than the one they had led in the impoverished highland province of Andamarca (located in the department of Junín). In his native community Guillermo's father had owned a few scattered plots of land totaling about 1.5 hectares. The family produced potatoes, vegetables, and corn, but not in sufficient quantities to feed themselves. Their landholdings, Guillermo says, "*no alcanzó*" (did not "reach" or were not adequate) as a basis for subsistence. They lived in constant hunger and were "without decent clothes and shoes."

With so many mouths to feed (eight children in all), Guillermo's father left home during certain parts of the year to seek outside employment. Often he would work for two or three months in the copper and zinc mines of the Cerro de Pasco Corporation, an American company that had mining interests throughout the central Peruvian highlands. Alternatively, he might find temporary work as a day laborer on one of Andamarca's several large haciendas. One year, however, an enganchador from Satipo came to Guillermo's village wanting to enlist workers for the coffee harvest in the montaña. Guillermo's father signed up with the enganchador and spent three months in Satipo. Upon returning, he spoke enthusiastically about the montaña and about the possibilities of finding work and cheap land there. Within a short while it was decided that the whole family would leave the sierra and resettle in Satipo.

Upon arriving, Guillermo and his family were not able to acquire a piece of land of their own because of the intense speculation and land grabbing that had taken place in the early days of the coffee fever. Instead, they went to work as laborers on the coffee estate of don Pedro Sánchez. Guillermo, who was sixteen when he moved to the montaña, worked together with his father and brothers in the clearing, planting, weeding, and harvesting of don Pedro's land. Each earned a daily wage for his work except during the harvest season, when he was paid according to the number of five-gallon cans of coffee beans he picked. But according to Guillermo, don Pedro was a bad patrón who abused and mistreated his workers. "When don Pedro wanted to pay us," says Guillermo, "he paid us. When he didn't care to pay us, there was nothing we could do to obtain our wages."

After Guillermo's father died, in 1961, the family gradually began to split up and drift apart. Guillermo left the farm of Pedro Sánchez and went to work for a man who lived in Marankiari, a zone of colonist settlement located about twenty kilometers east of the town of Satipo. In his new job Guillermo was an *operario*, a permanent farm hand who cultivated his employer's small (five-hectare) coffee grove in return for a monthly salary. But as the price of coffee began to drop, the landowner fell further and further behind in the payment of Guillermo's wages. In 1963 the owner finally decided to abandon the farm and to give all of his twenty hectares of land to Guillermo as compensation for his unpaid wages. In this manner Guillermo acquired the small farm on which he lives today.

During the worst years of the coffee bust (the middle and late 1960s) Guillermo thought about leaving the montaña and returning to Andamarca. He realized that the best he could do as a coffee farmer was to break even with the creditor/merchant or habilitador in Satipo who loaned him money in advance of each year's harvest. But after making several visits to his home town in the sierra, Guillermo decided that he would be better off to stay in the montaña and hope that conditions would improve. If nothing else, he would not starve in the montaña, because he was fortunate enough to have a few hectares of relatively flat, fertile land on which to cultivate subsistence crops (corn, manioc, bananas). Having married and become the father of four children, Guillermo wanted to be sure that his family could count on an adequate food supply.

Guillermo's current concern is with the harm that may be done to farmers like himself by the policies of the Velasco regime. Already, he says, the agrarian reform has caused much damage by creating a shortage of landless farm laborers. "Ten years ago," Guillermo claims, "peasants like myself had to practically beg the patrón to give us work at any price. But now that I am my own boss, I have to get on my knees and beg the few peones that I can find to come and work for me at good wages." Moreover, Guillermo says, the patrón once exercised full authority over his laborers and exacted from them the most work possible. Nowadays Guillermo cannot scold or even criticize his farm hands for laziness or disobedience because he knows that they will simply leave and find work elsewhere. Guillermo has also had problems with farm laborers who request an advance on their wages and then run away without having fulfilled their obligations. These signs of what is to come in Peru are, Guillermo concludes, very discouraging and lead one to expect only the worst from the military government.

Most recently, a problem has arisen with the state bank which has convinced Guillermo that the government is against him. In 1973 he borrowed money from the bank in order to carry out his plans to cultivate bananas on a commercial scale. According to a bank agronomist who was consulted on the matter, Guillermo owned about two hectares of land well suited to the cultivation of that crop. On this recommendation, the bank granted a loan for S/.12,000, or S/.6,000 for each hectare of bananas. Guillermo then cleared, burned, and planted the land in the manner recommended to him by the bank agent. Production fell far short of expectations, however, and the bank had to be informed of this problem. When the agronomist came out to inspect the grove, he scolded Guillermo for planting the banana trees too closely together and for failing to follow other directions. But Guillermo insists that the agronomist gave him bad advice to begin with and that he is now trying to cover up his mistakes by asserting that Guillermo did not follow instructions.

Worse yet, just as the banana grove began to produce, a landslide wiped out a large section of road between Guillermo's farm and the market center of Satipo. In all, the road was blocked for four months before the government finally sent out a few bulldozers to clear away the rubble and reopen the route. During those four months the better part of Guillermo's first banana harvest rotted for lack of access to a market. Guillermo's losses were substantial during this period, and as a result he has been unable to repay the loan in full. But the bank, he says, shows no sympathy and always blames the farmer when problems arise in the cancellation of a debt. Although he has asked for more money to continue cultivating his banana grove, the bank has refused his petition for credit on the grounds that he still owes on the first loan. "They say in the bank that I am irresponsible and lazy but I know and they know that this is not true." Meanwhile, the interest continues to accumulate on the unpaid portion of Guillermo's debt and there is no solution in sight.

Whether or not Guillermo eventually gets out of debt, the future holds little promise. At most he hopes that his children will have a somewhat better life with greater opportunities. The key to getting ahead in a rapidly changing society is, he says, a good education. Himself illiterate, Guillermo claims that innumerable abuses and injustices are suffered by those who are uneducated. "The bank officials know that I am helpless against them because I have no education or culture." The only way to

correct this situation, Guillermo explains, is to sacrifice everything for the education of one's children. Although he knows
the deficiencies of the rural one-room school that his children
now attend, he still dreams that someday one of his children will
attend a national university. At least that is the distant hope and
ambition that carries him through the long, hot days of work on
the farm.

Jacinta de Samaniego

It is not uncommon for a woman, most often a widow, to be
the head of a colonist household. Jacinta de Samaniego has been
running a farm and raising a family by herself for over three
years, ever since her husband died of tuberculosis. She is one of
six widows who own and operate farms in the Pérez Godoy
colony. Jacinta works like any male colonist, rising before dawn,
eating a quick breakfast, and heading for her fields with
machete and hoe just as the first daylight breaks. Her nine children, ranging in age from four to sixteen years, have learned to
fend for themselves. The oldest, a daughter, takes care of the
youngest children during the day and makes sure that the ones
who should be in school leave early enough to arrive on time.
When food is scarce, as it often is, the older children allow their
younger siblings to eat first. Tasks such as carrying water, washing clothes, cooking, and cleaning are assigned to the children
individually according to their capabilities. Although Jacinta and
her family live in dire poverty, there is a definite sense of confi-
dence and poise in their daily round of activities.

Jacinta, who was born and raised in the highland province of
Huancayo, came to Satipo with her husband in 1956, when she
was seventeen and he was twenty years old. Their hope was to
find a piece of virgin land on which to settle and begin a farm.
But like many other poor Indian peasants who came to Satipo
during the coffee fever, Jacinta and her husband soon discovered that all of the lands surrounding the colony were claimed.
Consequently, they sought employment on one of the estab-

lished coffee estates of the region, temporarily postponing the search for a farm of their own. Jacinta's husband found work as a permanent farm hand or operario on the coffee estate of don Ramón Castro. There they resided for six years in a small hut provided by the patrón, living on wages that barely covered their subsistence needs.

Finally in 1963 Jacinta and her husband learned that a group of landless colonists such as themselves was organizing to invade an abandoned estate. They immediately sought to join the group and to participate in its plan to take over the land and divide it into small farms. When the occupation and settlement of the land took place, the Samaniego family was present and claimed a parcel of thirty hectares. Thus they were among the original twenty-eight families who founded the colony of Pérez Godoy.

Although Jacinta and her husband lost fourteen of their thirty hectares in the government reorganization of the colony, they at least received legal title to the other sixteen hectares. As government-certified landowners, they became eligible for credit from the state bank. Since they needed money to maintain and improve their coffee grove of six hectares, they sought and obtained a series of loans for farm development. Serious problems arose in the repayment of these loans, however, owing to the steady fall in the price of coffee through the 1960s and early 1970s. The meager earnings from each year's harvest were not sufficient to support the Samaniego family and to pay the bank as well. Today Jacinta still owes the bank more than S/.100,000, and the figure steadily rises as interest accumulates.

Moreover, she is a widow now and must manage these debts and handle other matters that were once the responsibility of her husband. It is difficult, she says, for an illiterate peasant woman such as herself to carry out business dealings with bank employees, town merchants, and farmers' cooperative officials, many of whom would readily take advantage of her inexperience to cheat her in some way. For example, recently she has been involved in a dispute with the man who owns the farm next to hers, whom she accuses of having encroached on her land.

When she went to the government land office in Satipo to file a complaint and to demand justice, she was virtually ignored. When she pressed for an answer, she was told "to stop nagging and bickering like a woman." Jacinta claims that this is the kind of treatment she receives whenever she goes to town on business matters. "They know that I am a poor Indian woman with nine children and no husband and no friends or relatives to stand behind me. It is a very sad and lonely life that a widow leads here in the montaña."

The worst part of it, she feels, is the farmwork, the twelve hours that she spends in the fields each day. Although Jacinta has learned how to use the machete, the ax, and the hoe, and how to perform all of the tasks in the annual cycle of coffee production, she believes that this work should be done by men. "A woman's place," she says, "is not in the field but in the home with her children and her domestic occupations." When her husband was alive Jacinta worked in the chacra only rarely; most of her time was spent cooking, washing, and caring for her children. Forced by his death to step forward and take charge of the farm, Jacinta reluctantly accepted this responsibility. She expects that soon her older sons will be able to assist her and that eventually they will take over the farmwork entirely. In the meantime, she continues to be the sole provider for nine hungry children.

So poor is the Samaniego family (even by montaña standards) that each week marks a new quest for survival. Every Sunday Jacinta goes to Satipo with one of her older children to buy food supplies for the following week. At the time of my study she needed at least S/.600 to buy enough rice, beans, noodles, vegetables, and other items to feed her family for a week. But usually she has only S/.300 or S/.400 to spend in town and therefore cannot bring home enough food to last until the next Sunday. They make up for this deficit as best they can with the produce from their tiny garden of subsistence crops (principally bananas, papayas, and manioc). In addition, they raise a few chickens and guinea pigs that can be eaten on special occasions such as a birthday or a holiday. Sometimes, however, the family has nothing and must go hungry for days at a time. As inflation drives up the cost of foodstuffs relative to the income that Jacinta derives from coffee production, the hunger in her household is likely to become ever more acute.

Already several of her children show signs of malnutrition complicated by inadequate health care. A diet wholly deficient in protein accounts for the reddish hair, swollen joints, and general frailty noted in a few of Jacinta's younger children. These symptoms of kwashiorkor have combined with the effects of parasitosis to weaken the children severely. They have never seen a doctor because Jacinta has no money and because she does not believe that medical attention would be of any value at this point.

When I last saw Jacinta she informed me in a rather expressionless tone that her youngest child had died. Though legally she was required to report the death to local authorities and obtain a death certificate, she had not done so because she knew from past experience that they would charge her S/.500 for the certificate. Instead, she buried the child in the jungle and told none of her neighbors what had happened. When a child dies young, she explained, it goes directly to heaven even if it does not have a proper funeral.

Changing the subject slightly, Jacinta said that she had heard over the radio that the Peruvian government had declared 1975 to be the Year of the Peruvian Woman. "What does it mean?" she asked. "Does the government intend to help poor widows like me?" I replied that to my knowledge it was only a slogan that the government had adopted in conformity with the United Nations celebration of International Women's Year. Not really understanding my answer but knowing full well that no government assistance would be forthcoming, Jacinta sighed and said, "Every promise made to the poor people of Peru turns out sooner or later to be a deceit."

Teodoro Acuña

The farmhouse of Teodoro and Carmen Acuña is no ordinary
colonist dwelling. In contrast to the disordered, ramshackle appearance of most colonists' homes, the Acuña house is well constructed, tidy, and surrounded by a series of carefully kept
flower gardens. The impression is not one of wealth but rather
of stability, resolve, and direction. The man who emerges from
the house confirms this impression. He is friendly and smiling
though he shakes hands in an awkward and effusive manner,
the kind of handshake one might expect from a man of peasant
origin who is accustomed to bowing in the presence of important
persons and who has only recently, and with some nervous determination, adopted a greeting that seems more egalitarian.

My visits to Teodoro's farm, located in the Río Negro Valley,
about eight kilometers north of Satipo, were always well received. Teodoro referred to me as a "man of science" and insisted that my study would be of great value to a "backward
country like Peru." Before an interview could begin, Teodoro
insisted that the chair in which I was to sit had to be dusted and
coffee served, followed by an enormous plate of food that Carmen offered "with apologies." Before I had asked any questions,
Teodoro explained to me that he had never learned to read or
write but that he had studied things "empirically" and would be
glad to share this knowledge with me. He said further that he
hoped I would share my "advanced knowledge" with him because he wanted to "technicize his mind" (*tecnificar la mente*).
Although I never quite understood what he meant by that, I
believe that he derived as much satisfaction from our relationship as I did.

Teodoro grew up as an orphan in a Franciscan convent near
Huancayo. As a teenager he was adopted by a peasant family of
that region. This family, he says, was interested only in exploiting his labor and never gave him enough to eat. At the age of
seventeen he ran away from his foster home and went to the
mining center of La Oroya to look for work. There he met a

"gringo"[2] (an American official of the Cerro de Pasco Mining Corporation) who helped him find a job and a place to live. Teodoro worked for a total of eight years in the mines, beginning as an ore shoveler laboring deep underground and advancing to the position of machine operator with surface duty. "In general," he concludes, "the Americans treated me well and paid me better wages than I could have made anywhere else. From them I also learned about the marvels of science and technology."

When Teodoro heard about the montaña from friends who had visited and worked in Satipo, he began to entertain the prospect of moving there. He thought that his experience in the mines had made him "smarter than the average Indian" and that he stood a good chance to succeed as a montaña farmer. When he arrived in Satipo in 1960, at the age of twenty-five, Teodoro had only a little money and could not afford to buy a farm of his own. But he soon met a merchant who owned some property in the Río Negro Valley and who was looking for someone to work this land on a sharecropping basis. Teodoro agreed to this arrangement and the two men became partners in a coffee-farming venture. They took out a loan from the state bank for the development of eight hectares of coffee grove on a farm that consisted of thirty hectares in all.

Only a year after this joint venture had begun, Teodoro's partner died. Shortly thereafter Teodoro claimed full possession of the land and assumed full responsibility for the debt of S/.100,00 that was owed to the bank. The remainder of the story should by now be familiar: the falling price of coffee on the world market left Teodoro unable to repay the bank, a predicament that continues without resolution to the present day. Teodoro says that the high rate of interest (12 percent) charged by the bank made it impossible for him to catch up in his repay-

[2]Peruvians use the term "gringo" to refer to any person with white skin. The term is simply descriptive and does not have the pejorative connotation common in other parts of Latin America.

ment schedule. At least that is what he tells the bank officials when they threaten him with seizure of his property. "The bank personnel," he says, "harass us only in order to exact a gratuity or favor of some kind in exchange for placing our file at the bottom of the stack. Now I just ignore them or challenge them to take legal action against me."

Though he continues to cultivate coffee, Teodoro now earns a living mainly from the commercial production of bananas, papayas, and oranges. He is fortunate in having about five hectares of land suited to this purpose and in living close enough to the main highway so that trucks can enter his farm to load the harvest. Teodoro is also a constant experimenter. Several years ago he planted a few hectares of land in tobacco, a crop that he says had never been cultivated previously in Satipo. While the grade of tobacco that he produced was considered poor, it did stimulate local interest and led to further experiments by other colonists. Today there is a small but growing tobacco industry in the Satipo colony. In his latest venture Teodoro has planted several hectares of pasture and purchased a few head of cattle in the hope that he can slowly build a small herd. His cattle seemed to me to be very thin and sickly, however, and I doubt that this enterprise will be successful. Nevertheless, Teodoro now refers to himself as a *ganadero* (cattleman) and is mapping out even grander schemes for the future.

This is not to say that Teodoro is blindly optimistic. He has grave concerns about the changes that have taken place since the Velasco military regime came to power. "Socialism is a lie," he says, "an excuse for some corrupt generals to seize power and make themselves rich in a hurry." Teodoro likes to ridicule the government's agrarian reform slogan: "Peasant, the patrón will no longer eat of your poverty" (Campesino, el patrón no comerá más de tu pobreza). A slightly different version of this slogan is offered by Teodoro: "Peasant, the socialists will now eat of your poverty." Though Teodoro has no kind words for any previous government, civilian or military, he feels that the Velasco regime is the worst he has lived under.

Farm laborers are scarcer than ever before, inflation is higher than ever before, and taxation is heavier than ever before. All of these problems can be attributed, Teodoro believes, to the policies of the "revolutionary" government. Moreover, Teodoro says that the socialists want eventually to eliminate all private property in agriculture and establish farming communes. Such a system would be intolerable, Teodoro claims, because it would destroy his ambition to build a better future for himself and his family. "If a man does not know that what he is working toward will be his own, then he will never work at all."

My most lasting impression of Teodoro Acuña is of one Sunday afternoon when he came to my house in Satipo to tell me about the military government's most recent blunder. He said that the regime was sponsoring a national folklore contest in which groups representing folk traditions from all parts of the nation would compete in a large festival in Lima. Instead of reviving antiquated customs and traditions, Teodoro argued, the government should be promoting science and technology. "Only science can give us machines to replace the farm laborers that we lost in the agrarian reform." Teodoro believes that folklore is useless and that it gives other nations the idea that Peru is still a nation of backward Indians. "We do not need folklore," Teodoro says, "we need machines."

Santos Ramos

Santos Ramos is the headman of a Campa village located about twenty-five kilometers north of Satipo. His community is an officially recognized native reserve composed of fifteen families living on approximately sixty hectares of land. The reserve is surrounded on all sides by colonist farms. As the leader of his small group of paisanos, Santos organizes their communal work sessions, settles their disputes, and perhaps most important, represents the community in its dealings with colonists, government officials, and other outsiders (such as an anthropologist or a missionary).

Santos, now in his late thirties or early forties, grew up in the same area where he lives at present. When he was a child, however, there were no colonists, only paisanos living by hunting and gathering "in the tradition of our ancestors." The first colonists to enter his native territory were land speculators who had purchased large tracts of virgin jungle from the state in the early 1950s, the era of Satipo's infamous coffee fever. Before that time the paisanos had traded sporadically with the colonists of Satipo, but the frontier of settlement had not advanced far enough to threaten Santos' community directly. Then suddenly the natives were confronted by colonists who told them that the state had sold the Campas' land and that the jungle no longer belonged to them.

The Campas, Santos says, were confused and frightened by the settlers' arrival. Many paisanos chose to flee farther into the jungle rather than confront the men who spoke and acted so strangely. Santos, however, was determined to stay and to learn what he calls "the ways of civilization." The leader who emerged among those Campas who had decided not to be pushed back by the colonists was Santos' father. A strong and respected Campa elder, Santos' father was also a shaman. In a trance induced by the native drug *ayavasca,* Santos' father had envisioned a future in which the Campas would receive in airplanes vast shipments of machetes, hoes, shotguns, metal pots and pans, and other material goods possessed by colonist society. The Campas should not run from the colonists, therefore, but should accept and adopt the ways of civilization and wait for the cargo to arrive.

Thus Santos and his father proceeded to negotiate an agreement or contract with a wealthy colonist from the coast who had purchased one thousand hectares along the Ipoke River. For his part, the colonist would set aside one hundred hectares of his land as a native reserve where a community of Campas who "wished to become civilized" might be established. For their part, the Campas agreed to work for the patrón in the clearing, burning, and planting of his land. As payment for their labor, they would receive a certain quantity of merchandise (machetes, rifles, and so on), the exact amount depending on the number of hectares prepared and planted. This arrangement is typical of the modus vivendi that was reached between the Campas and the coffee patrones of Satipo during the 1950s and early 1960s.

When Santos and his father founded a Campa community of approximately thirty families on land that had been ceded to them by their patrón, a new way of life began. The nomadic habits of the Campas, their aboriginal practice of changing settlement sites every few years, came to an end. And while they continued to hunt, fish, and gather, they began to rely much more heavily on agriculture as a means of subsistence. The need to be near the patrón at all times of the year so that work obligations could be fulfilled virtually dictated a sedentary, horticultural existence. Santos explains these changes by saying that they became necessary when the Campas decided to become "civilized" (a term he uses often).

The patrón borrowed large sums of money from the state bank in order to start a coffee plantation. In all, some fifty hectares of land were planted in coffee. The labor force that served this plantation included peasant immigrants from the sierra as well as the group of Campas led by Santos and his father. But while the Campas got along well with their boss (whom they describe as a "good patrón"), they frequently came into conflict with the Indian peasants from the highlands. Santos claims that the Indian laborers took liberties with Campa women, stole goods from the natives, and created many other problems with their disrespectful and abusive behavior. In the years since this first bitter encounter, relations between the Campas and the serranos have not improved.

Today the patrón is gone (a victim of the bust in coffee prices), Santos' father is dead, and the Campa village of which Santos is now headman faces a difficult and uncertain future. After the patrón left in 1965, many Campa families deserted the community and retreated farther into the jungle (along the lower Perené and upper Tambo rivers) where colonists had not yet arrived. At present only fifteen families remain on the native reserve that was established by the patrón and which is now an officially recognized Campa settlement. Before government recognition was achieved, however, the Campas lost approximately forty of their original one hundred hectares to colonists from the highlands who settled nearby and encroached forcefully on the natives' land. Santos says that the scant land resources that the community owns today cannot support even fifteen families. There is also a danger, he believes, that the serranos will try to steal more land from the Campas.

In the past, Santos explains, the Campas never knew how to defend themselves because they were unfamiliar with the ways of civilization. By "civilization" Santos generally means the customs, language, and governing agencies of the larger Peruvian society. Santos gives as an example of Campa naiveté the fact that his own generation did not know how to claim land at the government land office in Satipo. "We were all illiterate," he says, "and we could not make out the papers needed to file a claim." Instead, the Campas obtained from their patrón a piece of land to live on and never attempted to secure legal title to their property until the patrón had left and neighboring serranos had begun to steal native lands. "Now we know better," Santos claims, "and we must act with determination to protect our rights."

One of Santos' strongest convictions is that his children and their generation should attend school and should learn to read and write Spanish. As yet, however, there is no school in Santos' village. Several years ago the community, under Santos' leadership, constructed a large Campa-style house to be used as a school building. They even equipped it with desks and a crude blackboard, the way they had seen communities of colonists do. But the Campas' petition requesting the Peruvian Ministry of Education to send a teacher to the village has thus far been ignored. Although it has been more than two years since the petition was submitted, there is still no answer. Santos continues to hope that a teacher will be sent in the near future. In the meantime, he worries greatly about the possibility of yet another generation of Campas growing up in the shadow of the civilized world.

This is not to say that Santos would like to see the Campa children lose their native language and culture in the process of being educated in a different tradition. Rather, he would like the children to acquire the basic skills needed to live in a civilized world while retaining and preserving the beliefs and values of Campa culture. Santos says that there are bilingual teachers in a few Campa villages and he believes that this is a good idea. "We speak only Campa to our children," Santos explains, "and we do not want them to forget our language and our customs. We will not let them become lazy and drunken and disrespectful like the serranos." But Santos knows well that neither he nor anyone else can direct or control the course of change as it affects the younger generation. In any case, Santos feels that it is his responsibility to prepare the Campa children for the future even if such action may result in a weakening of native cultural tradition. The alternative of retreating into the wilderness to escape colonization becomes more unrealistic every day.

Pedro Cacique

To reach the farm of Pedro Cacique one must venture well off the beaten path. His farm is located almost twelve kilometers from the main highway and is accessible only by a narrow, muddy logging trail. This route was first opened in 1973 and it is now possible for a jeep or truck to enter the Cheni canyon, where Pedro lives. Before that time, Pedro brought in his supplies and took out his coffee harvest on his four mules. Even today Pedro must rely on his mules during much of the rainy season, when constant landslides block portions of the road.

Pedro has lived in this remote zone since 1963, the year he bought eighty hectares of virgin land from the state. Although he migrated to Satipo in 1958, he spent the first five years working for various patrones and saving money in order to buy some land of his own. Before 1958, Pedro lived in Moyobamba, in the department of San Martín, a zone of montaña settlement similar to Satipo. His parents were colonist farmers in Moyobamba but they had little land and were very poor. As a young man Pedro heard that Satipo was a new frontier settlement where lands were abundant and a coffee economy was booming. With his experience in montaña agriculture, Pedro thought that he would do well in Satipo, where most of the colonists had little knowledge of the jungle.

The fact that Pedro has not done well (or at least not so well as he anticipated) is due, he says, to forces and circumstances beyond his control. "I built one of the best coffee plantations in all of the Satipo region," Pedro claims, "and then the bottom fell out of the coffee market." Pedro did indeed develop a coffee grove of high quality and high yield. Until recently he produced around twenty quintals of coffee beans per hectare of cultivated land (about twice the average yield of a colonist farm). But what appeared to be a success turned into a failure as a result of deteriorating market conditions. Today Pedro is one of the hundreds of colonists who owe large sums of money to the state bank and who have little hope of ever paying their debts.

Pedro often says that the bank at least should discriminate between those settlers who used their credit to build good coffee groves and other colonists who spent the money unwisely and not in the manner prescribed in their loan contracts. According to Pedro, there was much cheating and misuse of bank funds during the coffee fever. His recommendation, then, is that colonists who, like himself, acted responsibly and failed honestly should be excused from their debts; the swindlers should be tracked down and forced to repay all of the money that they "stole" from the bank. This would be, Pedro believes, the only equitable solution to the problem. Years of experience in the montaña, however, have taught Pedro not to expect equitable solutions.

The small farmers of Satipo, he contends, have suffered countless abuses at the hands of bank officials, merchants, lumbermen, and other "exploiters." For example, Satipo's merchants purchase the produce of colonist farms at extremely low prices and transport it to Lima for resale at a substantial profit. Whether it is coffee, bananas, citrus fruits, papayas, or any other product of montaña agriculture, the system of buying cheap and selling dear is, in Pedro's eyes, always the same. "For this reason," Pedro explains, "we established the Coffee Cooperative of Satipo." The coffee growers of the region were tired of having their product marketed by a handful of merchant exporters who conspired among themselves to keep prices low. "We wanted to organize a cooperative that would export our coffee directly, enabling us to avoid the intermediaries and thus obtain higher prices for our crop."

But the cooperative, Pedro continues, has been plagued from the beginning with corrupt and inefficient administrators who have prevented the institution from fulfilling its avowed purpose. Pedro says that since the cooperative was formed in 1966 there have been many "scandals," most of which have involved elected officials who accepted bribes from coffee export companies based in Lima. Moreover, the government has never given the cooperative a license to export its own coffee, thereby forcing the colonists to make arrangements with these private export firms. Although within the past year (1974) changes have been introduced in the cooperative system, these reforms, Pedro is convinced, will not help the farmers' cause. "The government is trying to take over our cooperative by saying that we have managed our own affairs poorly and that we need state supervision and control." While Pedro agrees that the cooperative functioned poorly in its first years, he believes that a government takeover will only make matters worse. "When the government sells our coffee on the foreign market," Pedro asserts, "they will make an even greater commission than that of the merchant-thieves we are accustomed to dealing with."

Like most colonists, Pedro mistrusts the government and believes that it can do great harm and little good. He feels that there is already too much bureaucracy and state regulation in Peru and that under the Velasco regime these tendencies have increased. As an example he cites the recent social security law (*ley de jubilación obrera*), which he contends is nothing more than a plot designed to tax the poor people of Peru in order to fill government coffers. Pedro says that his workers do not want the social security tax deducted from their wages because they know that they will never receive any benefits under this program. As an employer, however, Pedro is required by law to deduct 2 percent from his workers' earnings and to contribute 4 percent of his own funds. According to Pedro, many laborers have left his farm when they learned that the social security tax would be taken out of their wages. In addition, Pedro has been fined several times by the social security office in Satipo for not keeping his records in proper order or for not paying on time or for some other reason. Pedro has decided to defy the authorities the next time they fine him. "We can pay taxes all of our life," he adds, "but we know that we will never receive medical care or a pension from the state when we grow old. It is all a fraud."

Pedro's lack of faith in his government is matched by his lack of faith in the future development of the Peruvian nation and its people as a whole. "We Peruvians," he declares, "are a people too easily exploited, too backward and uneducated to defend ourselves. Have you not noticed," Pedro asks, "that even though all of us colonists are opposed to the policies of our government, we cannot organize to express our dissatisfaction?" Pedro says that a colonist will express his beliefs openly to his family and friends but becomes shy and docile in the presence of local authorities. In Pedro's opinion a nation cannot develop when its people are like sheep who always yield before their master. If the settlers of Satipo were organized and united, he argues, they could effectively oppose the government and could determine for themselves the course of development and change in the montaña.

But instead of facing the real source of their problems, Pedro continues, colonists turn against each other and become engaged in an endless series of petty disputes. Pedro himself has been involved in a number of these conflicts and he knows how bitter and divisive they can be. One such dispute, which currently occupies much of his time, is over access to and ownership of the lumber reserves of the Cheni canyon. Although Pedro believes that these problems could be worked out harmoniously by the settlers concerned, egotism and self-seeking prevent a resolution. "The Peruvian people," Pedro says, "are vicious and unprincipled egotists." In the montaña every man seeks to gain and prosper at the expense of his fellow colonists. "We Peruvians," Pedro concludes, "are a disgraceful lot."

Juan Paredes

For the anthropologist far from home and more than a little bored with rural community life, a visit with Juan Paredes is a refreshing experience. Juan is the sort of man who, under other circumstances, might have been a great teacher and scholar. Though confined by lack of opportunity to the status of colonist farmer, Juan has become an acute observer and analyst of the world and of humanity. Through the newspapers that he buys in town and through the radio broadcasts that he listens to in his spare time, Juan keeps abreast of all the latest world news. In our interviews Juan would usually divert our attention from the local to the international scene: the Vietnam War, the Watergate scandal, the presidential elections in France, and other matters that one would ordinarily consider far removed from the concerns of a Peruvian jungle settler.

Surprisingly, Juan's background does not differ markedly from that of other frontier settlers. He grew up in a small town in one of the coastal valleys of Peru, where his father was a peasant sharecropper. There Juan completed five years of primary education before his parents took him out of school to help on the farm. But having learned the fundamentals of reading and writing, Juan continued to cultivate these skills on his own in the hope of resuming his studies at a later date. Although that hope has never been realized, Juan still reads and studies in his free time, and he is always eager to express and exchange ideas.

Juan first came to Satipo in 1955, to visit one of his older sisters who had married and moved to the montaña with her husband. As Juan explains it, he liked the montaña so much that he decided to stay and work as a day laborer on his brother-in-law's coffee farm. Having lived only on the barren and desert-like coast of Peru, Juan first thought of the jungle as a rich and infinitely promising land. His enthusiasm was further sparked by the coffee boom. The wages he made on his brother-in-law's farm were several times higher than the wages earned by an agricultural laborer in Juan's home town. All of these advantages convinced Juan that, in his own rather bold phrasing, "the future of Peru lay east of the Andes."

The bust in the coffee industry and the economic decline of the colony during the 1960s have greatly subdued Juan's once optimistic outlook. His explanation of what happened to the bright future he once foresaw is simple yet discerning. Too many speculators, he says, came to Satipo with the idea that they could make a quick and easy fortune in coffee. They calculated how many hectares of land they would plant and how many quintals of coffee they would produce per hectare. Then they multiplied the total number of quintals they planned to produce by the market value of a quintal in the boom year of 1954. On paper it appeared that each of these speculators would be able to repay the state bank and still make a handsome profit. But all of the predictions and calculations proved to be incorrect for two major reasons: the number of quintals that could be produced per hectare was much lower than expected and the world market price of each quintal fell far below the 1954 peak. As a result, the "paper millionaires," as Juan calls them, went bankrupt and abandoned their estates.

Juan acquired his own farm of fifty hectares in 1962, well after the coffee bust had begun. One might expect, therefore, that Juan would have had little interest in starting a coffee grove on this land. Since his farm was located far from town, however, in an area that at that time had no road connections, coffee was the only cash crop that he could produce. Unlike any other crop grown in the montaña, coffee can be stored for long periods without rotting and can be transported efficiently by mules even where there are no roads. All other products of montaña agriculture must be marketed swiftly, before they can spoil. Thus a settler who owns a farm that is not situated on or near the main highway has little choice but to cultivate coffee for a living. Such was the case with Juan Paredes; he became a coffee grower by necessity rather than by design.

Nevertheless, Juan managed to survive the worst years of Satipo's economic depression without getting into debt. He never borrowed money from the state bank and he accepted only as much credit from local merchants as he would be able to repay. Although he has lived through some very lean years, he is proud of the fact that he is not now in the position of so many other settlers, who, as Juan would say, "have their ass in hock to the bank."

Furthermore, today Juan depends much less on coffee because he has direct access to the urban market by means of a new road completed in 1975. The road actually bisects his farm and places him in the best possible position to cultivate a variety of crops for the Lima market. Juan says, however, that after thirteen years of cultivation his land is depleted of its nutrients and does not yield good harvests. At present Juan is taking advantage of the new road by cutting and selling the valuable timber that remains on a small part of his land. Juan burned away most of his commercial timber years ago, when there was no road by which to reach a sawmill. At present he seems to be slowly exhausting, in terms of both lumbering and farming potential, the few resources that are left in his land. The road has come a bit too late for Juan to prosper from it.

But Juan is not a man who likes to talk about his own problems, which in any case are not so great as those of most settlers. He is much more interested in and concerned about the problems of the world in general: the fierce competition between capitalism and communism, the inferior status of the Third World nations, the spread of international terrorism and civil warfare. These topics fascinate Juan, and he will discuss them into the early hours of the morning if he can find a willing audience. Juan has a sense of humor with respect to the world's manifold problems. Upon concluding one of his vivid descriptions of, say, hunger in Africa, he is likely to throw his hands in the air, laugh, and say, "The world is all screwed up, my friend, but what can one do?"

Juan's beliefs do not fit into any of the familiar ideological molds. Rather, he delights in pointing out the absurdities in the world and in demonstrating how, if people ever came to their senses, most problems could be overcome. "Just think," Juan often said to me, "if we Peruvians were to have the money that your country spent in the Vietnam War, could we not work miracles here in the montaña?" Another of Juan's favorite targets for attack is the practice of poor nations such as Peru spending enormous sums of money for sophisticated military weapons. "Our air force has Mirage jets," Juan complains, "while our farmers have only the crudest tools to work with." Juan believes that the arms race in the Third World takes money away from agriculture, education, and other vital areas where investments are badly needed.

A concept such as imperialism is, in Juan's mind, overly simplistic and entirely inadequate as an explanation for Peruvian underdevelopment. Juan says that after the fall of the Incas, Peru became a weak and divided nation. The Incas, he maintains, were able to unite the various peoples of Peru into a strong and progressive society, a feat never accomplished before or since. Peru's failure to develop in the present century is, Juan feels, largely the fault of internal disorganization and a lost or "wandering" mentality. Juan contends that Americans and other foreigners are not to blame for this structural and intellectual malaise.

In searching for their own solutions to their own problems, Peruvians must eventually return, Juan argues, to the Inca system of social integration. Juan believes that it is in this tradition that the spirit of the Peruvian nation will be discovered and rekindled. "Imported ideas," Juan says, "have never worked well in Peru." Thus, while Peruvians must attempt to learn all they can from the experiences of other nations, they must strive even harder to forge a national identity and consciousness of their own. "As you can see here in the montaña," Juan explains, "we Peruvians are not one in spirit." The nation, in his view, needs to build a new moral order based on the old Inca model.

The Myth of Peasant Like-Mindedness

These seven life stories illustrate, among other things, some of the ways in which individuals cope with the burden of poverty. Today all of Satipo's farmers live in some condition or degree of poverty. Yet the colonist population is characterized by a remarkable diversity of experience, thought, and behavior. One purpose of this chapter has been to reveal the significant heterogeneity of persons and lives that are concealed behind the common surface of rural poverty.

Unfortunately, individual diversity has not been a prominent theme in the social-scientific study of impoverished rural communities. Since 1852, when Karl Marx asserted that peasants form a "class" in the same way that potatoes in a sack form a sack of potatoes, little progress has been made in recognizing differences in personality, philosophy, and motivation among the rural poor. It is assumed that throughout the world poverty evokes similar moral and behavioral patterns of adaptation. This adaptive system, often referred to as the "culture of poverty," structures family relations, time orientation, value systems, spending patterns, and so on. The idea seems to be that long-term poverty creates an undifferentiated mass of people whose principal achievement is survival.

The individuals described in this chapter are definitely not part of an undifferentiated mass, nor are their lives devoted to a mere quest for survival. The testimony rendered by seven key informants shows that while there are common problems, common interests, and common concerns among the settlers, there is not a common mentality. Among these seven individuals we find a dauntless entrepreneur (Teodoro Acuña), a worldly philosopher (Juan Paredes), a wistful reactionary (Pedro Sánchez), and a hopeless cynic (Pedro Cacique). The list of character traits to be found among the colonists of Satipo is practically coterminous with the range of human personality attributes.

Thus the seven biographical portraits presented in this chapter serve to expose the first half of a popular misconception concerning the cause-and-effect relationships of poverty. According to this misconception, poverty, by narrowing options, begets like-mindedness, and like-mindedness, by inhibiting innovations, perpetuates poverty. We have seen that poverty does narrow options and impose limits on individual advancement. But we have also seen that the poor do not develop a common mentality as a result of their common plight. The following chapter will expose the second half of this misconception. There we shall see that the perpetuation of poverty in Satipo can be explained in accurate and comprehensive terms without resorting to such fanciful notions as peasant like-mindedness. The source of poverty in Satipo lies not in the minds of the settlers but in the nature of the colony's attachment to the national economy and society.

7

Two Systems
of Exploitation

The buying, transporting, and reselling of montaña produce is a highly profitable business in which the colonists do not participate. A network of merchant middlemen and a massive state bureaucracy stand between the colonists and the ultimate consumers of the food crops they produce. No matter which marketing channel a farm family chooses, they find themselves unable to obtain a margin of profit that would allow them to rise above the level of bare subsistence. In the opinion of most colonists, this double bind poses an insurmountable obstacle to the development of agriculture in Satipo.

The study of marketing arrangements adds an important dimension to the understanding of agricultural development. Unfortunately, research in this area has been hampered by the assumption that land reform is the key to rural development in such countries as Peru, where for centuries land has been monopolized by a privileged few. Yet in the underdeveloped nations land reform has repeatedly failed to stimulate farm production or significantly to raise the living standards of the rural poor. This fact demonstrates the naiveté of earlier theories

203

of agrarian development and indicates a need for new insights into the complex set of socioeconomic relations that render peasants poor and powerless. The evidence now available seems to indicate that the Inter-American Committee for Agricultural Development was in error when it asserted in 1966 that "in the less developed countries, land is the principal source of wealth. As a result, the distribution of rights to territorial property primarily determines the degree to which persons and groups have access to the wealth of such nations. . . . Land tenure is considered the strategic factor in agricultural development" (CIDA 1966:xxix; my translation).

Perhaps the most puzzling outcome of land reform is that rights to and ownership of territorial property have not, as the Inter-American Committee for Agricultural Development would have predicted, given peasants greater access to the wealth of their nations. Equally puzzling is the fact that in the reformed agrarian communities the wealthiest individuals often own no land at all. The "land equals wealth" hypothesis is turned upside down in such countries as Peru, where it is now the poor that are landed and the rich that are landless. If we are to understand this paradox, we must turn our attention to aspects of rural development that have been overshadowed by the land reform issue. The marketing system is one of the more promising areas for investigation.

In an analysis of how marketing systems affect economic opportunity in agrarian societies, Carol Smith (1977) shows that the unequal distribution of wealth in the highlands of western Guatemala is explained by exchange relations rather than production relations. She says that land, labor, and tools, the basic means of production, are owned by the producers themselves. The reason that producers are poor is that they do not control the marketing process. A small nonproducing elite controls the channels through which farm produce reaches domestic and foreign markets. Smith reveals that economic opportunities exist not in the production of foodstuffs but in the buying, transporting, and reselling of what others have produced. She concludes that it is commercial relations and not, as is commonly supposed, land-tenure relations that provide a basis for creating and maintaining vast differentials in wealth among the highlanders of western Guatemala.

By examining rural stratification systems through marketing arrangements, Smith has made an important contribution to the study of agricultural development. Her argument is particularly appropriate to the case of Satipo. Since the mid-1960s the colonists of Satipo have owned their own land, tools, and labor (the means of production). They own land as a result of their spontaneous invasions of mostly abandoned estates. They purchase the simple tools of montaña agriculture (machete, ax, and hoe) at hardware stores in town. The family is the basic labor force. Yet Satipo's farmers have not improved their economic standing by gaining ownership of the means of production. Like their Guatemalan counterparts, the peasants of Satipo are victimized by a marketing system that is controlled by a nonproducing elite.

The problem faced by Satipo's farmers can be stated quite simply: the producer of foodstuffs is exploited by the people who control the marketing channels. The rural producer and the urban consumer are separated by a vast network of mediating agents and agencies. These mediators keep prices low in the fields and high in the city, thereby ensuring a wide margin of profit for themselves. The colonists are barely able to meet their operating costs with the miserably low prices they receive for their produce. Settlers have neither the means nor the incentive to expand or improve their farms under the present marketing system. The stagnation of agriculture in Satipo is due in large part, therefore, to the exploitive nature of the national market economy.

Exactly how and by whom the farmers of Satipo are exploited is the central question to be considered here. Although "exploitation" is a term used rather freely (and loosely) in the social sciences (Dalton 1974), its meaning should become quite clear in the case at hand. Basically, it means that colonists are forced to sell their farm produce for a fraction of its value on the urban market, thereby generating a large surplus of wealth that falls directly into the hands of those who act as middlemen. These middlemen, as I explained earlier, are of two kinds: private entrepreneurs, known locally as *comerciantes* or *intermediarios,* and state bureaucrats.

In recent years the government bureaucracy has grown at the expense of the private entrepreneurial sector, and this pattern is likely to continue. Under the "revolutionary" military government, state agencies assumed an exclusive right to market certain crops that previously had been bought and sold by individuals and a few companies. Coffee and rice are two crops produced in Satipo that, according to laws adopted in 1971, could be sold only to a government agency called EPSA (Empresa Pública de Servicios Agropecuarios). Any private transactions involving these crops were declared illegal. Thus, whereas the private sector is still a vital force in the market economy, it is losing ground to an emerging state bureaucracy.

The Private Entrepreneurial System

One would know just by sitting in the town plaza of Satipo on any afternoon that a lively commerce links the capital city of Peru to the frontier. Trucks arrive regularly from Lima carrying a wide variety of essential consumer goods: cement, tin roofing, gasoline, machetes and other tools, clothing, and such foodstuffs as sugar, cooking oil, and flour.[1] After unloading these goods at the farmers' cooperative or at one of a large number of local stores, the truck drivers head for the surrounding countryside in search of cargo for the return trip to Lima. When the trucks are reloaded with one of Satipo's several exports—lumber, coffee, bananas, papayas, citrus fruits—they set out immediately for the national capital.

[1]The actual volume of traffic varies according to the season (heavier during the dry summer months and lighter during the rainy season, when road conditions are bad). The distance from Lima to Satipo is around four hundred kilometers and in good weather the trip can be made in twelve to sixteen hours.

This trade link is at once the lifeblood of the Satipo colony and the source of its gravest problems. Without the urban market, frontier settlers would have no cash income with which to purchase tools and other basic supplies. The exchange of products between metropolis and hinterland is vital to the population of each. Yet in their dual role as consumers of manufactured or processed goods and producers of raw foodstuffs, montaña farmers participate in an economic system that offers them few opportunities for advancement. The colonists complain that the prices of both consumer goods and farm produce are unjust, the former being exceedingly high and the latter extremely low. Under the private enterprise system, those who control the marketing process can enforce this pricing structure and thereby engage the rural farmers in a virtually hopeless struggle to make ends meet. In order to understand exactly how the private enterprise system works, it is best to begin by studying the development of this sector of Satipo's economy during and since the coffee fever.

The first major private investments in the Satipo colony were made by a group of coffee-exporting companies. Beginning in the early 1950s, these companies sought to increase the production of coffee in Satipo by extending credit through their local agents to the farmers of the region. The coffee growers who received credit from a company representative or habilitador were obligated to sell all of their crop to the sponsoring firm. In effect, the money lent under the habilitado system was simply a cash advance on the income that the colonists would receive from their next harvest. When the coffee crop was delivered to the company office in Satipo, the amount owed by a farmer was deducted from his or her total earnings.

In Chapter 4 I discussed the habilitado system insofar as the relationship between the creditor/merchant and his clientele is concerned. In fact the dimensions of the system are far greater than this habilitador–habilitado relationship. The habilitador is most often not an independent financier but rather the local agent of a large company that seeks to lend money in exchange for the exclusive right to market the borrower's produce. The cash advance is the company's way of gaining clients, thus securing a share of the lucrative coffee market. During the boom years of the coffee industry many colonists who could not obtain a loan from the state bank sought and received smaller amounts of credit from the private coffee-export companies.

In some ways the commercial credit system was preferred over the state bank's lending program. According to the colonists, one of the chief advantages of the habilitado system is that it entails only a verbal agreement between lender and borrower, with none of the complex, time-consuming paperwork required for a bank loan. A newly established family that possessed neither title to its land nor any of the other legal documents demanded by the bank could obtain cash from an habilitador simply by promising to sell its crop to him. Moreover, the settlers paid no interest on the money borrowed from an agent of the export companies. The state bank, in contrast, charged 12 percent interest on all of its loans. Finally, the habilitador could be relied on to advance money when the settlers most needed it. The state bank was notorious for failing to deliver payments when they were due, a practice that often led to crop failures. For example, the bank frequently would provide the colonists with money to purchase insecticides only after the dry season (the period in which these chemicals should be applied) was over. In general, the habilitadores were much more flexible and better attuned to the farmers' needs than was the clumsy state bureaucracy.

From the colonists' point of view, the principal drawback of the commercial credit system was their obligation to sell their farm produce at a price designated by the lender. The habilitador always lowered the selling price of coffee for those who were indebted to him. In addition, some habilitadores were known to discount a colonist's earnings if the coffee beans were not completely dry or if the crop showed other minor defects. The farmers contend that company agents used any conceivable ruse to lower the value of the coffee delivered to them. Colonists could complain about this practice, but they remained committed to sell their coffee crop at the creditor's designated price.

The abuses of the habilitadores became worse as the world market price of coffee began to fall in the late 1950s and early 1960s. A steady decline in the profits of the export companies led to an even greater decline in the prices paid by those companies to the coffee producers. Colonists began to accuse the five principal export companies of conspiring to reduce the price of coffee in order to overcompensate for the world market bust.[2] Soon a movement was afoot to form a cooperative that would market the colonists' coffee directly, thereby bypassing the commercial exporters and eliminating their lucrative commissions. The Coffee Cooperative of Satipo was formed in 1965 but never succeeded in obtaining a license to export its own coffee.

When the military came to power in 1968, the export licenses of the private companies were revoked and the state became the sole marketing agent of the nation's coffee producers. At present only two of the original five export companies are still in business, and they are able only to buy coffee, sort it into grades according to quality, and resell it to the government at a small profit. As the role of the private coffee companies has diminished, the amount of farm credit offered to colonists under the terms of the habilitado system has fallen.

The first phase in the development of Satipo's free market economy, then, was characterized by the attraction of private capital to the colony in the form of commercial credit for coffee cultivation. It is fair to say that both as a source of credit and as a market outlet, this form of private enterprise was highly unsatisfactory as far as the farmers were concerned. Unable to finance their own farming projects or to market their own produce, the colonists clearly needed the assistance of the coffee-export com-

[2]The five major coffee export firms were Lan Franco, Propesa, Tealdo, Comersa, and Anderson-Clayton. The first four companies were owned by Peruvian investors; the fifth was a large North American corporation with many diverse business interests in Peru. Anderson-Clayton sold all of its commercial holdings and left Peru in 1971. Of the four Peruvian companies, two are now defunct and two continue to operate on a greatly reduced scale.

panies. But the terms under which the settlers received this assistance were so unfavorable as to foredoom their plans and goals. Colonists who have worked under the habilitado arrangement invariably complain of the abuses and injustices of the system. They say that the habilitador reduces his clients to the status of subsistence farmers who must struggle throughout the year merely to break even with their creditor.

The second phase of Satipo's free-market development overlaps the first. In 1960 the road leading to the colony from the Peruvian coast was reopened, ending a thirteen-year period of isolation brought about by the severe earthquake of 1947. The new land route connecting Satipo to the market centers of the highlands and the coast soon became an avenue of intense commercial activity. Most important, Satipo's monocrop system began to yield to a pattern of economic diversification, a change made possible by the reduced costs of land transport. Coffee had been the colony's lone export during the thirteen-year period when air transport provided Satipo's only link to the outside world. Because of high freight costs, no crop except coffee could be marketed profitably by the air route. This situation changed dramatically when trucks began to transport goods to and from the colony after 1960.

The new trade network made it possible for montaña farmers to produce bananas, papayas, citrus fruits, avocados, and corn for the urban market. Moreover, as the colony's dependence on coffee lessened, the power of the private export companies also diminished. A different class of entrepreneurs took advantage of the commercial opportunities presented by the reopened road. The marketing of fresh fruits and other produce was handled by a network of independent merchant middlemen and not by the companies that had monopolized the coffee trade. Nearly all of the trucks that began to transport perishable foodstuffs from Satipo to the market centers of Huancayo and Lima were individually owned and operated. This form of private enterprise has continued to grow and develop to the present day, whereas the large companies have virtually disappeared.

Today the prominent entrepreneurs of Satipo are the truck

drivers who bring consumer goods to the colony and return to Lima with farm produce. Typically, these merchants come from the central highlands, where they have worked in various small business endeavors before entering their present profession. Most of them have saved money over a period of years in order to make the down payment on a truck. Many more years of hard work are required before the truck is fully paid for. The drivers claim that if they are not idle for more than a few days per month, the trucks will pay for themselves and will return a modest profit to the owner. Because of the excessive wear due to bad road conditions, however, the trucks are frequently laid up for maintenance and repairs, a process that has become extremely slow in recent years as a result of a nationwide scarcity of automobile and truck parts. Furthermore, during the rainy season sections of the road between Lima and Satipo may be washed out or covered by landslides for as long as a week before repair crews can be summoned. These temporary road closings represent lost time and lost money for the truck drivers. If they are so unfortunate as to be obstructed for several days by a landslide while carrying a load of perishable produce, the whole truckload may be spoiled by the time it finally reaches the market. Such are the risks taken by all of the entrepreneurs who transport goods between Lima and the frontier.

The colonists take a rather less sympathetic view of the truckers' plight. In fact, colonists frequently assert that the merchant intermediaries are ruthless profiteers who conspire to keep the farmers in poverty. To prove their point, the farmers cite the prices that the truckers pay for several kinds of farm produce (see Table 9). These prices, the colonists contend, are far too low to allow producers to meet their costs of production and attain a satisfactory standard of living. According to the settlers, those who profit from montaña agriculture are not the primary producers but rather the intermediaries who control the marketing process. Even though the truck driver is only one link in a chain of merchant middlemen, it is he that interacts directly with the colonists and absorbs most of their criticisms and complaints.

Frontier farmers often do not understand the scope and com-

Table 9. Farm prices and urban consumer prices for several basic products of montaña agriculture, 1974 (in soles)

Product	Farm price	Urban consumer price
Bananas		
Seda	S/.1.8 per kilo	S/.20 per kilo
Isla	2.5 per kilo	22 per kilo
Biscocho	1.2 per kilo	12 per kilo
Morado	2.5 per kilo	24 per kilo
Papayas	30 per crate[a]	320 per crate
Oranges	30 per hundred	240 per hundred
Sweet lemons	20 per hundred	150 per hundred

[a] Each crate contains from 22 to 25 papayas.

NOTE: In gathering these data I first recorded the prices that Satipo's farmers were being paid for their produce, then made a trip to Lima and visited several neighborhood markets where the same produce was being sold at the retail level. The task of identifying which bananas, papayas, oranges, and lemons had come from Satipo was relatively easy as the vendors nearly always knew the origin of their produce. Often they would advertise their fruits as "papayas from Satipo" or "grapes from Ica." The province from which the produce comes is important to the consumer and plays a role in the determination of price. I was told by several vendors and buyers that Satipo's produce is generally of high quality and commands a good price on the urban market. The consumer prices are those I recorded at the Mercado Minorista de Surquillo, the central market of the neighborhood of Surquillo. The costs of these items would vary slightly at other neighborhood markets in Lima. My purpose is only to reveal the wide spread between farm prices and urban consumer prices.

plexity of the marketing system that their produce enters via the trucks that travel the Lima–Satipo route. Few settlers realize that the truck drivers, the men who exercise such firm control over local farm production, wield virtually no power at all in the urban arena. Nor are the colonists fully aware that their produce, once delivered by the truckers, passes through many channels before it finally reaches the consumer. What the farmers do know is that the price paid by the urban consumer for produce from Satipo is normally about ten times greater than the amount that the colonist receives at the first stage of the marketing process (see Table 9). This tenfold inflation between producer and consumer is a fact that is frequently and heatedly discussed by the settlers. By examining what happens to the fresh produce of Satipo once it is delivered in Lima, we can begin to see how and why the sharp price increase occurs.

Under Peruvian law all farm produce brought to Lima from the provinces must be sold in a central marketplace called the Mercado Mayorista, also known as La Parada. A truck driver carrying meats, vegetables, or fruits to Lima is required to sell his cargo to one of the wholesalers (*mayoristas*) who are licensed to do business in this market. There are 360 mayoristas, each with an assigned position or *puesto* within the marketplace. As a group the mayoristas exercise a legal monopoly over the food supply of an urban population of more than three million. Their strategic position within the marketing system allows them to realize enormous profits in the buying and reselling of farm produce.

A pillar of the national economy, the Mercado Mayorista has received far too little attention in the social-scientific literature on Peru. We know more about the regional and local markets of the highlands and their colorful traditions than we know about the nation's preeminent redistribution center. To my knowledge there has been only one study of La Parada (Patch 1967), and that study is concerned primarily with the role of Lima's main marketplace in assimilating immigrants from the sierra into the culture of the metropolis. Although Richard Patch offers some excellent insights into the sociology of the Mercado Mayorista, he does not examine the price-setting function of the market or the mechanisms by which the mayoristas control the nation's food supply. These latter two considerations are vital to an analysis of why Satipo or any other rural Peruvian community engaged in cash-crop farming cannot progress or prosper.

The Mercado Mayorista was created in 1945 for the purpose of regulating the nation's commerce in foodstuffs. Government leaders thought that a single central marketplace would facilitate the inspection of produce by health officials and would ensure more rapid and efficient distribution of food. The most significant change introduced under the Mercado Mayorista system, however, was the creation of a limited number of licensed wholesalers through whose hands all foods destined for urban consumers had to pass. Those merchants who managed to secure one of the 360 puestos within the market could virtually dictate the price of the produce they handled. Only men of considerable wealth and influence could hope to obtain one of the highly prized mayorista licenses. Bribery and corruption always played a major role in the licensing process.

Today the operation of the Mercado Mayorista is essentially unchanged. All trucks that enter Lima with farm produce must head directly for the city's one and only wholesale marketplace. There the truck drivers may negotiate with any of the mayoristas who will agree to buy their cargo. Very little bidding or bargaining occurs, however, because the mayoristas simply will not compete with each other for the truckers' produce. Most of the time a trucker knows what price he can obtain from the mayoristas and he seeks only to sell at that rate or perhaps a few cents more. In the end the truck driver has no choice but to accept whatever price he is offered. If he were to try to sell his produce to a neighborhood vendor or directly to the public, he would be arrested on the spot and forced to pay a heavy fine. There is, in other words, no way to circumvent the powerful mayorista middlemen.

Once the trucker–mayorista transaction is completed, a new set of middlemen enters into the marketing process. These are the *minoristas,* merchants from neighborhood markets who are licensed to buy farm produce from mayoristas and to resell it in their own communities. The mayorista's task consists merely in unloading the cargo of the truckers and dividing it into smaller quantities for resale to the minoristas. The latter, in turn, reload the produce into their trucks, cars, or bicycle carts and set out for local city markets, where other vendors are waiting. The mayorista earns by far the greatest profit in this series of exchanges. He may buy bananas, for example, at S/.5 per kilo and resell them for S/.10 to S/.12 per kilo. The minorista normally sells his produce to street or market vendors who deal directly with the public. As a rule, the profit of the minorista is less than that of the mayorista and greater than that of the final seller.

The profits earned at each stage of the marketing process combine to increase the price of farm produce by approximately

1,000 percent (see Table 9). Satipo's colonists have no share in this lucrative commerce even though it is they that make the entire enterprise possible. The fundamental irony of the marketing system is that the farmers, who invest the greatest amount of capital and labor, reap the least reward. The mayorista simply buys and resells at the wholesale level and takes in the largest portion of the food industry's profits. The earnings of the multitude of lesser middlemen who participate in the marketing process vary greatly but are generally far below the average income of the mayoristas.

In view of the obvious injustice of this system, it is somewhat surprising that the "revolutionary" government that came to power in 1968 did not assign top priority to the problem. The reforms introduced by the Velasco regime concentrated on land-tenure patterns and neglected market arrangements. The only incursions by the government into the marketing sphere were in the form of state agencies created for the purpose of buying and selling a few selected crops (such as coffee and rice). There have been no changes in the structure of the Mercado Mayorista. While the state established "official prices" for most types of farm produce in an attempt to control rising food costs, these prices were ignored by merchants at all levels of the market hierarchy. Since the laws were not enforced, the middlemen were free to raise prices at will.

Increasingly, however, groups of citizens have won the support of the national press for their complaints about the market structure. Thus far the urban consumers have protested more strongly than the farmers. The consumers would like to see the middlemen eliminated so that food prices could be brought down to a more affordable level. They share a common interest with the farmers in this regard. Although no real progress has yet been made, one program developed in 1974 by an organization of housewives and sponsored by the leftist newspaper *Expreso* did reveal what would happen if the mayoristas and other merchants were to be eliminated.

A campaign called *De la chacra a la olla* (from the field to the cooking pot) was begun in a few neighborhoods of Lima to dramatize the need for a closer link between the producers of foodstuffs and the consumers. Several community organizations requested local and national authorities to allow a series of open markets to be held at selected sites in Lima on Sunday mornings. The idea was to permit trucks arriving with fresh produce from the provinces to park at one of these sites and to sell their cargo directly to the public. With the backing of the newspaper *Expreso* (a strong supporter of the "revolutionary" government) the campaign organizers finally obtained permission to proceed with this experiment. Each Sunday for three months the residents of several working-class neighborhoods—Comas, Lince, Villa María del Triunfo—were able to purchase directly from the trucks that transported farm produce to Lima. The mayoristas and all of the lesser middlemen were bypassed. Figure 4 shows a political cartoon that appeared in *Expreso* in which the middleman is being "bridged" so that food costs may be lowered for the benefit of the housewife.

This experiment proved to be a great success for all concerned. The producers and the truck drivers found that they could increase their earnings and still provide fresh foods to the urban consumers at prices well below the prevailing market rates. Throughout the campaign foods were sold to the public at or below the government's official price schedule. According to *Expreso,* everything from potatoes to oranges to chicken and other meats could be purchased for from 50 to 80 percent less than their normal cost. The demand for foodstuffs at the Sunday open markets was actually more than the truckers could supply during the brief period in which selling was permitted. In fact, the campaign was so successful in demonstrating how farm prices could be raised and consumer prices lowered that a threat was posed to the powerful mayoristas. They responded by using their influence in the higher circles of government to have the program canceled. Only three months after the open-market experiment began, it was terminated by the military regime. Although no official explanation was given, this action was un-

De la chacra a la olla

Figure 4. Political cartoon: "De la chacra a la olla." A tearful "intermediary" complains, "They're 'bridging' me," as produce moves directly from the field to the housewife's cooking pot along a path labeled "price-cutting campaign." Reproduced by permission from *Expreso* (Lima), August 7, 1974.

doubtedly a result of intense and effective lobbying by the market middlemen.

As we shall see later, the Velasco government proposed eventually to eliminate the market entrepreneurs, though not in the manner hoped for by the public. Instead of supporting the highly popular open-market concept, the government planned to replace the private sector with state marketing agencies. Under this plan the middleman function would not be abolished but rather would be taken over by the state. The earliest signs of the way this system would work indicated that prices would not be significantly raised for the farmer or lowered for the consumer. The government succeeded only in antagonizing the middlemen (who stood to lose their businesses) and alienating the producers and consumers of foodstuffs (who advocated an open market with no state intervention).

The short-lived "De la chacra a la olla" campaign brought to the forefront of national attention a problem that affects farmers and consumers alike. The farmers' plight, however, has an added dimension in that, as we saw earlier, they are not only producers of raw foodstuffs for which they ordinarily receive an extremely low price but also consumers of manufactured or processed goods for which they pay dearly. The colonists' inability to stretch their income from farm production to meet their consumer needs inhibits any kind of progress, individual or communal. A brief analysis of the colonists as consumers should serve to portray the hopelessness of their economic situation.

The same trucks that transport fresh produce to Lima return to Satipo loaded with a wide range of basic consumer goods. Most of these goods will be sold in the town of Satipo, which in the years since the colony was founded has evolved into the region's major commercial center. The town's few dusty streets are lined with stores selling tools, clothing, and a variety of canned and packaged foods. Farmers from throughout Satipo province come to town at regular intervals (usually on Sundays) to buy their supplies. What and how much they buy varies from week to week but normally includes such foods as salt, sugar, beans, rice, and noodles; such tools as machetes, hoes, and axes; clothing (including required school uniforms for the children); and fertilizers, insecticides, and other farm supplies. Few colonists are able to buy anything beyond essential items and many settlers cannot afford even those.

Stated simply, the problem is that there is a wide disparity between the income colonists receive from the sale of their produce and the expenditures necessary to maintain the farm and the family. In recent years, the settlers contend, the price of farm produce has barely risen while the costs of manufactured items have soared. The colonists furnish numerous examples of this general trend. They say that machetes, for instance, quin-tupled in price, from S/.30 to S/.150 each, over a period of six years (roughly 1968–74). Many other tools used by the settlers in their daily work have also increased sharply in price. But the tools are not only more expensive than ever before, they are also of greatly inferior quality. Until 1972, nearly all such tools were imported from the United States and Europe. According to the colonists, those imported tools were of excellent quality and were reasonably priced. After 1972, however, the military gov-ernment prohibited the importation of many kinds of farm tools in order to protect recently established national manufacturers. The colonists claim that this is a disastrous policy because the Peruvian-made machetes, axes, and hoes are vastly inferior in quality and are far more expensive than the imported brands. A good American machete, the farmers often say, will last for at least two years, while a Peruvian machete is worn down in the course of a few months of hard work.

In the same six-year period in which machetes quintupled in price, the market value of banana, papaya, and coffee harvests increased little, if at all. From 1968 to 1974 the average farm price of bananas rose from S/.1.5 per kilo to approximately S/.2.0 per kilo. Colonists have their own way of gauging this widening gap between the value of their harvests and the value of consumer goods that must be purchased with the income from those harvests. They express this relationship in terms of the amount a farmer must produce in order to buy a given item. Thus a colonist may say that six years ago he could buy a shirt with 100 pounds of bananas while today he must sell 150 pounds of bananas to buy a shirt. Similarly, a settler may claim that with the cash earned from the sale of a quintal of coffee she is able to buy only half as much merchandise as she could six years ago. In short, the colonists must surpass their earlier production by 50 percent or more in order to be able to afford the same amount of consumer goods. But since greater productivity could come about only by means of larger investments, the farmers' efforts to increase production would be self-defeating (that is, the in-vestment would always be more than the return).

This problem grows worse each day and no short- or long-term solution is yet in sight. Some relief is offered by the farmers' cooperative of Satipo, which sells consumer goods to its members at rates slightly below those of local retail stores. But the savings made possible by the cooperative are rather insignificant in terms of the colonists' overall budget squeeze. The cooperative can do nothing to control the rapidly rising costs of manufactured and processed goods. Like any other store in Satipo, the cooperative must pass these inflated prices along to its customers. Many colonists actually prefer to patronize the commercial stores, which charge only about 5 percent more for consumer items than the cooperative and are often willing to give regular customers small amounts of credit, a practice that is strictly forbidden at the cooperative. Most colonists say that when the advantages and disadvantages of the cooperative are compared with those of the privately owned stores, neither alternative stands out as a clear favorite.

The inability of the cooperative system to help the farmers of Satipo in any significant way is a fact that supports the view that the agrarian crisis in Peru is of broad structural dimensions. Little can be done at the local level to correct the situation. Unlike the redistribution of lands, the restructuring of the internal marketing system cannot be accomplished from below. The task of transforming the structure of market relations in Peru belongs to the national government. After coming to power in 1968, Velasco criticized the private enterprise system and the market relations it fosters. His military regime introduced reforms aimed at reducing the role of the merchant middlemen. As we shall see, however, the remedy prescribed for the capitalist malaise created a great deal of controversy and dissension in its own right.

The State Bureaucratic System

The Peruvian government first became actively involved in the development of Satipo in the early 1950s, when a local branch office of the state agricultural bank, the Banco de Fomento Agropecuario, was established. Since that time, and especially since 1968, the state's role in charting the course of Satipo's growth has steadily increased. In some cases, such as in the construction and maintenance of the region's main highway, the actions of the state have been well received and much appreciated by the settlers. Other state projects, such as the agricultural credit program and more recently the national marketing program, have created many problems and have aroused feelings of bitterness and hostility toward the government. Anyone who talks to the colonists of Satipo today will discover that the latter sentiments are the ones more often expressed. Essentially, the farmers believe that the government has done far more harm than good in the various projects it has undertaken. The following account of the history of state intervention in Satipo strives faithfully to reflect the settlers' point of view. This background information is crucial to an understanding of why the military government was so unsuccessful in its attempts to reform the marketing system and thereby to win the support of the nation's farmers.

The colonists' misgivings about government participation in Satipo's growth are primarily a result of their experiences with the state agricultural bank. From the outset the salient feature of state bank policy was the highly formalized and complex set of regulations that governed the processing of loan applications. A bureaucracy that extended from the bank headquarters in Lima through a series of regional branches to the local Satipo office was involved in every decision to grant or deny credit to a colonist. Even before a loan could be requested a settler had to present several legal documents as credentials: a certificate of landownership, a certificate of good conduct from the police, a social security card, and so on. Once these papers were in order, the farmer submitted a formal application for credit to local bank officials. Because of the numerous bureaucratic channels through which the application had to travel, the length of time required for loan approval was seldom less than a year and was often much longer. A colonist who inquired as to the status of a loan application was told that it was being processed and that he or she should come back in a week or two weeks or a month to see if any progress had been made. Each successive inquiry usually brought the same reply and left the colonist in doubt as to whether a loan would ever be forthcoming.

It is not surprising, then, that many farmers chose to seek commercial credit from Satipo's coffee merchants, the habilitadores. The protracted wait for state bank credit proved, in many instances, to be worse than the abuses of the habilitado system. On the same day a farmer could both request and receive a loan from one of the local agents of the coffee-export companies. As we have seen, this cash loan agreement amounted to an advance sale of the borrower's coffee crop to the creditor. Under the bank lending program, in contrast, borrowers were free to sell their crops to the highest bidder. Obviously, the advantages and disadvantages of each credit system had to be carefully weighed by the colonists.

If the state bureaucracy was on the whole a bungling, inefficient, and painfully slow-moving apparatus, there were nevertheless certain ways to spur it into action. Personal influence and favoritism entered into the determination of credit allocations, as did outright bribery. This is the second major characteristic of state bank procedures that I wish to emphasize. The speculators who came to Satipo in the early 1950s to buy land and to build coffee estates were able to make the bureaucratic machinery operate a little more smoothly than normal in granting their loan requests. Preferential treatment was accorded by bank employees to those settlers who agreed to kick back a small percentage of the loan in exchange for an expeditious completion of the bureaucratic procedures. Prosperous and influential speculators obtained nearly all of the larger grants of bank credit in this fashion. The small farmers of Satipo frequently had no personal contacts at the state bank, nor could they afford to pay bribes out of the limited credit fund they hoped to receive.

Another serious fault of the state bank was its lack of foresight and understanding in directing the agricultural development of Satipo. In Chapter 3 I explained how the bank's lending policy encouraged a monocrop system on the frontier. This policy was firmly adhered to despite repeated warnings from many colonists that a coffee-market bust was inevitable and that the bank should attempt to lessen the colony's dependence on coffee by providing credit for a variety of new crops. Even when world market prices began to fall, the bank would not recognize its mistake, but rather attempted to recover all of its investments (with interest) despite the colonists' inability to pay. The settlers felt that the state bank should absorb at least a part of the heavy losses suffered by the coffee industry. When the bank showed no leniency and no willingness to renegotiate the loan agreements, a general climate of resentment and antagonism began to build among the settlers. The government was seen as the culprit in a plot to prevent the farmers from ever getting out of debt.

To this day, in fact, the bank insists on collecting overdue debts that have grown to several times their original value as a result of accumulated interest. Most of the major debtors have abandoned their farms by now, defaulting on their loans and leaving their land to be repossessed by the bank. The state bank, in turn, does nothing with this land until a new colonist or group of colonists attempts to settle there. Then the bank informs the settlers that the land they have occupied "owes to the bank." In order to remain on the property, the new colonists must agree to pay off the previous landowner's debt with accumulated interest. Since nearly all of the region's best farmland is "indebted" in this manner, the colonists have little choice but to accept the bank's conditions. The debt, it should be noted, has no relation to the actual value of the property in question. In most cases the coffee groves that were planted by the original owner are overgrown by jungle and are useless to the new settler. Rather than selling land according to its value, the bank transfers debts inflated by interest from farmer to farmer.

It is rare to find a colonist who does not have problems with the state bank. Frequently a farmer who assumes the debt of an earlier settler is unable to repay the loan and must in turn abandon the land. It is then likely that the farm will be repossessed, reabandoned, and so on ad infinitum. I found pieces of land that had been transferred five or six times in this fashion. Needless to say, the colonists are extremely bitter about the situation and have repeatedly asked government authorities to find a workable solution. Thus far the government's only concession has been to freeze interest on the uncollected debts that remain from the era of coffee fever. This policy went into effect in 1973 but has done little to ameliorate the colonists' financial difficulties. Since no profit can now be made in agriculture (owing to the problems discussed in this chapter), no one has money with which to settle accounts with the state bank.

In the years since it opened for business in Satipo, the state bank has established a rather dubious record of achievement. The colonists view the bank as a corrupt and poorly managed institution whose goal, official propaganda notwithstanding, is to profit from rather than serve the public. Furthermore, the same kinds of criticisms that are made against the state bank and its officials also apply to the agrarian reform office, the social security office, and other government agencies. Their own experiences have led the settlers to feel that government action, no matter what its stated purpose, is generally inimical to their best interests. For example, in Chapter 4 we saw some of the serious economic and social problems that arose as a consequence of the government's reorganization of the Pérez Godoy settlement. The results of similar agrarian reform projects in various parts of the Satipo region have been equally discouraging. On the whole, the government is seen as having hindered local development even when its intentions were basically good.

Understandably, then, the colonists were reluctant to endorse a government plan announced in 1971 to reform the nation's internal marketing system. Experience had taught the settlers to be highly skeptical of such seemingly beneficial proposals. Even though the colonists wanted to have the merchant middlemen eliminated, they could not believe that a state takeover was the best means to this end. Many farmers felt that in tampering with the existing market system, the government would only make it worse. Skepticism grew when it was learned that the state itself would assume the function of a marketing agent. The colonists had hoped that they would be allowed to market (via the cooperative) their own farm produce.

Only a few months after the government decided to intervene in the buying and selling of foodstuffs there were clear indications that the settlers were correct in assuming that they would gain little from the market reforms. What went wrong with this program is essentially what went wrong with previous state endeavors: growing bureaucracy, inefficiency, corruption, and a fundamental misunderstanding of the wants and needs of the colonist population. The new state agency assigned to carry out the marketing of farm produce earned a reputation similar to that of the state bank. This agency, the Empresa Pública de Servicios Agropecuarios (EPSA), became the sole marketing agent for two of Satipo's most important crops (coffee and rice) and the major buyer and distributor of a third (corn). A brief account of EPSA's performance in the marketing of these crops should help to explain why the agency came to be viewed so unfavorably by the farmers.

Ominously, one of EPSA's first projects in Satipo was carried out in conjunction with the state bank. Under this joint program it was agreed that the state bank would provide credit for the cultivation of corn and that EPSA would purchase the harvested grain at a rate of S/.5.5 per kilo. The government wanted to promote corn production in the montaña in order to reduce the national grain shortage. The government was certain that if it provided financial backing and a guaranteed selling price that would allow the farmers a modest margin of profit, its project would succeed. Precisely for the lack of credit and the unstable (but generally low) market price of corn, this crop had never been cultivated on a large scale in Satipo. The small amount of corn that the colonists did produce was used by the settlers themselves to feed their chickens, ducks, and other domesticated animals. The government's program was designed to generate a local corn surplus that could be taken out of the colony.

In the project's first year approximately 500 colonists agreed to participate. They were allowed S/.6,000 for each hectare of corn that they intended to plant. While most of the farmers said that S/.6,000 was not sufficient to cover the actual costs of production, there were no major arguments over this matter. The participants in the project calculated how many kilos of corn their land would yield per hectare and concluded that at S/.5.5 per kilo they could repay the bank and still realize a profit. For the most part, then, the program progressed smoothly for the first few months.

At harvesttime, however, several sharp disputes took place between the farmers on the one hand and the state bank and EPSA on the other. The most severe clash began when the local EPSA office announced, shortly before the harvest was to commence, that a mistake had been made when the official selling price of corn had been quoted. The figure that had been given, S/.5.5 per kilo, was not the price to be paid in Satipo but rather the price to be paid for corn delivered in Lima. EPSA claimed that there had been a "misunderstanding" between the local office and the national headquarters. As a result of this confusion, the farmers who had expected to receive S/.5.5 per kilo would in fact receive S/.3.0 per kilo for corn delivered to the EPSA warehouse in Satipo. Only if farmers paid to have their own corn transported to Lima would they receive the original "guaranteed" price. But since the cost of transport was about S/.2 per kilo, farmers had little incentive to have their grain trucked to Lima.

The colonists claimed that EPSA's "mistake" was a deliberate deception. They were convinced that the government had conspired against them. Had they known that the selling price of corn would be S/.3 per kilo, few of the colony's farmers would have participated in the project. At that price a settler would be fortunate merely to break even at harvesttime. But the 500 farmers who had already committed themselves to the project and who had sizable loans to repay had no alternative but to proceed with the corn harvest. Ironically, they could be held to their loan contracts whereas EPSA could not be held to its part of the original agreement. Since EPSA had made only a verbal promise to purchase the shelled corn at S/.5.5 per kilo, the colonists had no legal grounds on which to challenge the agency's sudden shift in policy.

The selling price of corn was not the only point of controversy in the ill-fated project. The farmers had been told at the beginning of the program that they would be able to rent corn-shelling machines from EPSA. Without such machines the task of separating the grain from the corncob is extremely slow and difficult. But when the harvest had been completed and the colonists were ready to shell their corn, EPSA informed them that it had no machines to rent. According to the agency, the machines had been ordered from the United States but had not yet arrived. And so the farmers were forced to spend as much as a week shelling their corn by hand, a tedious job that a machine could have done in a few hours.

Yet another argument developed between EPSA and the farmers during the actual sale of the corn crop. EPSA would not accept the corn unless it had been dried in the sun for at least four days. If the colonists delivered corn that had more than the minimum allowable moisture content, they were sent away and told to dry the grain more thoroughly. The farmers, who had never before been required to meet such exacting standards, believed that EPSA only wanted to reduce the weight (and hence the value) of the corn by insisting that it be completely dry. To make matters worse, the crop was harvested in December, at the start of the wettest part of the rainy season, when there were few clear and hot days during which the corn could be spread out on the ground to dry. Many farmers, rather than attempt to meet the government's low-moisture requirement, sold their grain to town merchants or to the numerous truck drivers who bought and sold farm produce. The middlemen paid only S/.2.3 to S/.2.5 per kilo, but they were willing to buy corn that had been rejected by EPSA.

In short, the corn project sponsored by EPSA and the state

bank was a failure in every respect. The colonists' initial suspicion of government plans to "reform" the marketing system proved to be well founded. The corn venture not only was unprofitable; it left most of the farmers unable to cancel their debts at the state bank. As usual, the bank showed no leniency toward those who could not repay their loans in full. The farmers who canceled only a part of their debt were placed on the bank's black list and were ineligible for any future credit. Black-listing was a long-standing bank practice that was preserved by the military government despite the farmers' pleas for its abolition. The policies and procedures of the "revolutionary" government, as revealed in the corn project, differed little from those of previous regimes.

Nor was the government's credibility boosted by subsequent attempts at market reform. EPSA's takeover of the rice trade is an excellent case in point. In 1973 the government declared that too much speculation and profiteering had taken place in the marketing of the nation's rice supply. Consequently, the merchant middlemen would no longer be allowed to buy and sell rice. The government conferred on EPSA the exclusive right to purchase rice from the producers, to clean and hull the grain, and to transport and resell it on the urban market. Presumably this system would bring about a more rational and efficient distribution of the rice harvest, a change that would benefit producers and consumers alike.

For a variety of reasons, however, the change was definitely not in the colonists' best interest. In the first place, most of the rice produced in Satipo is destined not for the market but for the farm family's own consumption. Rice is one of an assortment of subsistence crops that are cultivated on a small scale for domestic consumption only. Colonists seldom plant more than a hectare of land in rice. According to the farmers, the high labor and capital expenditures needed to produce rice on a commercial scale are not justified in the montaña environment because of the low yield and the poor quality of the grain that is obtained. Nevertheless, a small plot of rice can contribute significantly to

the family's food supply without involving an excessive investment in time or money.[3] Rice plays an important role in the
frontier economy even though it is not among the region's principal cash crops.

Before the reforms imposed by EPSA, three merchants in
Satipo owned and operated rice-hulling machines. A farmer
could take grain to one of these merchants and have the hulls
removed for a fee of S/.1 per kilo. After the rice had passed
through the machine, it was weighed and the corresponding fee
was assessed. The colonist then returned home with as much rice
as the family needed, selling any excess to the merchant at the
going market rate.

This system was highly satisfactory to the rice growers of the
region because it allowed them to process a basic part of their
food supply at a very low cost. In addition, enough surplus rice
was produced to satisfy the needs of those colonists whose land
would not support rice cultivation. Local supply, in other words,
was able to meet local demand. Unlike most other foodstuffs,
rice was neither exported from nor imported to the colony. This
simple fact is important because it meant that the usual chain of
middlemen was not involved in the handling of rice. The only
middleman was the town merchant who purchased the surplus
of the rice producers and sold it to the nonproducers at a relatively low margin of profit. The system of rice production and
distribution was perhaps the only system that worked to the
colonists' advantage.

Nevertheless, EPSA was assigned to take control of the nation's
rice industry and convert it into a more "rational" and "efficient"
enterprise that would better serve the "public interest." As its

---

[3]It must be recalled here that many colonists, such as those who belong to the
Pérez Godoy community, do not have land that is suitable for the cultivation of
rice or any other subsistence crop. These settlers must use the income they
derive from coffee cultivation to buy the foodstuffs that they themselves cannot
produce. Perhaps as many as half of Satipo's farmers are in this category. The
other half own at least a few hectares of land on which they can raise subsistence
crops.

first act EPSA declared that the private operators of rice-hulling machines would no longer be permitted to carry on their business. Henceforth only the state would be licensed to engage in the buying, processing, and selling of rice. Satipo's farmers were told that they could sell their rice only to EPSA, that EPSA would operate the region's only rice-hulling machines, and that hulled rice could be purchased only from EPSA. It should be noted that this set of procedures contained a subtle yet extremely significant difference from the manner in which business was conducted under the old system: the farmers now had to sell their rice to the state and then buy it back, whereas before they had paid the merchant a flat rate to hull their grain.

EPSA adopted a nationwide policy that set the price of unhulled rice at S/.5 per kilo and the price of hulled rice at S/.11 per kilo. The farmers of Satipo had no alternative but to sell their grain at the former rate and purchase it at the latter. As a result, the rice-hulling service that earlier had cost S/.1 per kilo now (as of 1974) cost S/.6 per kilo. This arbitrary and highly injurious state policy provoked strong but futile protests by the colonists. They sent several commissions to plead their case before EPSA officials in Lima, all to no avail. The government could not even be persuaded by the argument that the new hulling fee would discourage most of the region's farmers from planting any rice at all. Although EPSA's stated purpose was to promote agricultural development, it remained indifferent to the imminent decline in rice production in Satipo.

After the reforms went into effect, rice cultivation declined steadily. The farmers said that it was too expensive to produce rice under the regulations established by the government. The major disincentive was, of course, the sharply increased hulling fee. Adding to the problem was EPSA's refusal to buy rice that was not thoroughly dried or not of high grade. Often a colonist would bring rice to the EPSA warehouse only to have it rejected as being too moist or too low in quality. The rice was going to be consumed only by the colonist's family and they did not care about its quality or its moisture content, but EPSA's policy was not geared to these considerations. From the colonists' viewpoint, the agency's rules were as inflexible as they were unjust. A few colonists managed to avoid the EPSA bureaucracy by hulling their rice at home by means of a crude pounding technique. But by this method several hours of hard work are required to hull a few kilos of rice, an investment in time and labor that most settlers do not consider worthwhile. On the whole, Satipo's farmers reacted to the EPSA reforms by replacing rice with other subsistence crops.

The final blow to EPSA's credibility came in late 1974, when all of the agency's highest officials were arrested and accused of embezzling millions of soles in a series of fraudulent marketing schemes. The "EPSA scandal," as it came to be called in the national press, is too complex to be analyzed here. But the fact that some of the charges of corruption involved EPSA's coffee- and rice-marketing programs made the scandal of particular interest to Satipo's farmers. They learned, for example, that the coffee that EPSA had classified as third grade when it was purchased in Satipo was later sold as first grade on the international market. The settlers had been deceived into thinking that their coffee was of a much poorer quality than it actually was. Apparently the EPSA officials kept for themselves the profits that the reclassification of coffee automatically produced.

But as we have seen, corruption was not the only cause of EPSA's failure as a pilot project designed to show the effectiveness of the state as a marketing agent. From the outset EPSA formulated policies without any regard for the special needs and interests of the colonist population. No attempt was made to consult the farmers so that their opinions might at least be known by the designers of the agency's various marketing projects. Consequently, the subsistence strategies of many colonists were placed in jeopardy by thoughtless and ill-conceived "reforms." More often than not, the supposed beneficiaries of market reform became its victims. As the colonists see it, the government's alternative to the private entrepreneurial marketing system created many new problems while solving none of the old.

How Exactly Are Colonists Exploited?

At the beginning of this chapter I said that the nature of national market integration places the farmers of Satipo in a double bind, exploited by a network of merchant middlemen on the one hand and a powerful state bureaucracy on the other. I hope I have shown where exactly the colonists stand within the overall structure of market relations and how exactly they are exploited in that context. My conclusion is that the market economy as it is now instituted subverts individual achievements in agriculture and retards the development of the Satipo colony as a whole. The stagnant, depressed state of the Peruvian frontier is best explained in terms of the exchange relations that prevail between the settlers and the agents of national commerce.

The choice that colonists make between the two credit and marketing channels available is really no choice at all. Either way they turn, toward the merchant entrepreneurs or toward the state bureaucrats, the farmers find themselves in no position to negotiate a fair deal. They simply take what is offered and dare not complain. They are fortunate if the income they receive from the sale of their produce is sufficient to meet their costs of production. The fact that most colonists are in permanent debt, either to a private creditor or to the state bank, reveals that the investment in agriculture often exceeds the return. As the costs of tools and other essential manufactured items continue to soar while farm prices remain constant, the farmers' hopes of ever getting out of debt, much less of achieving a degree of stability and prosperity, grow dimmer. The roles of the colonist as consumer and as producer cannot be played to the actor's advantage.

It should be noted, however, that the settlers have not been idle in the face of their mounting difficulties. They have attempted by various means to help their own cause, most notably through the formation of the farmers' cooperative of Satipo. But the cooperative has never succeeded in its efforts to challenge the forces that control the internal marketing system. In the first years after the cooperative was formed, the merchant middle-men fought the colonists in their attempts to obtain the right to market their own farm produce. Later, under an enigmatic "revolutionary" government, the state became the most vigorous and effective opponent of the cooperative. While approving of the cooperative system in principle, the government delegated all of the powers that the colonists seek to the state marketing agency, EPSA. An autonomous cooperative with authority to market its members' produce is clearly not what the military government wanted. Most farmers felt that the cooperative was doomed to become a purchasing agent for EPSA rather than a market force in its own right. These are the only terms under which the state would agree to recognize the local farmers' cooperative.

It appears that the state will increasingly intervene in the marketing of crops produced in Satipo and in the nation as a whole. To intervene successfully the state must find a means to give the people most affected by market reforms a voice in the determination of policy. The rural producers and the urban consumers have already demonstrated, through the brief "De la chacra a la olla" experiment, a popular approach to market reform. A nation beset by myriad economic problems that have repeatedly defied "revolutionary" solutions cannot afford to ignore viable initiatives from below. The evidence indicates that the Velasco government's market-reform program was ill conceived and that future programs should be based on a mutual understanding between the benefactors and the intended beneficiaries of reform.

8

Anthropology and the Frontier

In this book I have tried to interweave the external and the internal sources of distress in the Satipo colony. To weave is not to blend; the elements of my analysis are interconnected yet separable. By distinguishing between the basically external problem of economic exploitation and the basically internal problem of ethnic conflict, I hope to have explained their respective contributions to the present impasse in the colonization effort. In sum, it seems to me that whereas economic exploitation is the more fundamental obstacle to local development, ethnic conflict is the more immediate obstacle.

The settlers themselves often say that nothing will change in Satipo as long as the colony remains divided and disorganized. It is generally felt that a collective voice is essential to the pursuit of public as well as individual goals. Pressure-group tactics are seen as the only means of effecting basic changes in the market economy. Thus colonists recognize the need for popular mobilization even though they are undecided as to how it should be achieved. For them, as for me, the resolution, or at least the mitigation, of

Satipo's internal differences stands out as the most urgent of the several major tasks that lie ahead.

But there is no way to determine how or when common problems and concerns might begin to erode the ethnic barriers to collective action. I can only say that my own research produced no evidence that this erosion process has begun. The missing link in this heterogeneous pioneer settlement is still missing, although the search goes on. The colonists have not given up hope that someday they will be able to understand each other. Their past failures in communal understanding are painful lessons that have not been forgotten. Nevertheless, the stalemate in ethnic relations continues.

Naturally, I would like to be able to conclude this study with a set of proposals or suggestions for improving ethnic relations in Satipo. If I were not aware of the many subtle and complex issues involved, I might readily take up the challenge of social engineering. But the longer I studied and pondered ethnic conflict in Satipo, the more convinced I became of the need for cautious, considered judgments. In one sense the corpus of data that I have presented speaks for itself, providing insights into problems that are often oversimplified by well-meaning but naive community organizers. Furthermore, I hope I have shown that the colonists are indeed aware of the crisis in ethnic relations and that they are in fact working toward a solution, one of their own making. Certainly the best solution would be one devised neither by the government nor by the anthropologist, but by the colonists themselves. I believe that the efforts of the settlers to overcome their internal differences and to build a strong communal organization should not be interfered with.

Thus in this final chapter I shall not ignore but rather look beyond the crisis in ethnic relations, focusing on another major issue that I believe will ultimately decide the fate of the colonization movement. The issue, in essence, is whether Satipo's external source of distress lies in poor government planning and management or in basic contradictions and inequalities in the patterns of national growth. The answer to this question obviously has profound implications for future resettlement policies. In addition, I shall take another look at the theoretical and methodological issues that have guided my inquiry into the colonization process. In this manner I hope to bring together my contributions to anthropology on the one hand and to the policy aspects of frontier settlement on the other.

Toward a Middle-Range Anthropology of Development

This book offers a middle-range analytic perspective on the problems of economic and social change in Peru. Eric Wolf (1974:67) defines middle-range studies as those that fall "between theoretical efforts cast at a high level of abstraction and narrowly conceived local studies." The middle ground of theory and investigation is largely uncharted terrain; both the high and the low grounds of social research are better known. Ethnography has traversed the low ground, mapping its contours with admirable precision and detail. But in another sense the results of ethnographic surveys are disappointing. Together they resemble what Edmund Leach (1961:2) has called a "butterfly collection" of traits and customs, a collection that includes many rare and exotic types but which provides little insight into the patterns of social process. In contrast, the high ground of social research presents an intellectual landscape unbroken by ethnographic facts. Here societies pass through "inevitable" historical sequences, as from tradition to modernity, without a hitch or a complaint. On the high ground deductive reasoning places the facts at the service of theory; the data can be incorporated or discarded at will. The result is what Manning Nash (1965:312) has termed a "dance of spectral categories," a proliferation of free-floating models and of reified ideal-type constructs.

The middle ground between parochial ethnography and ecumenical theory is (or at least should be) more than a buffer zone; it is a promising field of study in its own right. Middle-range anthropology is concerned with discovering and explaining diachronic and synchronic patterns of social process. Ethnography is the *terminus a quo* of middle-range investigation, the point at which anthropologists begin to focus on the patterns in their data and to analyze the relationships among those patterns. By adhering to the data, by drawing only the conclusions that are warranted by their information, they avoid the kind of disembodied theorizing that characterizes much of modern social science. The ability to document social regularities with the hard-won facts of original empirical research is the forte of middle-range anthropology.

Another strength of this approach is that it lends itself to cross-cultural comparisons. More specifically, middle-range studies reveal the extent of variation in the developmental process as a whole. By systematically describing and comparing the patterns of social, economic, and political change in a wide range of emerging nations, anthropologists can steadily increase their understanding of the dynamics of development. Already anthropologists have begun to challenge such ideas as the "stages-of-growth" (Rostow 1961) and the other evolutionary sequences that have been extrapolated from the history of Western development and applied anachronistically to the contemporary Third World. In contrast to the elegant but ill-fitting theoretical designs of economics and macrosociology, middle-range anthropological models are tailored to the social configurations they purport to explain. While this practice may limit the scope of such models—perhaps to the extent that we speak only of "Latin American" or "African" developmental problems—it greatly enhances their explanatory power.

Middle-range anthropology is particularly well suited to the comparative study of specific growing points in the economic and social structures of the developing nations. One such growing point is the frontier. The colonization and settlement of new lands is a process that has played a major role in the history of certain developed nations and that continues to attract the interest and the imagination of the underdeveloped world. As I stated earlier, colonization stands at the forefront of Peruvian planning as a bold experiment whose results are expected to have a major impact on national development. Many underdeveloped countries are observing the Peruvian frontier experiment in the hope of finding a model of tropical settlement that might be emulated elsewhere.

My own purpose in observing a Peruvian frontier experiment was to analyze the patterns of growth and change in a new, formative community and to relate those patterns to the larger problems of nation building. I doubt that I could have found a better forum for the study of social change than the frontier. Peru's agonizing yet inconclusive search for a more dynamic form of national social and economic integration is a drama played out each day in the Satipo colony. The seemingly minute affairs of everyday living in an out-of-the-way frontier zone such as Satipo are nonetheless immensely revealing of a wide variety of problems that affect Peruvian society generally.

What, then, might we venture to say about the role of colonization in the highly desired but long-delayed transformation of the Peruvian nation? How does Satipo fit into the scheme of reorganizations, reforms, and reconstructions contemplated by the nation's leaders? Given the preference shown by Peru and by most other Third World countries for authoritarian rather than laissez faire models of growth, it seems unlikely that the frontier will develop spontaneously or chaotically. We have seen, for example, how a Peruvian government agency is now taking over the marketing of farm produce from Satipo. Colonists say that the government has moved rapidly into other areas as well: the control of the lumber industry, the appointment of political officials, the enforcement of tax laws, and the supervision of many other activities that were once either loosely regulated or left entirely to local determination. The economic and political absorption of the frontier has begun in earnest. This trend toward greater central government control is expected to continue.

Peruvian planners see the frontier as an area rich in possibilities. The region's natural resources—principally lumber and petroleum—figure prominently in the government's plans for national development.[1] The extractive phase of frontier economic expansion, which began with the rubber boom in the late nineteenth century, is far from complete. Satipo and the other outposts of montaña colonization are destined to serve as the headquarters of new efforts to discover and exploit the jungle's allegedly vast resources. These efforts are being organized and directed by the Peruvian government in conjunction with foreign companies capable of providing the necessary technology and expertise. Though short-lived and ultimately of little consequence, the extractive industries are being counted on to carry Peru through a difficult transitional period.

More important to Peru's long-term goals is the permanent settlement of the jungle region and the development of agriculture in this zone. The nation needs new farmland, a fact that has come to national attention in the wake of recent agrarian reform legislation. In 1969 a comprehensive agrarian reform law was passed and the implementation of this law has brought about major changes in the land-tenure system of Peru. The architects of the agrarian reform program soon discovered, however, that the land resources of the expropriated highland and coastal estates could not accommodate all of the eligible claimants. A government report (CENCIRA 1973:18–19) estimates the number of families eligible for benefits under the agrarian reform law at 1.2 million. The same report states that 300,000 families will be either incorporated into farming cooperatives or granted individual units of land. The remaining 900,000 families will not "participate" in the agrarian reform process because of a short-

[1]The search for major oil fields in the Peruvian tropical forest has only recently paid off. Extensive drilling for oil in the mid-1970s yielded a few disappointingly small discoveries. The construction of a pipeline from the jungle to the coast of northern Peru proceeded amid speculation that the amount of oil produced might not even pay for the pipeline's construction, the cost of which increased from the originally estimated $300 million to $900 million (Werlich 1978: 359). But the soaring price of oil on the world market since 1978 has produced profits where losses had been anticipated. In 1980 Peru expected to earn approximately $1 billion from its oil exports, which average 70,000 barrels a day.

ter 2 we saw that overpopulation in the montaña produces a vicious ecological cycle in which the land's resources are depleted more rapidly than they can be restored by fallowing. This cycle invariably culminates in sterile farmland and bankrupt farmers. It is imperative, then, that government planners not allow their desire to accommodate the displaced masses to tempt them to strain or exceed the carrying capacity of the jungle land.

In the community of Pérez Godoy we have an excellent example of what happens when the government yields to this temptation. As I explained in Chapter 4, the national government reorganized Pérez Godoy in such a way that sixty-four family parcels were created in an area that originally had held only twenty-eight. The amount of land owned by each family in the reorganized settlement was too small to permit rotation of fields or any other soil-management technique. Consequently, the land was overworked and rapidly depleted of its nutrients. As productivity levels fell, colonists began to sell or abandon their nearly worthless parcels, initiating a process of degeneration that continues in Pérez Godoy to the present day. It is easy to see how government planners, besieged by poor and landless immigrants, could overpopulate a zone without considering the long-range effect of that policy. Future colonization projects would do well to overcome this shortsightedness and attempt to establish an ecologically optimal form of montaña settlement.

Another area where the government could learn from its past mistakes is in the extension of credit by the state agricultural bank to farmers. The lending policy that fostered the coffee fever of the 1950s had disastrous consequences for the Satipo colony. First, it led to the emergence of a precarious monocrop system. Since the bank could not be persuaded to provide credit for a wide variety of crops, the colonists were left with no choice but to plant more and more land in coffee. Second, when the inevitable bust in the coffee industry began, the bank refused to negotiate with the financially stricken farmers. As we saw in Chapter 7, the repayment of debts to the state bank is a problem that still has not been resolved. The Peruvian government, if it were so inclined, could learn an important lesson from this painful experience and prevent its repetition in the future.

Yet another lesson lies in the poor performance of the state bureaucracy in its takeover of certain segments of the national marketing system. The problems that arose in the government's corn- and rice-marketing programs (discussed in Chapter 7) indicate that the bureaucracy is due for a major overhaul in the near future. The government's lack of flexibility and openness greatly reduces its effectiveness as an agent of change. In the trial-and-error process of jungle colonization, rigid guidelines and standardized procedures hamper progress. If the problems that have plagued the colonization movement thus far are to be avoided in the future, the machinery of government must become more fluid and pragmatic and must allow the colonists a voice in the determination of policy.

But perhaps these mistakes in government planning and procedures are not the real issue. A case could be made for the assertion that frontier development in Peru is thwarted not by bureaucratic incompetence but by structural contradictions in the patterns of national growth. It must be remembered that central government power has been felt only recently in Satipo; the colony was confused and stagnant before as well as after state intervention. Surely the present malaise was not brought about merely by bureaucratic bungling and mismanagement. Perhaps there is and always has been a design or motif in the interminable frustrations of the Satipo colony.

Internal Colonialism and the Peruvian Frontier

According to André Gunder Frank (1967), underdevelopment is an absolutely necessary condition for development. In order for such developed nations as the United States to exist, underdeveloped nations such as Peru must exist. The exploitation of the latter by the former generates, through a process that Gunder Frank calls "surplus extraction," development in the

metropolis and underdevelopment in the satellite. In contrast to modernization theorists, who view the underdeveloped countries as isolated and traditional, dependency theorists assert that these countries are fully integrated into the modern world system. The underdeveloped nations are poor because they are dominated by and dependent on the developed nations. Thus Gunder Frank (1967:9) contends that "economic development and underdevelopment are opposite faces of the same coin . . . they cannot be viewed as the products of supposedly different economic structures or systems, or of supposed differences in the stages of growth achieved within the same system."

The basic mechanisms of economic exploitation or surplus extraction are international trade and finance. The satellite produces and exports raw materials. The metropolis imports these raw materials, refines and manufactures them, and exports finished goods. Since the satellite itself has no significant industrial capacity, it relies heavily on imports of finished goods from the metropolis. The income that the satellite receives from the export of raw materials is returned to the metropolis via the purchase of manufactured goods and new technologies. Thus the terms of trade between metropolis and satellite create a constant drain on the natural resources and the export earnings of the underdeveloped nations. The same terms of trade create a solid industrial base and substantial capital reserves in the developed nations.

The financial structure that supports these terms of trade perpetuates the cycle of underdevelopment. The satellite economies need foreign investment and credit in order to develop and expand their own industrial potentials. But it is not in the interests of the metropolis to assist the satellite in its quest for a self-sufficient and diversified economic base. Thus the metropolis uses investment and credit as a means of further orienting the satellite economies to the requirements of export. This fact, coupled with the high cost of servicing loans and investments from abroad, prevents the underdeveloped nations from breaking out of the cycles of poverty and dependency. International loans and investments have the further disadvantage of allowing the metropolis directly or indirectly to shape government policy in the satellite nations. Because of their dependent status, the underdeveloped countries are not free to define and pursue their own economic, social, and political goals.

In each satellite nation, according to Gunder Frank, there is an intranational system of exploitation similar to the international system of dominance and dependency outlined above. The capital city of the satellite nation dominates its rural hinterland in the same way that the developed nations dominate the underdeveloped nations, and by the same mechanisms. In the domestic system of exploitation the national metropolis expropriates the economic surplus of its rural satellite regions and appropriates this surplus for its own development. As in the international sphere, commercial and financial transactions provide the basis for creating and preserving the economic advantage exercised by the capital city over its hinterland. Gunder Frank refers to the intranational process of surplus extraction and capital accumulation as "internal colonialism."

The concept of internal colonialism challenges the widely held belief that rural communities in the underdeveloped nations are poor because they are marginal or traditional or feudal. Peasants in fact have multiple links to national and international metropolises, and it is the nature of this linkage that renders peasants poor and powerless. Accordingly, the solution to rural poverty in the underdeveloped nations lies not, as modernization theorists contend, in the incorporation of peasants into the national society and economy. Incorporation is the problem, not the solution. Thus for rural development to take place, the present mode of incorporation must be radically transformed and the chain of dependency relationships broken.

Satipo is obviously not an isolated or marginal or traditional rural province. It is a frontier of active pioneer settlement that is destined to play a major role in Peru's quest for economic development. There is little reason to believe that Satipo's developmental problems could be solved by a more thorough incorporation of the frontier into Peruvian society. The Satipo region is by now fully incorporated and yet its manifold problems persist. Modernization in the form of improved roads, expanded markets, and increased government services has not benefited the colonists of Satipo. Moreover, these symbols of "progress" are in many ways the substance of underdevelopment and the vehicles of internal colonialism.

Modernization in Satipo has been accompanied by the establishment of a commercial and financial structure that has placed the local economy under the control of the national metropolis. The terms of trade between Lima and Satipo reveal the classic features of a metropolis–satellite relationship. Satipo exports farm produce to and imports clothing, building materials, tools, and other essential manufactured items from Lima. This exchange of commodities is weighted heavily in favor of the metropolis. As we saw in Chapter 7, powerful metropolitan interests depress farm prices and inflate the costs of durable goods. As a result, the earnings that Satipo receives from its exports are wholly inadequate to pay for its imports. Satipo cannot progress because its economic surplus is siphoned off by unfavorable terms of trade.

The manner in which farm production is financed further ensures that no surplus wealth accumulates on the frontier. The lending policies of the state bank and the coffee-export companies entangle the satellite in a complex web of indebtedness spun by the metropolis. Because of the unfavorable terms and conditions under which farm credit is granted, each year at harvesttime the Satipo colony finds itself unable to break even with its creditors. The costs of servicing debts to the state bank and of selling crops at below-market rates to the habilitadores are too high to allow Satipo to escape the cycle of indebtedness in which it has become mired.

The investment and credit policies of the national metropolis have also led to the formation of a monocrop economy. In Chapter 3 we saw that during the 1950s and 1960s the lending policies of the state bank encouraged the production of coffee and discouraged the production of all other crops. The coffee-export companies also promoted monoculture by lending money that could be repaid only in coffee. The development of a self-sufficient and diversified frontier economy was thwarted by the withholding of credit for all activities other than coffee cultivation. On the basis of the evidence presented in the preceding chapters, I believe that farm credit served as a means to gain control over the frontier and to exploit its coffee-producing potential. Rather than attribute the emergence of a fragile monocrop economy to shortsightedness or mismanagement, I attribute it to the machinations of internal colonialism.

Whenever the colonists have attempted to establish a new commercial and financial structure, their efforts have been subverted by the metropolis. In Chapter 7 I described a highly popular and successful experiment in market reform (the "De la chacra a la olla" campaign) that was canceled because it posed a threat to the wholesale merchants of Lima. Satipo's cooperative movement has been suppressed because it also has sought higher prices for local farm produce. The terms of trade between metropolis and hinterland would be altered if the farmers of Satipo were allowed to market their produce directly and to receive higher prices for it.

Satipo has been unsuccessful in its efforts to enlist outside assistance in combating the system of internal colonialism. The "revolutionary" government of the armed forces, the logical source of this assistance, introduced reforms that served only to strengthen the grip of the metropolis on the hinterland. Governmental regulation of the marketplace via EPSA did not change the basic terms of trade between Lima and Satipo. Nor did the "revolutionary" government aid the colonists by appointing local political leaders who, as we saw in Chapter 5, do not identify with the cause of frontier development. By selecting community leaders exclusively from the ranks of the vecinos notables, the central government ensures that the interests of the metropolis are protected. The actions of the "revolutionary" government, their avowed purpose notwithstanding, reinforced the intranational system of exploitation.

In my view the data from Satipo speak for themselves on the question of whether mistakes and mismanagement or internal colonialism account for the depressed state of the frontier. Satipo's manifold problems constitute a system rather than a random series of blunders. The national metropolis, in its triple function as a source of technology and durable goods, a provider of agricultural credit, and an outlet for the sale of farm produce, drains the economic surplus of the Satipo community and leaves the colonists with only debts to show for their industry and diligence. In other words, Satipo suffers not from neglect or poor planning or mismanagement, but from systematic domination under the guise of progress. By exposing this fact, dependency theory and the concept of internal colonialism establish a framework for the analysis and explanation of Satipo's dire economic predicament.

If dependency theory is valid in the case of Satipo, then it is reasonable to suggest that it might explain the plight of impoverished rural communities throughout Peru. In fact, the concepts of dependency and internal domination have already been employed in a small number of Peruvian community studies. One group of anthropologists (Matos Mar et al. 1969) has examined the structural conditions of dependency in four types of rural communities: the traditional haciendas of the highlands, the modernized haciendas of the coast, the indigenous communities, and the smallholder farming settlements. In each case they describe the regional pattern of dependency and attempt to relate this pattern to the general system of domination at the national level. Domination of the hinterland by the national metropolis constitutes, according to these anthropologists, the unifying element in the highly differentiated structure of Peruvian society. Their research shows that internal colonialism appears in many local forms and that it not only survives but flourishes under conditions of change.

The influence of dependency theory is also evident in a recent study of the forms of peasant cooperation and capitalist expansion in the Mantaro Valley of Peru (Long and Roberts 1978). The anthropologists who directed this study reject modernization theory and contend that "even the most remote village and the poorest agricultural laborer have been fully integrated into a hierarchical system whereby, at successive points, the metropolitan centers siphoned off economic surplus" (1978:300). Long and Roberts seek to overcome the centralist bias of dependency theory, however, and to reveal the "significant differences between neighboring villages in their internal social and economic differentiation, in their potential for political action, and in their economic diversification." Dependency theorists, according to Long and Roberts, overemphasize the extent to which the metropolis controls and organizes local-level processes. Long and Roberts show, for example, that cooperative organizations in the Mantaro Valley have at times advanced the interests of the peasants at the expense of the metropolis while at other times they have reinforced the ties of dependency and exploitation. The Mantaro Valley study demonstrates the need for more empirical testing, leading to the revision and refinement of dependency theory.

Although a growing number of scholars are seeking to understand the problems of economic and social change in Peru from a dependency perspective, some are skeptical of or opposed to this trend. I refer here to such anthropologists as Orlove (1977) and van den Berghe and Primov (1977), who examine the dependency model and conclude that it is either inadequate or misleading as an explanation of rural poverty in Peru. Their criticisms of and their alternatives to dependency theory are worth noting.

Orlove states that both the modernization and dependency paradigms are "typological" and "do not admit the range of responses of different societies to incorporation in the world-system" (1977:11). He believes that dependency theorists are overly concerned with the opposition between dominant and dependent societies and between dominant and dependent sectors of the same society. Like Long and Roberts, Orlove asserts that rural populations have far more vitality, diversity, and autonomy than dependency theorists give them credit for. Thus Orlove feels that dependency theory does not allow him the methodological and conceptual latitude he needs to describe and analyze the complex wool-export economy of southern Peru. He calls for a new model rather than a reformulation of either the dependency or modernization paradigms.

The "sectorial" model is Orlove's answer to the need for a more flexible approach to the study of rural transformations. His idea is to use such value-free terms as resources, activities, units, and sectors rather than such value-laden terms as metropolis and satellite in observing and describing rural economic formations. As a result, the sectorial model is strong where dependency theory is weak and weak where dependency theory is strong. Accuracy, precision, and objectivity in ethnographic research are Orlove's strengths. His weakness is a lack of understanding of the economic and political forces that created the empirical configurations he so masterfully describes.

In another recent study of the Peruvian highlands, van den Berghe and Primov (1977) question the validity and applicability of dependency theory. They believe that there is something to both modernization and dependency theories but that neither explains the severe underdevelopment of the Cuzco region. They are basically opposed to the idea that any single conceptual scheme could account for all forms and conditions of rural poverty. After surveying the history of Cuzco, van den Berghe and Primov conclude:

> The radical [dependency] thesis applies well to the colonial period. From the time of independence, the area became economically marginal and stagnant rather than externally exploited. The marginalization [modernization] thesis applies better to the nineteenth century. Only in the twentieth century, with the increasing emigration of surplus labor from the sierra and the greater economic integration brought about by better communication and transport, does the internal colonialism thesis begin once more to find some applicability, but only in a very limited sense. The area simply produces too little surplus to be worth exploiting. [van den Berghe and Primov 1977:29–30]

I find perplexing the conclusion that the dependency thesis applies only in a narrow sense to Cuzco because the region "produces too little surplus to be worth exploiting." If Cuzco was an internal colony during almost 300 years of colonial rule, as van den Berghe and Primov suggest, then it is not surprising that today the region is economically depressed and no longer appears to be a major target of surplus extraction. This finding does not seem to me to limit the applicability of dependency theory. The system of internal colonialism that stripped Cuzco of its gold, silver, and other natural resources has left a living legacy of poverty and despair. Gunder Frank points out that "the regions which are the most underdeveloped and feudal-seeming today are the ones which had the closest ties to the metropolis in the past. They are the ones which were the greatest exporters of primary products to and the biggest sources of capital for the world metropolis and were abandoned by the metropolis when for one reason or another business fell off" (1969:13).

The fact that the forces of internal colonialism are not so active in Cuzco today as they were in the sixteenth century is no indication that either Cuzco or Peru has loosened the bonds of dependence and domination. If, for example, new mineral deposits were to be discovered in Cuzco, the mechanisms of surplus extraction would once again be set in motion. The seeming disinterest in and abandonment of the southern highlands by the national metropolis would be reversed overnight. It is important to recognize, therefore, that Cuzco is encompassed by and subject to the Peruvian system of internal colonialism even though it now "produces too little surplus to be worth exploiting."

A region such as Satipo, in contrast, produces a surplus worth exploiting. When the commercial potential of this frontier zone was first demonstrated in the era of coffee fever, a process began that would ultimately convert an autonomously developing province into a dependent satellite of the national metropolis. Thus what was happening in Cuzco 400 years ago is happening under different circumstances in Satipo today. The colonial and the modern forms of internal domination are basically similar. The major difference is that at today's rate of surplus extraction it will not take 300 years to drain Satipo of its natural resources.

As we have seen, the fragile rain-forest environment already shows signs of succumbing to intensive commercial exploitation. If present trends continue, the national metropolis will soon have exhausted Satipo's economic potential.

In my view, then, internal colonialism is the primary obstacle to development in Satipo, Cuzco, and thousands of other Peruvian communities. Accordingly, any rural development program that does not directly confront the problem of internal colonialism is destined to fail. Peru's colonization program has failed for precisely this reason. The opening of virgin lands for settlement would seem to provide a nation with an excellent opportunity to experiment with new agrarian policies. But thus far the Peruvian government has wasted this opportunity. As a result, the system of internal colonialism is now firmly established in Peru's valued frontier zones.

In the light of the data I have gathered, it would be irresponsible to recommend any course of action short of a thorough transformation of the metropolis–hinterland structure of Peruvian economic integration. My study of Satipo's unrewarded quest for development leads directly to this conclusion. Progress in the areas of housing, education, health, or nutrition cannot occur without a restructuring of the terms of trade between Lima and Satipo. The effect of recent domestic "reforms" has been merely to substitute state abuse of power for private abuse of power. The system of internal domination remains intact. Moreover, under the new system colonists have come to understand more fully the relationship between metropolitan development and frontier underdevelopment. They see the power wielded by the national metropolis over their colony and they recognize that the growth of the former and the stagnation of the latter are directly related.

Peru's "revolutionary" government vigorously attacked the system of foreign domination while quietly reinforcing the system of internal domination. The quest for national autonomy tended to obscure the fact that the provinces remained subordinate to and dependent on the capital city. By adopting a de-

velopment strategy that perpetuated internal dependency relationships, Perú's leaders detracted from their gains in the international arena. Their misguided domestic policies demonstrated
that the external and the internal aspects of underdevelopment
are too closely related to be accorded separate and unequal
treatment. If, under new civilian leadership, 900,000 additional
families are to make a success of jungle settlement, the structure
of internal colonialism must be dismantled along with the structure of foreign domination. Even if the dismantling of these
structures proceeds only a step at a time, the steps must be
coordinated in their internal and external dimensions.

Bibliography

ADAMS, RICHARD N. 1970. "Brokers and Career Mobility Systems in the Structure of Complex Societies." *Southwestern Journal of Anthropology* 26:315-27.

ALBERTI, GIORGIO, and ENRIQUE MAYER, eds. 1974. *Reciprocidad e intercambio en los Andes peruanos*. Lima: Instituto de Estudios Peruanos.

BASADRE, JORGE. 1949. *Historia de la República del Perú*. Lima: Editorial Cultura Antártica.

BÉJAR, HÉCTOR. 1970. *Peru 1965: Notes on a Guerrilla Experience*. New York: Monthly Review Press.

BOLTON, RALPH. 1972. "Aggression in Qolla Society." Ph.D. dissertation. Ann Arbor: University Microfilms.

———— and ENRIQUE MAYER, eds. 1977. *Andean Kinship and Marriage*. Special Publication no. 7. Washington, D.C.: American Anthropological Association.

BOURRICAUD, FRANÇOIS. 1967. *Cambios en Puno*. Mexico: Instituto Indigenista Interamericano.

————. 1975. "Indian, Mestizo, and Cholo as Symbols in the Peruvian System of Stratification." In *Ethnicity: Theory and Experience*, ed. Nathan Glazer and Daniel P. Moynihan. Cambridge, Mass.: Harvard University Press.

BRUSH, STEPHEN B. 1977. *Mountain, Field, and Family: The Economy and Human Ecology of an Andean Valley*. Philadelphia: University of Pennsylvania Press.

BURCHARD, RODERICK E. 1974. "Coca y trueque de alimentos." In *Reciprocidad e intercambio en los Andes peruanos,* ed. Giorgio Alberti and Enrique Mayer. Lima: Instituto de Estudios Peruanos.

————. 1977. "Coca Use and the Management of Carbohydrate Metabolism Problems in the Andean Highlands and the Amazonian Lowlands." Paper presented at the annual meeting of the Florida Academia of Sciences, Gainesville.

CAMPBELL, LEON G. 1973. "A Historiography of the Peruvian Guerrilla Movement, 1960–65." *Latin American Research Review* 8(1):45–70.

CARNEIRO, ROBERT L. 1956. "Slash-and-Burn Agriculture: A Closer Look at Its Implications for Settlement Patterns." In *Men and Cultures,* ed. Anthony F. Wallace. Philadelphia: University of Pennsylvania Press.

CENCIRA (Centro Nacional de Capacitación e Investigación para la Reforma Agraria). 1973. "Continuación de las reflecciones del equipo de Alto Marañón sobre el marco teórico." Lima: unpublished manuscript.

CHILCOTE, RONALD H., and JOEL C. EDELSTEIN. 1974. "Alternative Perspectives of Development and Underdevelopment in Latin America." In *Latin America: The Struggle with Dependency and Beyond,* ed. Ronald H. Chilcote and Joel C. Edelstein. Cambridge, Mass.: Schenkman.

CIDA (Comité Interamericano de Desarrollo Agrícola). 1966. *Tenencia de la tierra y desarrollo socio-económico del sector agrícola, Perú.* Washington: Unión Panamericana.

COLE, JOHN W., and ERIC WOLF. 1974. *The Hidden Frontier: Ecology and Ethnicity in an Alpine Valley.* New York: Academic Press.

COLLIER, DAVID. 1976. *Squatters and Oligarchs: Authoritarian Rule and Policy Change in Peru.* Baltimore: Johns Hopkins University Press.

CONKLIN, H. C. 1959. "Population-Land Balance under Systems of Tropical Forest Agriculture." *Proceedings, 9th Pacific Science Congress* 1 (7):60–62.

COTLER, JULIO. 1967–68. "The Mechanics of Internal Domination and Social Change in Peru." *Studies in Comparative International Development* 3 (12):229–46.

CRAIG, ALAN K. 1972. "Franciscan Exploration in the Central Montaña of Peru." In *Historia, etnohistoria, y etnología de la selva sudamericana,* ed. Rosalía Avalos and Rogger Ravines. Lima: Instituto de Estudios Peruanos.

CRAIG, WESLEY W. 1967. *From Hacienda to Community: An Analysis of Solidarity and Social Change in Peru.* Ithaca: Cornell University Latin American Program Dissertation Series, no. 6.

DALTON, GEORGE. 1974. "How Exactly Are Peasants 'Exploited'?" *American Anthropologist* 76:553–61.

DAVIES, THOMAS M. 1974. *Indian Integration in Peru.* Lincoln: University of Nebraska Press.

DAVIS, SHELTON H. 1977. *Victims of the Miracle: Development and the Indians of Brazil.* Cambridge, Eng.: Cambridge University Press.

DENEVAN, WILLIAM M. 1972. "Campa Subsistence in the Gran Pajonal, Eastern Peru." In *Historia, etnohistoria, y etnología de la selva sudamericana,* ed. Rosalía Avalos and Rogger Ravines. Lima: Instituto de Estudios Peruanos.

————. 1973. "Development and the Imminent Demise of the Amazon Rainforest." *Professional Geographer* 25:130–35.

DEW, EDWARD. 1969. *Politics in the Altiplano: The Dynamics of Change in Rural Peru.* Austin: University of Texas Press.

DIETZ, HENRY A. 1978. "Metropolitan Lima: Urban Problem-Solving under Military Rule." In *Latin American Urban Research,* ed. Wayne A. Cornelius and Robert V. Kemper, vol. 6. Beverly Hills, Calif.: Sage.

DOBYNS, HENRY F., and PAUL L. DOUGHTY. 1976. *Peru: A Cultural History.* New York: Oxford University Press.

DOUGHTY, PAUL. 1968. *Huaylas: An Andean District in Search of Progress.* Ithaca: Cornell University Press.

————. 1970. "Behind the Back of the City: 'Provincial' Life in Lima, Peru." In *Peasants in Cities: Readings in the Anthropology of Urbanization,* ed. William Mangin. Boston: Houghton Mifflin.

————. 1976. "Social Policy and Urban Growth in Lima." In *Peruvian Nationalism: A Corporatist Revolution,* ed. David Chaplin. New Brunswick, N.J.: Transaction Books.

FERNÁNDEZ, RAUL A., and JOSÉ F. OCAMPO. 1974. "The Latin American Revolution," *Latin American Perspectives* 1 (1):30–61.

FIORAVANTI, EDUARDO. 1974. *Latifundio y sindicalismo agrario en el Perú: El caso de los valles de La Convención y Lares (1958–1964).* Lima: Instituto de Estudios Peruanos.

FORD, THOMAS. 1955. *Man and Land in Peru.* Gainesville: University Presses of Florida.

FORMAN, SHEPARD. 1975. *The Brazilian Peasantry.* New York: Columbia University Press.

FUCHS, ANDREW. 1978. "Coca Chewing and High-Altitude Stress: Possible Effects of Coca Alkaloids on Erythropoiesis." *Current Anthropology* 19 (2):277–83.

FURNIVALL, J. S. 1948. *Colonial Policy and Practice.* London: Cambridge University Press.

GEERTZ, CLIFFORD. 1963a. *Agricultural Involution: The Processes of Ecological Change in Indonesia.* Berkeley: University of California Press.

————. 1963b. *Peddlers and Princes: Social Change and Economic Modernization in Two Indonesian Towns.* Chicago: University of Chicago Press.

————. 1965. *The Social History of an Indonesian Town.* Cambridge, Mass.: M.I.T. Press.

GONZÁLEZ CASANOVA, PABLO. 1965. "Internal Colonialism and National

Development." *Studies in Comparative International Development* 1 (4):27–37.

GOODLAND, R. J. A., and H. S. IRWIN. 1975. *Amazon Jungle: Green Hell to Red Desert?* Amsterdam: Elsevier.

GUNDER FRANK, ANDRÉ. 1967. *Capitalism and Underdevelopment in Latin America.* New York: Monthly Review Press.

––––––. 1969. *Latin America: Underdevelopment or Revolution.* New York: Monthly Review Press.

HANDELMAN, HOWARD. 1975. *Struggle in the Andes: Peasant Political Mobilization in Peru.* Austin: University of Texas Press.

HANNA, JOEL M. 1976. "Drug Use." In *Man in the Andes: A Multidisciplinary Study of High-Altitude Quechua,* ed. Paul T. Baker and Michael A. Little. Stroudsburg, Pa.: Dowden, Hutchison, & Ross.

HOBSBAWM, ERIC. 1969. "A Case of Neo-feudalism: La Convención, Peru." *Journal of Latin American Studies* 1 (1):31–50.

HOLMBERG, ALLAN. 1960. "Changing Community Attitudes and Values in Peru: A Case Study in Guided Change." In Richard N. Adams et al., *Social Change in Latin America Today.* New York: Harper & Row.

ISBELL, BILLIE JEAN. 1978. *To Defend Ourselves: Ecology and Ritual in an Andean Village.* Austin: Institute of Latin American Studies.

ISBELL, WILLIAM. 1968. "New Discoveries in the Montaña of Southeastern Peru." *Archaeology* 21 (2):108–14.

JONGKIND, FRED. 1974. "A Reappraisal of the Role of Regional Associations in Lima, Peru." *Comparative Studies in Society and History* 16 (4):471–82.

KEITH, ROBERT. 1971. "Encomienda, Hacienda, and Corregimiento in Spanish America: A Structural Analysis." *Hispanic American Historical Review* 51 (3):431–46.

––––––. 1976. *Conquest and Agrarian Change: The Emergence of the Hacienda System on the Peruvian Coast.* Cambridge, Mass.: Harvard University Press.

LATHRAP, DONALD W. 1970. *The Upper Amazon.* New York: Praeger.

LEACH, EDMUND. 1961. *Rethinking Anthropology.* London: Athlone Press.

LEEDS, ANTHONY. 1965. "Brazilian Careers and Social Structure: A Case History and Model." In *Contemporary Cultures and Societies of Latin America,* ed. Dwight Heath and Richard Adams. New York: Random House.

LEHNERTZ, JAY. 1972. "Juan Santos, Primitive Rebel on the Campa Frontier." In *Historia, etnohistoria, y etnología de la selva sudamericano,* ed. Rosalía Avalos and Rogger Ravines. Lima: Instituto de Estudios Peruanos.

LOBO, SUSAN BLOOM. 1976. "Urban Adaptation among Peruvian Migrants." in *New Approaches to the Study of Migration,* ed. David Guillet and Douglas Uzzell. Rice University Studies 62 (3):113–30.

LOCKHART, JAMES. 1968. *Spanish Peru: 1532–1560.* Madison: University of Wisconsin Press.

————. 1969. "Encomienda and Hacienda: The Evolution of the Great Estate in the Spanish Indies." *Hispanic American Historical Review* 49 (3):411–29.

————. 1972. *The Men of Cajamarca: A Social and Biographical Study of the First Conquerors of Peru*. Austin: University of Texas Press.

LOHMANN VILLENA, GUILLERMO. 1949. *Las minas de Huancavelica en los siglos XVI y XVII*. Seville: Escuela de Estudios Hispano-Americanos.

————. 1957. *El Corregidor de Indios en el Perú bajo los Austrias*. Madrid: Ediciones Cultura Hispánica.

LONG, NORMAN. 1977. *An Introduction to the Sociology of Rural Development*. Boulder, Col.: Westview Press.

———— and BRYAN R. ROBERTS. 1978. *Peasant Cooperation and Capitalist Expansion in Peru*. Austin: Institute of Latin American Studies.

MACNEIL, MARY. 1972. "Lateritic Soils in Distinct Tropical Environments: Southern Sudan and Brazil." In *The Careless Technology: Ecology and International Development*, ed. M. Taghi Farvar and John P. Milton. Garden City, N.Y.: Natural History Press.

MANGIN, WILLIAM. 1959. "The Role of Regional Associations in the Adaptation of Rural Population in Peru." *Sociologus* 9 (1):23–35.

————. 1970. "Urbanization Case History in Peru." In *Peasants in Cities: Readings in the Anthropology of Urbanization*, ed. William Mangin. Boston: Houghton Mifflin.

MARGOLIS, MAXINE L. 1973. *The Moving Frontier: Social and Economic Change in a Southern Brazilian Community*. Gainesville: University Presses of Florida.

MARIÁTEGUI, JOSÉ CARLOS. 1971. *Seven Interpretive Essays on Peruvian Reality*. Austin: University of Texas Press.

MARTÍNEZ, HÉCTOR. 1969. *Las migraciones altiplánicas y la colonización del Tambopata*. Lima: Centro de Estudios de Población y Desarrollo.

MATOS MAR, JOSÉ. 1966. *Estudio de las barriadas limeñas*. Lima: Departamento de Antropología, Universidad Nacional Mayor de San Marcos.

————. 1969. "El pluralismo y la dominación en la sociedad peruana." In José Matos Mar et al., *Dominación y cambios en el Perú rural*. Lima: Instituto de Estudios Peruanos.

————, W. F. WHYTE, J. COTLER, L. K. WILLIAMS, J. O. ALERS, F. FUENZALIDA, and G. ALBERTI. 1969. *Dominación y cambios en el Perú rural*. Lima: Instituto de Estudios Peruanos.

MEGGERS, BETTY J. 1971. *Amazonia: Man and Culture in a Counterfeit Paradise*. Arlington Heights, Ill.: AHM Publishing Corporation.

MORÁN, EMILIO F. 1974. "The Adaptive System of the Amazonian Caboclo." In *Man in the Amazon*, ed. Charles Wagley. Gainesville: University Presses of Florida.

————. 1976. "Manioc Deserves More Recognition in Tropical Farming." *World Crops* 28 (4):184–88.

————. 1979. "The Trans-Amazonica: Coping with a New Environment." In *Brazil: Anthropological Perspectives,* ed. Maxine L. Margolis and William E. Carter. New York: Columbia University Press.

MURRA, JOHN. 1956. "The Economic Organization of the Inca State." Ph.D dissertation, University of Chicago.

————. 1961. "Social Structural and Economic Themes in Andean Ethnohistory." *Anthropological Quarterly* 34 (2):47–59.

————. 1970. "Current Research and Prospects in Andean Ethnohistory." *Latin American Research Review* 5 (1):3–36.

————. 1972. "El 'control vertical' de un máximo de pisos ecológicos en la economía de las sociedades andinas." In *Visita de la Provincia de León de Huánuco en 1562.* Huánuco: Universidad Hermilio Valdizán.

NASH, MANNING. 1965. *The Golden Road to Modernity.* Chicago: University of Chicago Press.

————. 1967. *Machine Age Maya: The Industrialization of a Guatemalan Community.* Chicago: University of Chicago Press.

ONERN (Oficina Nacional de Evaluación de Recursos Naturales). 1962. *Evaluación e integración del potencial económico y social de la zona Perené-Satipo-Ene.* Lima: Instituto Nacional de Planificación.

ORLOVE, BENJAMIN S. 1977. *Alpacas, Sheep, and Men: The Wool Export Economy and Regional Society in Southern Peru.* New York: Academic Press.

ORTIZ, DIONISIO. 1958. *Monografía de Chanchamayo.* Lima: Editorial San Antonio.

————. 1961. *Reseña histórica de la montaña del Pangoa, Gran Pajonal, y Satipo (1673–1960).* Lima: Editorial San Antonio.

PAN AMERICAN COFFEE BUREAU. 1966–72. *Annual Coffee Statistics,* nos. 31–36. New York.

PATCH, RICHARD W. 1967. "La Parada, Lima's Market: A Study of Class and Assimilation." *American Universities Field Staff Reports, West Coast South America Series* 14 (1–3):1–47.

PICÓN-REÁTEGUI, EMILIO. 1976. "Nutrition." In *Man in the Andes: A Multidisciplinary Study of High-Altitude Quechua,* ed. Paul T. Baker and Michael A. Little. Stroudsburg, Pa.: Dowden, Hutchison, & Ross.

PIKE, FREDERICK. 1967. *The Modern History of Peru.* New York: Praeger.

QUIJANO, ANÍBAL. 1971. *Nationalism and Capitalism in Peru: A Study in Neo-Imperialism.* New York: Monthly Review Press.

REDFIELD, ROBERT. 1941. *The Folk Culture of Yucatan.* Chicago: University of Chicago Press.

ROEL PINEDA, VIRGILIO. 1970. *Historia social y económica de la Colonia.* Lima: Editorial Gráfica.

————. 1971. *Los libertadores: Proceso social económico, político, y militar de la independencia.* Lima: Editorial Gráfica.

ROSTOW, WALT WHITMAN. 1961. *The Stages of Economic Growth: A Non-Communist Manifesto.* Cambridge, Eng.: Cambridge University Press.

ROWE, JOHN HOWLAND. 1947. "Inca Culture at the Time of the Spanish Conquest." In *Handbook of South American Indians,* ed. Julian Steward, vol. 2. Washington, D.C.: Government Printing Office.

_____. 1957. "The Incas under Spanish Colonial Institutions." *Hispanic American Historical Review* 37 (2):155-99.

SAUER, CARL O. 1950. "Geography of South American Indians." In *Handbook of South American Indians,* ed. Julian Steward, vol. 6. Washington, D.C.: Government Printing Office.

SHOEMAKER, ROBIN. 1976. "Colonization and Urbanization in Peru: Empirical and Theoretical Perspectives." In *New Approaches to the Study of Migration,* ed. David Guillet and Douglas Uzzell. Rice University Studies 62 (3):163-75.

SIMMONS, OZZIE G. 1965. "The *Criollo* Outlook in the *Mestizo* Culture of Coastal Peru." In *Contemporary Cultures and Societies of Latin America,* ed. Dwight Heath and Richard Adams. New York: Random House.

SIOLI, HAROLD. 1973. "Recent Human Activities in the Brazilian Amazon Region and Their Ecological Effects." In *Tropical Forest Ecosystems in Africa and South America: A Comparative View,* ed. Betty J. Meggers, Edward S. Ayensu, and W. Donald Duckworth. Washington: Smithsonian Institution Press.

SMITH, CAROL. 1977. "How Marketing Systems Affect Economic Opportunity in Agrarian Societies." In *Peasant Livelihood: Studies in Economic Anthropology and Cultural Ecology,* ed. Rhoda Halperin and James Dow. New York: St. Martin's Press.

SMITH, M. G. 1965. *The Plural Society in the British West Indies.* Berkeley: University of California Press.

SPALDING, KAREN. 1967. "Indian Rural Society in Colonial Peru: The Example of Huarochiri." Ph.D. dissertation, University of California, Berkeley.

_____. 1970. "Social Climbers: Changing Patterns of Mobility among the Indians of Colonial Peru." *Hispanic American Historical Review* 50 (4):645-64.

_____. 1974. *De indio a campesino: Cambios en la estructura social del Perú colonial.* Lima: Instituto de Estudios Peruanos.

STAVENHAGEN, RODOLFO. 1966. "Seven Erroneous Theses about Latin America." *New University Thought* 4 (4):25-37.

_____. 1973. "The Plural Society of Latin America." *Plural Societies* 4 (4):65-74.

STEARMAN, ALLYN MacLEAN. 1973. *San Rafael: Camba Town.* Gainesville: University Presses of Florida.

STEIN, WILLIAM. 1961. *Hualcan: Life in the Highlands of Peru.* Ithaca: Cornell University Press.

STRASMA, JOHN. 1976. "Agrarian Reform." In *Peruvian Nationalism: A Corporatist Revolution,* ed. David Chaplin. New Brunswick, N.J.: Transaction Books.

TSCHOPIK, HARRY. 1948. "On the Concept of Creole Culture in Peru." *Transactions of the New York Academy of Sciences* 10:252-61.

VAN DEN BERGHE, PIERRE. 1970. *Race and Ethnicity: Essays in Comparative Sociology.* New York: Basic Books.

_____. 1974. "The Use of Ethnic Terms in the Peruvian Social Science

Literature." In *Class and Ethnicity in Peru,* ed. Pierre L. van den Berghe. Leiden: E. J. Brill.

———— and GEORGE P. PRIMOV. 1977. *Inequality in the Peruvian Andes: Class and Ethnicity in Cuzco.* Columbia: University of Missouri Press.

VARESE, STEFANO. 1972. "The Forest Indians in the Present Political Situation of Peru." In *IWGIA Documents,* no. 8. Copenhagen: International Work Group for Indigenous Affairs.

————. 1973. *La sal de los cerros: Una aproximación al mundo campa.* Lima: Retablo de Papel.

————. 1974. "La selva: Viejas fronteras, nuevas alternativas." *Participación* 5:18–31.

WACHTEL, NATHAN. 1977. *The Vision of the Vanquished: The Spanish Conquest of Peru through Indian Eyes, 1530–1570.* New York: Barnes & Noble.

WAGLEY, CHARLES. 1953. *Amazon Town: A Study of Man in the Tropics.* New York: Alfred A. Knopf.

WALTON, JOHN. 1975. "Internal Colonialism: Problems of Definition and Measurement." In *Latin American Urban Research,* ed. Wayne A. Cornelius and Felicity Trueblood, vol. 5. Beverly Hills, Calif.: Sage.

————. 1976. "Urban Hierarchies and Patterns of Dependence in Latin America: Theoretical Bases for a New Research Agenda." In *Current Perspectives in Latin American Urban Research,* ed. Alejandro Portes and Harley L. Browning. Austin: Institute of Latin American Studies.

WARNER, W. LLOYD. 1953. *American Life: Dream and Reality.* Chicago: University of Chicago Press.

WEISS, GERALD. 1969. "The Cosmology of the Campa Indians of Eastern Peru." Ph.D. dissertation. Ann Arbor: University Microfilms.

WERLICH, DAVID P. 1978. *Peru: A Short History.* Carbondale: Southern Illinois University Press.

WESCHE, ROLF. 1971a. "Successes and Shortcomings of Recent Colonization in the Montaña of Peru." Unpublished manuscript.

————. 1971b. "Recent Migration to the Peruvian Montaña." *Cahiers de Géographie du Québec* 15 (35):250–66.

WHITTEN, NORMAN E. 1976. *Sacha Runa: Ethnicity and Adaptation of Ecuadorian Jungle Quichua.* Urbana: University of Illinois Press.

WOLF, ERIC. 1956. "Aspects of Group Relations in a Complex Society." *American Anthropologist* 58:1065–78.

————. 1967. "Levels of Communal Relations." In *Handbook of Middle American Indians,* ed. Robert Wauchope and Manning Nash, vol. 6. Austin: University of Texas Press.

————. 1974. *Anthropology.* New York: W. W. Norton.

WOOD, CHARLES A., and MARIANNE SCHMINK. 1978. "Blaming the Victim: Small Farmer Production in an Amazon Colonization Project." Paper presented at the symposium "Nutrition and Agriculture: Strategies for Latin America," annual meeting of the American Association for the Advancement of Science, Washington, D.C.

Index

The Peasants of El Dorado

Designed by G. T. Whipple, Jr.
Composed by The Composing Room of Michigan, Inc.
in 10 point VIP Baskerville, 3 points leaded,
with display lines in Baskerville.
Printed offset by Thomson Shore, Inc.
on Warren's No. 66 Text, 50 pound basis.
Bound by John H. Dekker & Sons
in Holliston book cloth
and stamped in Kurz-Hastings foil.

Library of Congress Cataloging in Publication Data

Shoemaker, Robin, 1949–
    The peasants of El Dorado.

Bibliography: p.
Includes index.
1. San Francisco de Satipo (Peru)—Social conditions.
2. Frontier and pioneer life—Peru—San Francisco de
Satipo. I. Title.
HN350.S26S54   985′.24   81-9742
ISBN 0-8014-1390-7   AACR2